GREEK-TURKISH RELATIONS IN AN ERA OF DÉTENTE

The conflict-ridden relations between Greece and Turkey have long occupied a problematic position in the western alliance, first in NATO then more dramatically within the context of the newly developing European Union and its defence initiatives. This book addresses crucial issues between Greece and Turkey from a crucial perspective.

Following three major earthquakes on both sides of the Aegean, the two countries have now experienced a public empathy towards each other and a significant diplomatic rapprochement. This agreement though has failed to resolve the Cyprus conflict, and is now at risk of reverting back to a series of conflicts. This book provides an up-to-date assessment of the current state of the Greek-Turkish rapprochement and its future development.

Greek-Turkish Relations in an Era of Détente will be essential reading for students and academics in the fields of politics and international relations, and in particular, those interested in EU enlargement and Turkish and Greek foreign policy.

This is a special issue of the journal *Turkish Studies*.

Ali Çarkoğlu is associate professor in the Faculty of Arts and Social Sciences at Sabancı University, Istanbul. His areas of research include voting behaviour, political parties, public opinion and Turkey-EU relations. He is the co-author, with Mine Eder and Kemal Kirişci, of *The Political Economy of Cooperation in the Middle East* (1998), and the co-editor, with Barry Rubin, of *Turkey and the European Union, Domestic Politics, Economic Integration and International Dynamics* (2003).

Barry Rubin is the director of the Global Research in International Affairs Center and of its Turkish Studies Institute (TSI). He is the editor of the journals *Turkish Studies* and the *Middle East Review of International Affairs*. His publications include *The Tragedy of the Middle East* (2002) and *Anti-American Terrorism and the Middle East* (2002). His most recent book is *Yasir Arafat: A political Biography* (2003).

GREEK-TURKISH RELATIONS IN AN ERA OF DÉTENTE

Edited by
Ali Çarkoğlu and Barry Rubin

Routledge
Taylor & Francis Group

LONDON AND NEW YORK

First published 2005 by Routledge
2 Park Square, Milton Park, Abingdon, Oxon, OX14 4RN

Simultaneously published in the USA and Canada
by Routledge
270 Madison Ave, New York, NY 10016

Routledge is an imprint of the Taylor & Francis Group

© 2005 Routledge

Typeset by Genesis Typesetting Ltd., Laser Quay, Rochester, Kent

British Library Cataloguing in Publication Data
A catalogue record for this book available from the British Library

Library of Congress Cataloging in Publication Data

A catalog record for this book has been requested

ISBN: 978-0-7146-8573-1

CONTENTS

Contents

NOTES ON CONTRIBUTORS

Othon Anastasakis is director of the South East European Studies Programme, St. Antony's College, University of Oxford. He received his BA in Economics from the University of Athens, his MA in Comparative Politics and International Relations from Columbia University, New York and his Ph.D. in Comparative Government from the London School of Economics. Previously, he was research fellow at the London School of Economics, Expert and Advisor on European Union matters at the Greek Ministry of Foreign Affairs, and taught at the National School of Administration in Athens.

Ali Çarkoğlu is currently an associate professor at the Faculty of Arts and Social Sciences in Sabancı University, Istanbul. He received his Ph.D. at Binghamton University-State University of New York in 1993. He co-authored *The Political Economy of Cooperation in the Middle East* with Mine Eder and Kemal Kirişci (1998), and recently co-edited *Turkey and the European Union: Domestic Politics, Economic Integration and International Dynamics* (2003) with Barry Rubin.

Ahmet O. Evin, a member of the Istanbul Policy Center, teaches at Sabancı University, Istanbul where he was the founding dean of the Faculty of Arts and Social Sciences. He previously taught at Bilkent University, Ankara where he headed the Department of Political Science and Public Administration.

Kostas Ifantis is an associate professor of International Relations at the University of Athens and a Visiting Fellow at ELIAMEP, Athens. In 2002 he was Fulbright Visiting Scholar at the J.F. Kennedy School of Government, Harvard University. He edited *Greek-Turkish Relations in the 21st Century: Escaping from the Security Dilemma in the Aegean* with Mustafa Aydin (forthcoming in 2004).

Kemal Kirişci is a professor at the Department of Political Science and International Relations at Boğaziçi University, Istanbul and holds a Jean Monnet Chair in European Integration. He received his Ph.D. from City University, London in 1986. He has published extensively in journals including *International Migration, Middle Eastern Studies* and *International Journal of Refugee Law*. His most recent book, co-authored with Barry Rubin, is *Turkey in World Politics, An Emerging Multiregional Power* (2001).

Christos Kollias is an associate professor of Economics at the Department of Business Administration of the Technological Education Institute of Larissa, Greece. He has previously held posts as a research fellow at the Centre of Planning and Economic Research, Athens (1995–98) and as an adjunct assistant professor at the Department of Economics, University of Crete (1994–95), where he has also taught as an adjunct lecturer (1992–94). He is the author of two books (in Greek), co-editor of two volumes, and has published papers in collective volumes and journals on issues of defense and public sector economics and Greek-Turkish bilateral relations.

Gülay Günlük-Şenesen is currently a member of the Faculty of Political Sciences, Istanbul University, Turkey. She received her BA and MA degrees in Economics from Boğaziçi University, and her Ph.D. from Istanbul Technical University. Her major areas of research are defense economics, input-output models and gender issues.

Ahmet Sözen was born in Cyprus and received his Ph.D. in Political Science from the University of Missouri-Columbia. During 1994 he was involved in conflict-resolution workshops organized by the Cambridge Management Group in association with the Harvard Negotiation Project, and became a trainer. Currently, he teaches at the Political Science and International Relations department in the University of Bahcesehir, Istanbul, and is the director of the Istanbul Strategic Research Center (ISTAM).

Introduction

BARRY RUBIN

In a world full of crises and problems, few seemed less solvable than the Greek-Turkish conflict. After all, this was not only an old and bitter quarrel, but it involved many different issues. Aside from historic mistrust, there existed the Cyprus and Aegean questions, for which no compromises appeared likely.

Suddenly, however, this historic rivalry seemed to melt away. The ostensible occasion were the earthquakes suffered by each country, which gave the opportunity to send condolences and material aid. Yet the real factor behind this dramatic shift was a rethinking of historic Greek policy by the government in Athens.

Rather than use the conflict for demagogic purposes, as had been pursued by predecessor politicians, Greece had undergone a major change in its thinking. A better future lay neither with international posturing nor by mobilizing popular support by stirring up passions about the Turkish threat. Rather, the strategy was to downplay these old, profitless quarrels and turn one's face towards a European future. Greece's success would rest on integration with Europe and economic achievement.

This was, to say the least, a mature decision—and one well worthy of emulation elsewhere—based on putting the needs and interests of the Greek people first. For its part, Turkey was quite ready to take a similar course, made easier for Ankara by the fact that in both cases, the Aegean and Cyprus, it had possession of the territory under dispute.

What Greece did have, however, was its position as the gatekeeper that could keep Turkey out of the European Union (EU). On this point, too, Greece changed its tactics, ending a previous policy of making Turkish membership more difficult. Now, the argument was that if Turkey was part of the EU it would moderate its behavior in a way consistent with Greek interests. At the same time, Greece advocated early membership for the Greek-controlled republic of Cyprus as a major benefit for its co-ethnics there, and perhaps also as a way of putting additional pressure on Turkey to agree to a solution for the divided island.

The détente policy between the two countries, therefore, did not lead to the instant solution of their disputes and problems, but it did suggest a healthier, more mutually beneficial arrangement of priorities. The shift in Greek-Turkish relations is a useful development to study, both because of its intrinsic importance but also as a useful case of conflict resolution initiated by local parties based on a clear vision that the struggle no longer serves their interests. Of course, the relevant issues are also going to be important questions for future European and EU politics as well as for US foreign policy and a range of other considerations. This is the subject of this special issue of Turkish Studies—"Greek-Turkish Relations in an Era of Détente."

One of the most important elements in Greek-Turkish relations is that of US policy, which has sought to reduce the conflict but has often tilted towards the Turkish side. US policy has viewed the conflict as a waste of effort in view of far more important priorities—historically the US-USSR conflict and more recently US efforts against radical and terror-supporting states in the Middle East. Kostas Ifantis provides an analysis of current US policy in the region in "Strategic Imperatives and Regional Upheavals: On the US Factor in Greek-Turkish Relations."

We also consider the major new potential conflict in their bilateral relations: the two countries' diametrically opposed views of the Balkan situation. In the conflicts in Bosnia-Herzgovina and Kosovo, Greece supported Christian, Slavic Yugoslavia while Turkey backed the Muslim, Turkic Bosnians and Kosovars. In contrast to other questions, this division placed Turkey on the side of the European (and American) policies and Greece into an opposing position. The issue is explored by Othon Anastasakis in "Greece and Turkey in the Balkans: Cooperation or Rivalry?"

Ahmet Sözen looks at the major single issue that continues to create Greek-Turkish friction, assessing the various attempts to solve the thorny Cyprus conflict in "A Model of Power-Sharing: From the 1959 London-Zurich Agreements to the Annan Plan." Two contributions examine the military budgets of the two countries regarding their responses to past frictions and current détente. Gülay Günlük-Şenesen provides "An Analysis of the Action-Reaction Behavior in the Defense Expenditures of Turkey and Greece," while Christos Kollias focuses on "Greek Defense Spending in Perspective."

Two other contributions tackle the all-important question of mutual perceptions, with Ahmet Evin considering "Changing Greek Perspectives on Turkey: An Assessment of the post-Earthquake Rapprochement" and Ali Çarkoğlu and Kemal Kirişci studying "The View from Turkey:

Perceptions of Greeks and Greek-Turkish Rapprochement by the Turkish Mass Public." Ali Çarkoğlu also provides a concluding look at these issues.

We hope that these essays provide a revealing and original glimpse of Greek-Turkish relations at a moment of relative détente and cooperation, while also showing the remaining issues of contention, which might derail this welcome era. This volume is in itself an example of amicable Greek-Turkish cooperation and we wish to thank all those involved in it. This work is based on cooperation between the Global Research in International Affairs (GLORIA) Center's Turkish Studies Institute and the Turkish Economic and Social Studies Foundation (*Türkiye Ekonomik ve Sosyal Etüdler Vakfı*—TESEV) and on a workshop on the topic held at Sabancı University. We wish to thank all those involved in both institutions and especially Ali Çarkoğlu of Sabancı University and Elisheva Rosman, Özgül Erdemli and Ehud Waldoks of the GLORIA Center.

The current work is a special issue of *Turkish Studies* and, given the importance of the issues under discussion here, is also being published in book form (thanks are due to Ahmet Dalmann and Ufuk İlman of *Hürriyet* for helping us locate the cover image). We also would like to thank Vicky Johnson of Frank Cass for her assistance in publishing this project.

Changing Greek Perspectives on Turkey: An Assessment of the post-Earthquake Rapprochement

AHMET O. EVİN

Since 1999, Greek-Turkish relations appear to have undergone a positive change. A wave of sympathy in Greece for the victims of the Izmit-Gölcük earthquake of August 17, 1999, and the swift response to the disaster by the Greek government, as well as nongovernmental relief organizations, received broad media coverage in Turkey and gave rise to a warm sense of appreciation in Turkey. Less than a month later, the Turkish side responded in kind. The rescue work by Turkish relief organizations—notably the highly professional voluntary group, AKUT—was greatly appreciated in Greece in the aftermath of the September 7, 1999, Athens earthquake. Once again, broad media coverage in both countries reflected and reinforced a strong sense of mutual sympathy. It seems that Greek-Turkish relations took an unprecedented turn in the wake of the earthquakes that hit both sides of the Aegean.

Was it, in fact, the earthquakes that engendered a fundamental change in Greek perceptions of Turkey and the Turks? Or, did the earthquakes merely constitute catalysts for precipitating a significant process of change, the time for which had come? Indeed, there had been a significant but modest move towards a Greek-Turkish rapprochement prior to the 1999 earthquakes. Nonetheless, it was after the seismic disasters that the relations took a significant turn for the better. Yet, the question remains whether the post-1999 rapprochement does represent an irreversible process of change and an increasing improvement of relations between the neighbors.

It is with the foregoing questions in mind that an assessment will be made in this essay of the recent rapprochement between Greece and Turkey, with a particular emphasis on the nature of the changes in Greek perceptions of Turkey. The changes in outlook as well as policy will be considered against the historical background of Greek-Turkish relations.

An attempt will be made to project a realistic perspective on the basis of the progress achieved thus far in the process of rapprochement as well as the challenges that remain to be addressed.

A SHARED HISTORY

Greece and Turkey, chiefly due to historical reasons, pose a particularly difficult set of problems for each other. Turks and Greeks shared the same geographical area for a millennium, but their coexistence in that space does not seem to have resulted in a positive memory of a mutual experience.[1] To the contrary, a deep feeling of adversity seems to have permeated relations between the two countries ever since Greece's independence at the beginning of the nineteenth century.

Paradoxically, it is their shared history that has separated Greeks and Turks from one another, a shared history that has been remembered and interpreted in a widely divergent manner on opposite sides of the Aegean Sea. After Greek independence, formally recognized in 1832, Ottoman rule came to be increasingly viewed as a period of unrelenting oppression during which Greek culture, identity and national expression was repressed and frozen in time. It is true that Greek independence was achieved after eight years of struggle to overthrow what the Greeks have called *Tourkokratia*, a word that refers to Ottoman rule over Greece with the connotation of repressive dominance.[2] But the social mobilization that accompanied the nation-building program of the Greek state propagated the notion of "four hundred years of Turkish yoke," during which the history of Hellenic peoples was perceived to have come to a standstill— only to be animated after their liberation.[3] Greek nationalism, reinforced by the revolutionary ardor of the romantic era, thus rejected even the possibility of a shared history with Turkey and, in the process, successfully suppressed memories of any common experience. This included, for example, the common experience of taking part, with Turks as well as other Christian-born subjects, in no less an important vocation than imperial administration. The leaders of the Greek independence movement, be they the warriors themselves or their intellectual supporters, had every reason to obliterate the memory of the Greek elites who had served as members of Ottoman ruling classes, while at the same time they had good reason to perpetuate vivid memories of the Greek Church in captivity and of the Greek community's valiant struggle to free itself from the cruel Ottoman overlords.

For the Turks, on the other hand, Greek independence represented the beginning of what would become the traumatic experience of losing an empire. The Greeks were the first of the Ottoman subject peoples to gain full independence, which, in itself, had far reaching consequences insofar as Ottoman reforms and modernization were concerned. Because their loyalty came to be suspect, the Phanariot Greeks,[4] for example, who had been entrusted with handling the Empire's foreign relations, were replaced with Turks who were given a Western education expressly for the purpose of preparing them to serve in those positions for which the Ottomans had customarily recruited non-Muslims.

While Greek independence did not detract from the Turkish ruling elite's commitment to Ottomanism, it nevertheless resulted in a somewhat unclear and confusing perception of the Greek Orthodox *millet*—both as Ottoman subjects and subjects of a separate sovereign state that claimed Ottoman territory. Throughout the remainder of the nineteenth century, Turkish reformers sought the means to sustain Ottoman cosmopolitanism through establishing a strong, centralized modern state and then legitimizing that state by proclaiming it to be a constitutional monarchy.[5] For their part, the founders of the independent Greek state focused on instilling a strong sense of national identity, not only in the subjects of the new independent state but also in the Greek peoples throughout the Ottoman Empire. It was during the debates leading to the promulgation of the 1844 Constitution that the phrase *Megali Idea* (the Great Idea) was coined; it soon came to be adopted as the fundamental principle of the modern Greek state, as well as the overriding goal of all Hellenes. That goal was none other than to unify the Greek populations throughout the Ottoman domains by freeing the entire Hellenic homeland from Turkish occupation.

Turkish reformers received a rude awakening only after the full impact of Balkan nationalism was sustained and the Ottoman territories in Europe were lost one after the other in rapid succession until the Empire finally collapsed at the end of the First World War. By that time, Turkish nationalism had come to replace the frustrated goal of pan-Ottoman cosmopolitanism, and the Turkish nationalists came to associate their "shared history" with deception and betrayal on the part of the Greek subjects of the Ottoman Empire.

The Greek designs on Turkey, as exemplified particularly by the Greek occupation of the Aegean region after the First World War, made an indelible mark on the Turkish collective memory. While Greece has not posed a serious security threat to Turkey since 1923, a deep-seated suspicion of Greek motives has continued to influence Turkish perceptions. The *Megali Idea* has remained a Turkish obsession in the same way that Turkish rule has remained a Greek one, still remembered as "four hundred years of slavery." Its lasting impact on the Turkish psyche derives from its powerful association with the dismemberment of the Ottoman Empire, a traumatic experience that for many Turks still serves as a good reason for being suspicious of other nations' intentions. The partitioning of Turkey after the First World War according to the 1920 Sèvres Treaty and the subsequent occupation of Western Anatolia by the Greeks in pursuit of the *Megali Idea*, served to reconfirm Turkish suspicions and led to the so-called "Sèvres syndrome," a widely shared belief that the partitioning of Turkey reflected Europe's territorial ambitions.

Instead of fostering a cosmopolitan understanding between them, the long familiarity between Greeks and Turks resulted more in a mutual sense of suspicion and mistrust that has continued to affect the foreign policy considerations of both Athens and Ankara. The obsessive lack of confidence between the parties has created—and continues to create— significant constraints on the formulation and conduct of a coherent foreign policy. As a result, the bilateral relations between these countries emerge as an independent variable within the broader foreign policy objectives of each country.

In the recent past, Turkey has suspected that Greek intentions were to constrain and isolate Turkey politically and geostrategically, and attempt to diminish its international importance. Indeed, throughout most of the 1990s, after a brief period of détente, Greek policy towards Turkey was one of containment that included keeping Turkey out of the European Union (EU). Turkish suspicions, furthermore, were largely proven correct when the fugitive PKK leader Abdullah Öcalan was apprehended in the Greek ambassador's residence in Nairobi. Insofar as Turkish public opinion was concerned, that scandal proved conclusively the Greek government's complicity in supporting the separatist aims of a terrorist organization. Greece was perceived as assisting in the dismemberment of the modern Turkish state, just as it had done during the period of Ottoman dissolution.

Greek suspicions of Turkey, on the other hand, were grounded in the apprehension of its larger and militarily stronger neighbor. The 1974 Turkish intervention in Cyprus had revived the notions of Ottoman domination and the Turk as the violent oppressor of the Greek population of Cyprus. Since the 1960s, practically all Greek governments were guided by a similar consideration in actively opposing US and NATO (North Atlantic Treaty Organization) military assistance to Turkey.[6]

A significant similarity between Greece and Turkey is that the foreign policies of both countries with respect to one another have been highly influenced by popular and populist constraints as well as public opinion. Perceptions based on selective memory and, particularly in the case of Greece, emotions have guided not only policy but also tactical responses—with altogether disappointing results. Until recently, the burden of history prevented a fresh start in building a constructive relationship that would benefit both countries.

THE RAPPROCHEMENT

The events of 1999, it seems, have finally signaled a new beginning for Greek-Turkish relations. The radical change, particularly on the Greek side, could not have been precipitated by the earthquakes alone. The process of rapprochement, then, began before the earthquakes. On May 30, 1999, the foreign ministers of Greece and Turkey, Andreas Papandreu and Ismail Cem, met in New York and set concrete, uncontroversial and achievable targets for cooperation in the fields of culture, education, commerce and tourism.[7] The meeting was arranged in response to Turkish Foreign Minister Cem's letter of May 24, 1999, to Papandreu, proposing cooperation against terrorism. But the real turning point in the relations between the two countries, according to several observers, "was the capture in 1999 of Abdullah Öcalan" in Kenya.[8] The Greek government wished to distance itself from the scandalous circumstances of Mr Öcalan's apprehension and it did not want to be perceived internationally as a supporter of terrorism against a NATO ally. For Greece, improving relations with Turkey was an effective and appropriate way out of the quagmire. NATO intervention in Kosovo also provided opportunities for cooperation.

The earthquakes did not mark the beginning of the new détente, but they served to reinforce and accelerate the careful, well-orchestrated, but nevertheless self-conscious process of gradual rapprochement that had already been set in motion. The disasters served to focus attention on their shared geography and shared feelings of sympathy, and led to an understanding of a common destiny. They constituted effective catalysts for helping to break away from ideologically defined roles. The sustained state of tension that had continued since the Imia/Kardak crisis of 1996 gave way to euphoria.[9]

To what extent was that feeling of euphoria a harbinger of subsequent developments between the two countries? Today, four years after the earthquakes, there are planes full of people flying between Athens and Istanbul. The increased traffic—as a result of official and unofficial meetings, student exchange programs, joint research projects and tourism—points to a significant interest, among both peoples, in achieving a greater degree of familiarity with their neighboring society. This beehive type of activity, actively supported by international organizations as well as foundations, is said to reflect "a positive entrapment," which, by its very nature, will not permit relations to slide back into a state of polarized animosity.

Although optimists are prepared to claim that Greek-Turkish relations have been liberated from their historical and cultural constraints of mutual suspicion, skeptics convincingly question whether such deep-seated perceptions can be fundamentally changed within just a few years. There is no doubt that significant progress has been made since 1999 towards establishing a positive climate of cooperation, but significant challenges nevertheless remain in the way of achieving a sustainable and lasting détente.

PROGRESS ACHIEVED

The key accomplishment in this period of rapprochement has been the achievement of a spirit of cooperation and positive dialogue. On an official level, the meeting in 1999 between the two foreign ministers—the first one in 40 year—constituted a significant beginning. Since then, ministerial-level meetings and consultations between Greek and Turkish political leaders have become commonplace. Cooperation among local governments and municipalities, as well as higher educational institutions and voluntary organizations, has almost reached saturation point. The public opinion on both sides has benefited from increased cooperation among journalists; impartial media coverage has significantly contributed towards a common understanding of bilateral issues. Cultural exchanges, furthermore, have served to enhance the quality of communication—as well as the understanding—between the parties. The political dialogue and cultural exchanges have been paralleled by increased interest in economic cooperation among businessmen and bankers—the result of which will be assessed in a separate section below.

Intensified cooperation at the informal, nongovernmental and professional levels has led to increasing openness, frankness and ease in carrying out discussions between the parties. Collegial dialogue is no longer confined to Chatham House-type of private, closed-door meetings or networks of Track II diplomacy. The fact that multiple networks are now operational, that their meetings are open to media coverage and that they attract official support would seem to indicate that the influence of ideological constraints is diminishing and no longer interfering in civic cooperation. Concomitantly, the constructive involvement of the media, as mentioned above, has led to a broader space for collegial debate. More significantly, the influence of populist views seems to have diminished in the public opinion, leaving room for political decisionmakers to take realistic steps towards rapprochement. Turkish political leaders, for example, have responded favorably to proposals for initiating and expanding confidence-building measures.

Despite the broad differences of opinion with respect to the two most complex bilateral issues—Cyprus and the Aegean—official Greek policy towards Turkey has radically changed. Greek foreign policy statements have assumed a distinctly positive tone regarding neighborly relations with Turkey, while, since the 1999 Helsinki European Council, the Greek government, particularly the foreign ministry, has been consistently supportive of Turkey's EU candidacy.

CHALLENGES TO THE RAPPROCHEMENT

However, serious challenges remain to be addressed. Prior to the rapprochement, Greek-Turkish disputes centered around four major points of contention: The Aegean Sea; the Cyprus question; the status of ethnic minorities in Western Thrace; and Greek official action within the EU. Of these four issues, the latter two have been resolved since the rapprochement, but the first two remain and still carry the potential to sour relations, or, worse, to reverse the current spirit of cooperation.

First, regarding the Aegean disputes, Turkey places the blame squarely on Greece for obstructing a resolution founded on a mutual understanding based on respect for international treaties. The Greek policies, Turkey claims, evince a strong tendency to view the eastern Aegean as a Greek sea, in total disregard of Turkey's rights and interests as one of the two coastal states. Ankara's understanding, based on the *status quo* established by the 1923 Lausanne Peace Treaty, is that the bilateral Turco-Greek relationship in the Aegean Sea must be guided by three cardinal principles: 1) the Aegean is a common sea between the two countries; 2) the freedom of the high seas, and that of the air space above it, should be respected in accordance with point 1; 3) any extension of territorial waters by any party should be based on mutual consent between the parties and should be implemented in a fair and equitable fashion.

The basic premise of the Lausanne Treaty, according to Ankara, is to grant the coastal states limited areas of maritime jurisdiction and leave the remaining part of the Aegean for the common benefit of both countries. Although the continental shelf concept had not been foreseen in 1923, the

Lausanne Treaty—by virtue of establishing a political balance between Greece and Turkey and harmonizing the vital interests of both parties—claimed to provide an appropriate guideline for establishing an overall equilibrium of rights and interests in the Aegean Sea.[10]

Turkey's position is that an equitable delimitation agreement must be reached between the two parties by means of dialogue and negotiation in order to satisfy the security and economic interests of both parties in the Aegean Sea. As further evidence of legal support for its position, Turkey refers to a 1982 decision by the International Court of Justice (ICJ), which states that "delimitation is to be effected by agreement in accordance with equitable principles and taking into account all relevant circumstances."[11] Greece, however, also refers to the same decision of the ICJ to reject Turkey's pleading of special circumstances that prevail in the Aegean and argument that the continental shelf rights of the mainland extend into the Aegean Sea. Greece believes that the delimitation of the continental shelf rights of the Aegean islands would cede sovereign rights to Turkey to the west of several Greek islands, thus enclosing those islands in a Turkish jurisdiction zone.[12]

Two other major issues concerning the Aegean dispute are those related to territorial waters and airspace. Under the present six-mile limit, Greek territorial waters comprise approximately 43.5 percent of the Aegean Sea; Turkey's share amounts to 7.5 percent; international waters comprise 49 percent. If Greece were to expand its territorial waters to 12 miles, it would acquire sovereign rights over 71.5 percent of the Aegean, while the proportion of international waters would decrease to 19.7 percent. In the event of a 12-mile limit, Turkish territorial waters in the Aegean would merely increase to 8.8 percent of the Aegean Sea.

As far as the airspace issue is concerned, Turkey objects to what it sees as a deliberate Greek policy of limiting freedom of flight for Turkish military aircraft in international airspace over the Aegean. Greece's continued insistence in seeking submission of flight plans by military aircraft to the Greek government, Turkey argues, is in contravention of international law—specifically of Article 3, paragraph (a) of the Chicago Convention, which specifies that "the Convention shall be applicable only to civil aircraft and shall not be applicable to state aircraft."[13] Greece's definition of a ten-mile sovereign airspace over six-mile coastal waters also continues to be a source of serious friction. Although Turkey's refusal to accept Greece's claim of a ten-mile airspace is consistent with international agreements on this subject, movements of Turkish military aircraft within the ten-mile airspace are recorded as violations by Greece. Furthermore, Greece perceives such Turkish flights over the Aegean as deliberate acts of aggression for the purpose of intimidation.

Finally, Turkey also objects to what it describes as the Greek lack of respect for the demilitarized status of the Aegean islands. Turkey claims that this is in direct contravention of the legal and contractual obligations of Greece as stipulated in Article 14 of the 1949 Paris Treaty, which states that "these islands shall be and remain demilitarized."[14]

On the second point of contention, the Cyprus question, the Republic of Cyprus (RoC) was established in 1960 on the basis of the 1959 Zurich and 1960 London Agreements. The island's transition from a colony to a republic, however, did not lead to the formation of a fully independent, sovereign state. The tutelary rights of Great Britain, Greece and Turkey over Cyprus were enshrined in the 1960 London Agreement, which gave all three signatories powers as guarantors. Cyprus' very treaty of independence reinforced the special relationships Greece and Turkey had with their corresponding ethnic constituencies on the island.

Well before the island gained its independence, the Cyprus issue had become a popular and, worse, a populist, issue in the domestic political agendas of both Greece and Turkey. Greek activists and extremists called for *enosis* (union) of the island with Greece, while Turkish popular sentiments were reflected in the slogan "either division [of the island] or death." Moreover, Turkey was alarmed by the vulnerability of the Turkish Cypriots, who comprised approximately one-fifth of the island's population in 1960. The continued guerilla activity by *Ethnikí Orgánosis Kipriakoú Agónos* (EOKA—National Organization of Cypriot Struggle),[15] the paramilitary force headed by General Theodoros Georgios Grivas—a fanatic *enosis* supporter, was followed by the destabilization of the island's fragile political order and the *de facto* separation of the Turkish community from the Greek majority in 1960.

While Turkey nearly intervened in events on Cyprus in 1964 and 1967, Ankara eventually did so after seeing its worst fears of *enosis* confirmed in the 1974 *coup d'etat* masterminded by Athens and carried out by a fanatic Greek Cypriot, Nicos Samson. In Turkey, *enosis* was powerfully associated with the *Megali Idea* and, hence, with a Greek plan for ethnic cleansing. The 1974 intervention, Turkey believed, was not only justified on a humanitarian basis to protect a kindred group from extermination but was also firmly based on treaty rights accorded to Turkey as a guarantor power. This intervention by Turkey led to a *de facto* partitioning of the island; the northern part, separated from the rest of the island by a Turkish military presence, declared independence in 1983 as the Turkish Republic of Northern Cyprus (TRNC). The TRNC, however, is not recognized by any government or international organization other than Turkey and it is politically and economically dependent on Ankara.[16]

Shortly after the 1974 intervention, the so-called colonels' junta that had been ruling in Greece collapsed and Greece returned to democracy. Greece's political stability was ensured with its accession in 1981 to the European Economic Community (EEC), as the European Union was then named. These fundamental changes had little impact on Greek-Turkish relations and no impact on the Greek or Turkish policy regarding Cyprus. Turkey justified its Cyprus policy and defended the legitimacy of its 1974 intervention on the basis of the 1959 Zurich and 1960 London Agreements. Basing its case on the same agreements, Turkey has also been arguing that Cyprus cannot join any international political or economic union of which both Turkey and Greece are not members.

Political developments in Europe, notably the emphasis on the consolidation of democracy in the context of the EEC's southern enlargement in the 1980s and the corresponding changes in international public opinion, place the Cyprus situation in a different light. The fact that the TRNC failed to achieve international recognition significantly detracted from Turkey's arguments in defense of its military presence in northern Cyprus as the only means to protect the Turkish Cypriots from harm. As a result, in the eyes of European public opinion, the Turkish presence in Cyprus increasingly came to be viewed as a military occupation. Turkey, meanwhile, continued to maintain the *status quo* while arguing that an agreement between two equal, sovereign states in Cyprus would be the key to achieving a lasting solution.

The formal accession of Cyprus to the EU in May 2004 changes fundamentally the circumstances of the dispute.[17] All arguments in favor of the *status quo* have lost their relevance with the EU's decision to admit Cyprus as a member state with or without a settlement with Turkey and the unification of the island. Therefore, if the entry of Cyprus into the EU is a blatant violation of the 1959–60 agreements, as Turkey claims, would the Turkish troops on the island, after the accession, constitute a Turkish military occupation of EU territory, as several European observers have suggested? The Turkish reaction to Cyprus' membership would have been stronger had it not been for the fact that Turkey was formally given candidate status at the 1999 Helsinki European Council with active support from the Greek government and that Turkey had redefined its relations with Greece as "one of close cooperation, alliance and confidence."[18]

The Cyprus dilemma encapsulates all of the historical and cultural factors that have affected Greek-Turkish relations. At the root of the Turkish objections to the Annan Plan lie deep suspicions regarding Greek and European motives for the EU enlargement into the eastern

Mediterranean.[19] Turkish public opinion is divided on this issue, with the hardliners claiming that Europe will pursue its own strategic interests at the expense of those of Turkey. Active supporters of Turkey's EU membership, on the other hand, have little reason to perceive the EU as an adversary—a potential threat to Turkey's security interests in the region— and would like to see progress towards the settlement of the Cyprus issue.

With respect to this issue, Turkey's stated objective has been the achievement of a bi-communal and bi-zonal federal settlement, based on the sovereign equality of the Turkish and Greek Cypriot states. The Turkish position has been that a just and lasting settlement of the Cyprus issue can be achieved through negotiations between the Turkish and Greek Cypriot peoples; Greece's official position is that a lasting solution must provide for "the establishment of a federal, bi-zonal and bi-communal state, with a single sovereignty and international personality, as well as a single citizenship."[20]

Turkish suspicions center on the fear of the dilution of Turkish identity on the island in the event of unification, a position held by the present leadership of the TRNC but eschewed by the opposition. Turkish liberals point out that the Annan Plan puts forth a positive framework for reaching a fair and equitable solution, especially since it addresses all of the important issues raised by Turkey since 1974. They also agree with EU observers and experts that reaching a negotiated settlement prior to Cyprus' entry into the EU would be of greater benefit to Turkish Cypriots because derogations from Community Law that would be embodied in the Treaty of Accession at their request would provide for long-term guarantees for the Turkish community in Cyprus.[21]

However, neither the president of the TRNC nor Turkish policymakers in general are convinced of the benefit of reaching an agreement. As recently as August 2003, Turkey was moving to reinforce its special relationship with the TRNC, proposing a plan, for instance, to establish a customs union with the TRNC—which would contravene Turkey's agreements with the EU and adversely affect relations between them.[22]

While the Aegean and, particularly, the Cyprus disputes continue to present formidable challenges in the way of complete normalization of relations between Greece and Turkey, these challenges are not insurmountable. Both of these issues, it is understood, will cease to exist once Cyprus, Greece and Turkey become EU member states. The lingering doubt that also detracts from the full force of Turkey's political commitment to EU membership is: will Turkey be left out after "allowing a unified Cyprus in"? The question is one as much of realpolitik as perception and imagination. The essential first step to reach a lasting solution is to imagine Turkey as an EU member state, a step that seems to have been taken by Athens, if not by Greek public opinion yet. That step requires a mental exercise that must be urgently undertaken by Ankara as well as the major Western European capitals.

ECONOMIC FACTORS

The evolving economic relations between Turkey and Greece are often taken as a litmus test indicating the degree of political stability achieved in the process of détente. Since 1999 there has been a significant increase in business contacts between the two countries and a corresponding eagerness in both the Greek and Turkish business communities to expand trade and seek cross-border investment opportunities, as well as to enter into joint venture arrangements. The Greek-Turkish Business Forum has been actively promoting economic cooperation and partnership among small- and medium-sized businesses as well as major companies.

As Turkey's richest neighbor with the highest per capita income and correspondingly developed consumer orientation, Greece offers significant opportunities for Turkish exporters. Indeed, Turkish exports to Greece have been consistently increasing. In the four years from 1999 to 2002, for example, annual Greek imports from Turkey increased by 55 percent. The rapprochement, however, cannot be said to have influenced the pattern of trade between the two countries. In fact, Greece's imports from Turkey increased faster in the mid-1990s than after 1999: in the four-year period 1994 to 1998, Turkish exports to Greece increased by 119 percent (see Table 1).

Likewise, Greek exports to Turkey do not seem to have been affected by political relations between the two countries. Significant increases in Turkish imports at times when the Turkish lira has been overvalued have been followed by a sharp fall in the value of Greek imports at times of crisis and devaluation in Turkey. The overall trade balance between the two countries reflects a significant surplus in favor of Turkey.

From a realistic perspective, however, the trade between the two countries does not appear to be significant for the economy of either country. Over the past four years, for example, trade with Greece has represented around one percent of Turkey's total foreign trade, whereas trade with EU member states represented roughly half of Turkey's total imports and exports. Given the lower volume of Greece's overall foreign trade as compared to that of Turkey, trade with Turkey represented around five percent of Greece's total imports and exports in any given year. In 2000, for example, in comparison to Greece's total foreign trade of 15,221

TABLE 1
TURKEY-GREECE FOREIGN TRADE (MILLION USD)

Year	Exports	Imports	Surplus/Deficit	Volume	Exp/Imp
1994	168.7	105.1	63.6	273.8	1.6
1995	209.9	200.7	9.2	410.6	1.0
1996	236.5	285.0	-48.5	521.5	0.8
1997	298.2	430.8	-132.6	729.0	0.7
1998	369.2	319.7	49.5	688.9	1.2
1999	406.8	303.0	103.8	709.8	1.3
2000	437.7	430.8	6.9	868.5	1.0
2001	476.1	266.3	209.8	742.4	1.8
2002	573.8	323.6	250.2	897.4	1.8

Source: State Institute of Statistics (*Devlet İstatistik Enstitüsu*—DIE).

million USD and Turkey's foreign trade of 82,278 million USD, the volume of trade between the two countries is a mere 868.5 million USD. Nor is there an established pattern of trade dependency between the two countries. Iron, steel and cotton, readily available from multiple sources, represent the main commodities of trade between Greece and Turkey (see Table 2).

The magnitude of cross-border investments is also modest when compared to the foreign direct investments both countries attract. However, there are increasing numbers of relatively small investments made by entrepreneurs eager to expand their operations to the neighboring

TABLE 2
TURKEY-GREECE FOREIGN TRADE BY SECTOR 2000–2

Exports	USD	%	Imports	USD	%
2000					
OVERALL	**437,725,190**	**100**	OVERALL	**430,812,980**	**100**
Iron and Steel	112,155,330	25.6	Cotton	153,450,282	35.6
Aviation	41,230,418	9.4	Mineral Fuel	131,394,402	30.5
Cotton	30,033,931	6.9	Plastics	26,273,499	6.1
2001					
OVERALL	**476,095,465**	**100**	OVERALL	**266,253,783**	**100**
Iron and Steel	127,736,415	26.8	Cotton	113,607,183	42.7
Cotton	28,583,284	6.0	Mineral Fuels	52,404,536	19.7
Cauldrons, Machines	27,797,961	5.8	Plastics	24,114,169	9.1
2002					
OVERALL	**573,787,151**	**100**	OVERALL	**323,627,497**	**100**
Iron and Steel	77,219,680	13.5	Cotton	117,922,024	36.4
Automotive and					
Related Industries	48,433,230	8.4	Plastics	47,538,182	14.7
Cauldrons, Machines	37,597,947	6.6	Mineral Fuels	29,648,649	9.2

Source: State Institute of Statistics (*Devlet İstatistik Enstitüsu*—DIE).

market. At the end of 2002, for example, there were 71 Greek companies operating in Turkey. The total capital investment made by these companies, less than 25 million USD, represents less than 0.5 percent of foreign direct capital investment in Turkey.

It was the Turkish capital markets that initially offered significant potential for major investments, particularly in the banking sector. The anticipated growth of the Turkish financial markets, and low equity pricing in the Istanbul Stock Exchange, began attracting private equity funding from Greece as early as 2000. Several Greek banks proceeded to set up joint-venture schemes or pursued other means to invest in the Turkish equity market in anticipation of regional economic integration now that political impediments to economic cooperation had been removed. However, the anticipated level of investment in this sector was not achieved, due to the acute economic crisis in which Turkey found itself early in the following year.

There is nevertheless significant potential for enhanced economic cooperation between Greece and Turkey. The 2001 Turkish economic crisis, it is hoped, was merely a temporary setback. Now that the banking sector has been disciplined and strengthened by an independent regulator, there exists even greater potential for Greek capital investment in Turkey. There is also ample room for profitable cooperation in the tourism sector, which has also been significantly affected in the past several years as a result of hostilities in the region. If Greece represents a rich consumer market, Turkey represents a very large one. Market integration on a regional scale will be the key for achieving enhanced economic benefits as well as sustained stability.

CONCLUSION

It could be said, in the final analysis, that there has been a fundamental change in the Greek outlook on Turkey, both at the official level and, perhaps to a lesser degree, in public opinion. This change is evidenced best by Greek support for Turkey's EU membership. This radical turnabout in the Greek policy pertaining to this issue reflects a sense of responsible realism more than a change of heart. The new generation of Greek political leaders has come to realize that a self-confident and stable Turkey as an ally would be in Greece's best interests. Moreover, Greece's new policy is rational, credible and convincing in that it is based on national interest.

The Greek leaders have gone a long way towards promoting Greece's long-term interests by adopting a strategy of engaging Turkey. Turkey isolated, as previous Greek governments would have liked to see it, would have remained in an adversarial position to Greece and would have continued to be perceived as a serious threat. Old scenarios based on perceived notions of national security did not look upon borders as a limitation but as a means of protection. In reality, however, keeping Turkey out of the EU would have placed Greece on the remote fringes of Europe. Bringing Turkey in, on the other hand, will serve to expand Greece's economic and geostrategic interests.

For these reasons, Greece is expected to continue supporting Turkey's European vocation. It was the self-confidence and sense of security that Greece was able to find as a result of its own EU membership that enabled it to begin a process of rapprochement with Turkey in the first place. EU membership led not only to a higher standard of living in Greece but also to a higher quality of life. A widespread appreciation of the quality of life brought to the forefront the need for promoting a positive environment at home and in the region rather than perpetuating and finding satisfaction in an atmosphere of tension and mistrust.

The key to Greece's rapprochement with Turkey, I would strongly argue, lies in the transition of Greek politics from a Hobbesian to a Lockean context rather than in seismic factors.[23] The most significant result of the rapprochement was the change in cultural perceptions. In supporting Turkey's EU candidacy, Greece admitted for the first time, if not Turkey's European identity then its compatibility with that identity. The greater emphasis now placed on the similarities rather than the differences between Greeks and Turks best exemplifies the progress made since the rapprochement.

NOTES

1. "Coexistence" refers to the sharing of a common geography with a minimum degree of cultural integration between separate communities that have, and wish to keep, their distinct ethnic, confessional, and/or cultural characteristics; my definition derives from H.R. Trevor-Roper, "A Case of Coexistence," *The New Statesman and Nation*, May 14, 1957.
2. "*Tourkokratia*" "covers a period of from four to six centuries, in some cases as early as the 1300s and as late as 1922, depending on which geographical area of Greece one has in mind. A more restricted version of this term can be applied to the period from 1453, when the Turks conquered Constantinople, to 1821, when the Greek War of Independence started." Vamik D. Volkan and Norman Itzkowitz, *Turks and Greeks: Neighbors in Conflict* (Huntington: Eothen, 1994), p.71.
3. See, for example, Richard Clogg, *A Concise History of Greece* (Cambridge: Cambridge University Press, 1992), pp.47–99.
4. The Phanariot elites were the lay officials and rich Greek families which surrounded the Patriarch of Constantinople. See Hugh Seton-Watson, *Nations and States: An Enquiry into the Origins of Nations and the Politics of Nationalism* (Boulder, CO: Westview Press, 1977), pp.110–17. The translators of the imperial Divan, who constituted an influential corps of Ottoman foreign service officials, were drawn from this elite circle: "This translatorship ... became a virtual monopoly of a coterie of Istanbul Greek families who retained their hold

from the mid-seventeenth century until 1821." Carter V. Findley, *Bureaucratic Reform in the Ottoman Empire* (Princeton, NJ: Princeton University Press, 1980), p.77. See also Steven Runciman, *The Great Church in Captivity: A Study of the Patriarchate of Constantinople from the Eve of the Turkish Conquest to the Greek War of Independence* (Cambridge: Cambridge University Press, 1968), pp.364–9.

5. "Ottoman cosmopolitanism" refers to the culturally integrated composition of the ruling classes co-opted from among Muslim and non-Muslim subjects who have undergone elite socialization. As loyal state elites, they would form a different class from that of the separate communities of subjects living in a state of coexistence.

6. The Greek opposition to US military assistance to Turkey was particularly effective in lobbying the US Congress. The Congress, for example, passed in December 1974 a rule of law amendment to the 1961 Foreign Assistance Act, against the recommendation of the administration—particularly that of Henry Kissinger, then Secretary of State. As a result, an arms embargo was placed on Turkey, effective from February 5, 1975, that lasted for three years. In addition, at the insistence of the US Congress, the appropriation of military funds for Greece and Turkey was for many years on a seven-to-ten ratio. The Turkish government has regarded this formula as inequitable given Turkey's population, six times that of Greece, and its correspondingly higher NATO commitments.

7. See Republic of Turkey, Ministry of Foreign Affairs website, Dış Politika, Türk-Yunan Ilişkileri (Foreign Policy, Turco-Greek Relations), <http://www.mfa.gov.tr/turkce/grupa/yunan.4.htm>.

8. S. Gülden Ayman, "Springtime in the Aegean," *Private View* (Spring 2000), p.56.

9. A crisis between Greek and Turkish naval forces appeared around the islet of Imia on January 27, 1996, when a group of Turkish journalists from the *Hürriyet* newspaper flew to the islet from Izmir by helicopter, took down the Greek flag raised there by the nearby island community of Kalymnos, and raised the Turkish flag. The newspaper published photographs from the mission. See "The Imia/Kardak Rocks Dispute in the Aegean Sea," *Boundary and Security Bulletin*, Vol.4, No.1 (April 1996–Jan. 1997).

10. According to international law, the Aegean Continental Shelf is comprised of the seabed and subsoil of the submarine areas that extend beyond the territorial seas of the two countries into the high seas. The Aegean high seas lie beyond Greece's and Turkey's territorial waters and are open to all states of the world. See "International Legal Status of the Aegean," <http://www.saeamerica.org/en/useful/aegean_issue/shelf.html>.

11. See "Case Concerning the Continental Shelf (Tunisia/Libyan Arab Jamahiriya)," *International Court of Justice Reports 1982*, <http://www.icj.law.gla.ac.uk/idecisions.htm>.

12. For further reading on the Aegean territorial waters and continental shelf, see Theodore C. Kariotis (ed.), *Greece and the Law of the Sea*, Aegean Institute of the Law of the Sea and Maritime Law (The Hague: Kluwer Law International, 1997), and Aldo Chircpo, Andre Gerolymatos and John O. Iatrides, *The Aegean Sea After the Cold War: Security and Law of the Sea Issues* (London: Macmillan, 2000). For a Greek view, see particularly Anastasia Strati, "Greece and the Law of the Sea: A Greek Perspective," in Chircpo *et al.* (2000), pp.89–102. For Turkish and Greek perspectives on issues such as the legal status of the Aegean islands, militarization of the islands, questions of the Dodecanese, rights concerning the continental shelf, territorial waters and airspace, see <http://www.turk-yunan.gen.tr/English/aegean/index.html> and <http://www.minpress.gr/aegean/english/index_uk.html>.

13. Chicago Convention on International Civil Aviation, signed on December 7, 1944; see <http://www.iasl.mcgill.ca/airlaw/public/chicago/chicago1944a.pdf>, Sept. 16, 2003.

14. The International Legal Status of the Aegean; see <http://www.idis.gr/people/arvan9.doc>.

15. "Underground nationalist movement of Greek Cypriots dedicated to the expulsion of the British from Cyprus (achieved in 1960) and the eventual union of Cyprus with Greece." See "EOKA," *Encyclopædia Britannica*.

16. F. Stephen Lerrabee and Ian O. Lesser, *Turkish Foreign Policy in an Age of Uncertainty* (Santa Monica, CA: Rand, 2003), p.78.

17. The Accession Treaty with respect to the ten new members was signed at the Athens Summit on April 16, 2003.

20   *Greek-Turkish Relations in an Era of Détente*

18. Republic of Turkey, Ministry of Foreign Affairs website, Turkish Foreign Policy, Greece, <http://www.mfa.gov.tr/grupg/gb/default.htm#GREECE>.

19. UN Secretary-General Kofi Annan's proposal to reunite the Greek and Turkish communities segregated for 30 years, creating a Swiss-style devolved government with broad and effective power-sharing. "Annan Plan For Cyprus Settlement Full Text," <http://www.tcea.org.uk/ Annan-Plan-For-Cyprus-Settlement.htm>.

20. Concerning the Greek policy, see Hellenic Republic, Ministry of Foreign Affairs website, Foreign Policy, South-Eastern Europe, The Cyprus Issue, "The Need to Find a Just, Viable Solution," <http://www.mfa.gr/english/foreign_policy/europe_southeastern/cyprus/viable_ solution.html>.

21. William Wallace, *Reconciliation in Cyprus: The Window of Opportunity*, Mediterranean Programme Report, Robert Schuman Centre for Advanced Studies (Florence: European University Institute, 2002), pp.9–10.

22. Customs Union Framework Agreement Signed Between Turkey and TRNC after the sixth meeting of the TRNC-Turkey Partnership Council on August 8, 2003, in Girne (Kyrenia). See Turkish Republic of North Cyprus website, <http://www.trncinfo.com/TANITMADAIRESI/ ARSIV2003/ENGLISHarcive/AUGUST/110803.htm>.

23. See Ali Çarkoğlu and Kemal Kirişçi, "The View from Turkey: Perceptions of Greeks and Greek-Turkish Rapprochement by the Turkish Mass Public," in this volume.

Strategic Imperatives and Regional Upheavals: On the US Factor in Greek-Turkish Relations

KOSTAS IFANTIS

The aim of this contribution is to evaluate the significance and the impact of the American grand strategic presence in the Greek-Turkish subregional system. It attempts to re-evaluate the course of relations between Washington, Athens and Ankara in the context of the post-September 11, 2001, and post-Second Gulf War international system. Recognizing the complexity of the relationships, the analytical focus highlights the variety of relevant actors and discusses their relative power and influence. This contribution emphasizes the security sphere within the context of four interlocking environments: the evolution of US foreign policy priorities and preferences, especially after the September 11 terrorist attacks; the individual bilateral arenas and their interlocking nature; the dynamic domestic political arenas, which are shaped by an aggregation of internal and external influences, the most important of which is the European Union (EU); and the wider global environment insofar as it impinges on the triangular relationship.

It is the combination of—and the interaction between—these four environments that underpins Turkish-US-Greek relations. The discussion deals, in turn, with identifying the fundamental characteristics of the triangle as they were shaped through post-Second World War history, with the focus on US-Greek and US-Turkish relations. Second, the analysis underlines the impact of the post-cold war and post-September 11 systemic change on the international and regional roles, positions and behavior of the three actors as well as on the transitional constellations of power, along with the nature of the issues that dominate the agenda and the resulting policy problems. Finally, the discussion attempts to assess the latest phase in the evolution of Turkish-US-Greek relations—the period marked by the end of the cold war as well as other (related) developments that have been shaping the international and regional strategic field, notably September 11 and its impact upon the United States. At the same time, Turkey's drive to join the EU and the 2003 American intervention in Iraq seemed to have influenced the triangular relationship heavily.

THE COLD WAR YEARS

In the aftermath of the Second World War, Greece and Turkey attracted Washington's attention almost simultaneously and because of similar strategic considerations, despite the fact that American perceptions of the two countries were quite different. Greece had been a wartime ally and had suffered gravely during the Nazi occupation, while Turkey had remained neutral. After the first skirmishes of the cold war, official US attitudes towards the two countries were dictated entirely by the assumptions and requirements of the containment doctrine. Both countries were considered vital and mutually reinforcing outposts of the Western security and defense structure that the United States was anxious to establish and lead.[1] At both the political and military level, the sense of unity of purpose was genuine, as was the desire to cooperate inside and outside of NATO (North Atlantic Treaty Organization). Moreover, Greek and Turkish leaders were keenly aware of their powerful patron. The result was often the appearance of servile behavior—especially in Athens—and the image of the United States bossing around its two junior partners.[2] Yet, beneath the surface, American relations with Greece and Turkey were never easy and were hindered almost from the onset by nationalist sensitivities and, from the 1950s onward, the growing feud over Cyprus. The failure of Washington to orchestrate and sustain a cooperative momentum between Athens and Ankara indicates that US leverage over the two was circumscribed throughout the cold war.[3] In the case of Greece, the year 1947 marked the beginning of an era in which the country was greatly, if not absolutely, dependent on the United States. Greek governments "in the 1947–55 period faced a condition of structural dependency *vis-à-vis* the United States that could be referred to as a patron-client relationship."[4] In the post-1974 period, the Cyprus crisis, the collapse of the military regime, EU membership and eight years of socialist government in the 1980s fundamentally altered the nature of the bilateral relationship.[5]

The 1974–81 New Democracy governments made a strategic decision to consolidate Greece's democratic institutions and to reformulate its long-range political, economic and security policies towards a European context in order to pave the way towards accession to the European Community (EC). Apart from the fact that EC membership served Greece both as a diplomatic lever and as a restraining mechanism, it also operated as a means of altering the nature of Greek-US relations from extremely hierarchical to a more balanced one. Europe offered a powerful alternative to Greek foreign policymakers and gradually led to the normalization of Greek-US relations through Greece's participation in the European integration process, particularly in a period during which Western Europe as a whole had been actively addressing the issue of rebalancing its relationship with the United States.

Similarly, in the 1980s, the Greek Socialists' (PASOK) foreign policy decisions and actions converged with those of their New Democracy predecessors and opened up, perhaps for the first time in the post-war period, the prospect of a grand national consensus regarding foreign and defense policy. The maintenance of the regional balance of power became an overriding priority. Prime Minister Andreas Papandreou recognized that the vital interests of Greece continued to require that its ties to the United States and its place in the Atlantic framework be given the highest priority. In effect, that meant the re-establishment of what Theodore Couloumbis has termed a "linkage policy" *vis-à-vis* the United States.[6] According to Athens, the smooth development of Greek-US relations could only be achieved through Washington actively persuading Ankara to abandon what Athens perceived as "revisionist" policies in the Aegean and to reverse these policies in Cyprus. Although for the United States any disturbance in its relations with Turkey was unthinkable—given Turkey's role in American containment strategic planning, there seemed to be a tacit acceptance of the necessity to preserve a stable balance of power in the Aegean. In essence, it was the adoption of a policy of conflict management and conflict limitation to tolerable levels of tension so as to maximize the potential leverage on Greece and, to a lesser extent, on Turkey.

In Turkey's case, similarly, the country's post-Second World War foreign policy had been inescapably linked to both the United States and the Soviet Union. Relations with the latter had been one of the cornerstones of Mustafa Kemal's foreign policy, and Moscow consistently reminded Ankara of that fact. However, Turkey remained suspicious of the USSR in light of a history of hostility and warfare, a common frontier that was the longest of any NATO member, and Moscow's undiminished desire to control the Bosporus and the Turkish Straits. Since 1945, according to the dominant strategic analysis, regional space was organized on the basis of Turkey and Greece as the indispensable components of NATO's southeastern flank.[7] During the 1960s, this close relationship began to show strain, and in the 1970s tensions were further exacerbated. However, the biggest shadow over US-Turkish relations was cast, not by developments in the Middle East or by Soviet aggressiveness, but rather by Cyprus and the multitude of Aegean issues that continue to fester to this day.

Overall, Turkish cold war foreign policy displayed remarkable continuity. Indeed, Turkey's external relations were marked by a long-term perspective and by a strong sense of realism.[8] In the post-Second World War era, Ankara was enthusiastic in its efforts to forge links with the West. Cold war geopolitics determined that the United States was the key security partner for Turkey; hence this relationship became the central focus of Ankara.[9] However, in the 1960s a large part of the population became sharply critical of US policy over Cyprus and other issues. During that time US-Turkish relations were clearly less tied to the axioms and imperatives of solidarity that had characterized their relations in the early postwar years.[10] Moreover, by the 1970s, Turkey was pursuing a policy of rapprochement with the Muslim countries of the Middle East as well as the Soviet Union. By the late 1970s, the Soviet Union was aiding 44 different development projects in Turkey that received more Soviet economic assistance than any country in the Third World except Cuba.[11]

During President Reagan's first term in office, relations between the United States and Turkey improved markedly under the renewed systemic pressures of US-Soviet confrontation. Appropriations for Turkey's defense needs sharply increased and American assistance in its various forms throughout the 1980s amounted to well over 1 billion USD per year.[12] In the military sector, the Pentagon estimated in 1983 that bringing Turkish forces up to minimum NATO standards would take 18 billion USD over 13 years.[13] For the United States, Turkey's central importance through the years stemmed from the fact that it was an indispensable strategic factor linking the West with the turbulent Middle East and was a stepping stone or a barrier to gaining and sustaining access to the region.[14]

THE NEW INTERNATIONAL SETTING

The latest phase in the development of Turkish-US-Greek relations was marked by the end of the cold war and continues to be shaped by the other monumental events influencing the international and regional strategic environment, notably September 11. The profound change in the conduct of US foreign and security policy, vividly expressed in the 2003 US military intervention in Iraq, is examined in the following pages. At the same time, Turkey's drive to join the EU seemed to have a strong impact on the nature of the triangular relationship and the dynamic security bargain that exists. The main question is, to what extent have behavior, policy preferences, strategic priorities and constellations of power been affected by the evolving international and regional security restructuring? Again, the issue of the United States is of paramount importance.

Post-September 11 USA: Unilateralism and Militarization

American predominance is the central feature of the current geopolitical setting. Systemic unipolarity does not make for a particularly egalitarian world, as September 11 reminded us quite violently. Nevertheless, it is the superstructure that determines the main forces that shape the international system.

The central strategic questions that have confronted Washington since the end of the cold war have remained relevant, although the September 11, 2001, terrorist attacks have radically altered the strategic setting. They are: What are the principal threats to American interests? How can those interests best be defended? What combination of economic, diplomatic and military instruments should be used to protect and advance US interests? These are the enduring questions of US strategy, even if they are often obscured by political rhetoric and heated debate over particular military policies and weapons programs.[15]

Successive post-cold war US administrations have attempted to craft a coherent policy by pursuing a strategy that promotes American power, position and primacy in order to enhance the capacity of the United States to exercise influence abroad. Strong American interventionism since the end of the cold war has marked Washington's commitment to an active internationalist agenda, even without a geopolitical and ideological rival. This American globalism is compatible with a set of principles that have come to be associated with world order, stability and vital US interests.

The United States is the only state with the capacity to try to exercise global political leadership, at least in the short term. It is unquestionably the most powerful country in the contemporary system. At 329 billion USD the 2002 US defense budget was larger than the combined defense budgets of the nine next biggest defense spenders worldwide. Today, the United States spends close to 40 percent of world defense expenditures, while the 48 billion USD increase sought by the Pentagon for the 2003 defense budget allocation is some 14 billion USD more than that of the total defense budget of the United Kingdom, which has the world's third-largest defense budget. In fiscal year 2003 the United States will spend 3.5 percent of its GDP on defense, whereas Britain will spend only 2.6 percent, France 2.4 percent and Germany 1.5 percent.[16]

The United States possesses the most capable and mobile forces in the world, especially in critical areas such as airlift and sealift—which can carry forces to trouble spots around the globe. Furthermore, US superpower status is by no means confined to the military dimension. The United States still has the largest and most vibrant single national economy. The combination of the two drives—political and military—to form a strategy of "engagement and enlargement" has become the lynchpin of US foreign and national security policy. No other country or combination of countries can hope to challenge it within a generation. The 1991 Gulf War, the 1995 and 1999 Balkan campaigns, as well as the 2001 Afghanistan intervention and the spring 2003 war against Iraq have been impressive American exhibitions of its "capacity" to go to war and have demonstrated that military power is not obsolete. Although there can be no absolute US dominance, "order" can be premised on the total primacy of the United States in areas like the wider Middle East—where military power has always served as a major arbiter of events with implications far beyond the region.

For President George W. Bush, his predecessor, President Bill Clinton's foreign policy lacked coherence, clear priorities and a sense of what was important to US interests and security. From the outset, the new administration clearly indicated its intention to pursue unilateral strategies. This approach has been identified by many as the unifying theme running through most of the Bush administration's foreign policy initiatives. Indeed, the most profound effect of September 11 has been the reordering of Washington's international engagement coupled with the reinforcement of the administration's strident unilateralism. America's attempt to make its own international rules is the most vivid example of unilateralism. As Kenneth Waltz has observed, "New challenges have not changed old habits … Fighting terrorists provided a cover that has enabled the Bush administration to do what it wanted to do anyway."[17] The result has been to enhance American power and extend its military presence in the world. The war on terrorists has enabled the United States to establish bases on Russia's southern border and to further its encirclement of Russia as well as China.

Secretary of Defense Donald Rumsfeld announced that if necessary to pursue the war against terror, the United States will move militarily into 15 more states.[18] The basic fact of post-September 11 international politics is that America's relations with the rest of the world are undergoing fundamental changes. Washington is so powerful that those changes are affecting the international system much more drastically than the terrorist attacks themselves. According to Nicole Gnesotto, urgency, militarization and unilateralism characterize the US response to the strategic challenge of international terrorism.[19] The urgency refers to the fact that the disruption of US strategic priorities was immediate and violent. As a result, the war against terrorism has become the highest priority.

All other issues, including the Greek-Turkish disputes, have thus been relegated to secondary importance. The militarization of the US response to terrorism is highlighted by the defense expenditure figures cited above. These figures disclose the American obsession with military technology and power. This obsession seems to be the American reaction to terrorist threats,

> so much so that this military choice sometimes appears to be its sole policy. The speeding-up of missile-defense programs takes the place of diplomacy in the fight against nuclear proliferation; the basis for building alliances or coalitions becomes the number of divisions and other military assets that allies might be able to contribute.[20]

Intoxication with power has resulted in unilateralism very quickly becoming the guiding foreign and security policy principle in Washington. In addition to the sense of heightened danger, the plausibility of the unilateral option has led to a growing emphasis on pre-emption and preventive war as the main tools of US strategy. This has been the most striking development—and the most disturbing for America's allies. Washington seems to be unprepared to compromise either its means or its objectives to achieve its strategically imperative goals. In February 2002, Deputy Secretary of Defense Paul Wolfowitz declared that from now on it would be "the mission that determines the coalition; the coalition must not determine the mission."[21] The concept of "coalitions of the willing" seems to be replacing historical alliances as the core of US global strategy. As Gnesotto has put it, "this cult of unilateralism spills over from the political sphere into that of military strategy," thus affecting America's discourse and attitudes regarding its allies. On the political level, the "either you're with us or against us" Bush doctrine has made the debate among allies with less than identical security priorities extremely difficult.[22]

There has been, therefore, a US global strategic advance with a very strong element of continuity: a global foreign policy inspired by unilateral realpolitik efforts to prevent other states from challenging US security and primacy. Global activism, the centrality of military power and its application, and a strong, US-dominated NATO in the framework of European security and stability, are the fundamentals of American post-cold war foreign and security policy through which the Turkish-US-Greek interaction should be viewed.

THE TURKISH-US-GREEK TRIANGLE

Considering the effects that the dramatic turbulence had on the United States, Turkey and Greece, a central question is the extent to which the change has been cyclical or cumulative. The general course of events is well known, as are the policy problems. What must be assessed here are the implications of the new structural changes, and the extent to which assumptions about continuity and change are valid. A central question relates to the nature of change: are there more fundamental structural and systemic differences which must be recognized when considering future trends and patterns of behavior within the Turkish-US-Greek arena? In this context, the 2003 Gulf War and the Turkish-American "clash" as a result of the war are particularly important. When discussing these aspects, the focus is not on the long-term implications, which are difficult to assess and related to the broader issue of the renewed and more-autonomous-than-ever US strategic presence in the region. Rather, the point to be made concerns the changing nature of short-term Turkish-US relations and the extent to which Turkish foreign and security policy options have been enhanced or diminished as a result, as well as its impact on the Aegean. For Turkish-Greek relations, the overall framework organically involves the process of Turkey's evolution towards the EU as well. The strength of the post-1999 rapprochement between Athens and Ankara largely depends on the prospects for Turkey's EU membership and the modernizing effect of Brussels.

The Turkish Context Post-Cold War

According to Duygu Sezer, the collapse of the USSR "has had enormous adverse repercussions on an entirely different front: cohesion in the Western world. For Ankara, this has meant less confidence in the willingness and ability of major NATO allies to continue business as usual with Turkey."[23] Developments in the East outpaced whatever meager prospects Turkey might have enjoyed in Western European eyes.[24] America's traditionally strong military relationship with Turkey was called into question and economic and military assistance programs were reduced and eventually zeroed out. Even cash purchases of arms and equipment became subject to congressional holds. In short, the changing geopolitical environment in the late 1980s and early 1990s presented Turkey with many new challenges. These included a fragmentation of power along its northern and northeastern borders following the strategic withdrawal of Soviet/Russian power; the multiplication of political actors in the wider Eurasian region; the emergence and, in some cases, intensification of local conflicts with the potential to escalate into larger regional conflicts; and the absence of an easily conceived and articulated threat, "further isolating Turkey from mainstream European political and economic developments."[25]

At that time, the quest for a new role, that of peacemaker and regional stabilizer, began. President Özal went on to define Turkey as a model for the region because of its unique combination of characteristics: Islamic, democratic, secular and, above all, stable in the midst of a disintegrating region ranging from the Balkans to the former USSR to the Middle East. The Gulf War simply revalidated Turkey's self-definition and role in this context.[26] Security debates in the United States and Europe acknowledge Turkey's geopolitical significance and the need to reinvigorate relations with Ankara. But there has been relatively little progress in defining what a new agenda for strategic cooperation between Turkey and the West should include. It seems that the relationship between Turkey and the West still lacks a clear sense of direction; uncertainty remains as to what big issues parties can work for, or against, in a new strategic environment.

Special reference must be also made to the concept of Turkey as a "pivotal state." Turkey fulfills all the requirements of a pivotal state: population, location, and economic and military potential. Its defining quality, though, is the potential to affect regional and international stability. Turkey's significance lies not only in its geostrategic value, but also in the destabilization and uncertainty that the (even remote) possibility of its decline might result in.[27]

The regional balance, and—for that reason—the geostrategic value and role of Turkey, will continue to depend on a number of factors, which seemingly contribute—albeit unevenly—to either enhancing or diminishing Turkey's role in regional and world politics in the framework of US foreign policy and security interests. The most important of these factors is Turkey's relations with the United States and its position in the wider American security strategic plan, shaped by the future development of: 1) relations between the United States/West and Iraq (and Iran), especially after the successful campaign against Baghdad and the occupation of Iraq; 2) relations between the West and Russia as well as the general foreign and security policy goals of Moscow; 3) Turkish-Russian relations, especially in the strategic environment of the Caucasus and Central Asia. It will also be subject to: 4) continuation and intensification of the conventional arms race in the region and the horrifying prospect of the proliferation of weapons of mass destruction (WMD); 5) the prospects for stability of Central Asian countries and the security of the oil routes; 6) the future of the EU-Turkish relationship and the prospects of membership. Finally, 7) the issue of Turkish national power itself, with reference to not only the military dimension but mainly to the political, economic and social development of the country.

This final factor, the issue of Turkish national power, is of critical importance and is connected to the management of internal political, economic and social uncertainties. The 1999 general elections produced a nationalist coalition of the right and the left, with a sharp decline in support for centrist parties and for the Islamic political agents. The consolidation of military influence in defense of the secular state, which began with the removal of the Welfare Party (*Refah Partisi*—RP) from power and its banning from Turkish politics also means that the Turkish military remains a key interlocutor on foreign and security policy issues.[28] Three years later, the Turkish general election of November 3, 2002, transformed the country's political landscape dramatically. None of the members of the outgoing governing coalition won seats in the new parliament. Since taking office in 1999, the coalition had been tarnished by a series of corruption scandals; additionally, during its time in office, the country experienced the worst economic recession in 50 years.[29] In the elections in 2002, the Justice and Development Party (*Adalet ve Kalkınma Partisi*—AKP), formed in mid-2001, came to power with 34.3 percent of the vote and a massive majority of 363 seats in the 550-member parliament. The center-left Republican People's Party (*Cumhuriyet Halk Partisi*—CHP), after its disastrous performance in the 1999 election, emerged as the second party with 19.4 percent of the vote and 178 seats. Another nine seats were won by independents, with all other political parties failing to cross the ten percent threshold.[30] The indications of transition turbulence are strong and have been identified and assessed at an early stage:

> The "democratization process" that has been intensified by the decisions taken at the European Summit in Helsinki, and elaborated on a short and medium-term basis in the Accession Partnership that followed, will seriously affect Turkish domestic politics in many ways. Specifically, democratization is expected to be the driving force behind turbulence in Turkey's domestic politics, which is highly likely to undermine the country's democratization project and affect its external behavior. This turbulence in domestic politics will mainly concern the eruption of a set of domestic shocks at the state and society level, being portrayed as elite turbulence, societal turbulence and economic turbulence.[31]

In this regard, the future conduct of Turkish foreign policy, and the future of Turkey as a security partner for the West, might be driven to some extent by domestic developments. "Even if the overall direction of Turkish policy remains steady and pro-Western, Turkey's ability to play an active role in adjoining regions ... will depend on political stability in Ankara."[32] That entails a smooth modernization phase with a clear European future for Turkey. The policy implications for Washington and Athens are profound.

The Greek Context

For Greece, the end of the cold war and the resulting global transformation forced an urgent need to learn and readjust. Cold war stability was replaced by post-cold war uncertainty and turbulence, which affected the country's northern neighborhood. Less than orderly political transitions, bankrupt economies, sharp ethnic conflicts and border disputes on Greece's northern periphery threatened and challenged regional stability and vital national interests.

Throughout the post-1974 period, Greece's national strategy had been based on containing what Greek elites and public opinion perceived as the "threat from the East." The end of the cold war added to the Greek security dilemma by replacing a static regional environment with a tremendously unstable one. Athens had to deal with the disintegration of Yugoslavia and the other complex issues of the region brought about by the end of the cold war. Greek governments failed to formulate a coherent and effective Balkan policy and thus failed to play an important role in the resolution of the crisis. Instead, for at least half of the 1990s, Greece, to a certain extent, became part of the problem. Athens' inability to grasp the complexity of the situation was colossal. The complexity of actors, roles, policies and perceived interests resulted in a considerable security anxiety in Greece, which led to a policy without basic direction, coherence and well-assessed goals.

The situation reversed itself in the mid-1990s when Greece seemed to rediscover its role and expand its capabilities to respond successfully to the regional challenges. In the post-Dayton era, Greek foreign policymakers have been attempting to play a stabilizing role in the Balkan region by formulating a more comprehensive and cooperative approach to the region's problems. The endeavor to define and pursue an appropriate strategy continued, with considerable success, in the Kosovo crisis. Although plagued by problems of structural adjustment and with a serious deficit of healthy, export-led growth, Greece's upgraded role in southeastern Europe is based on its strong economic performance. Solid progress over the second half of the 1990s has guaranteed Greece's participation in the European Monetary Union—the "hard core" of the European integration process—as well as a constructive and continuing presence on the regional scene. A stable and dynamic economy is broadening its foreign policy perspectives and enhancing its capabilities as a partner for stabilization.

Greek policy towards Turkey, however, represents, strategically, the most impressive response to the new setting. The perception of the "Turkish threat," a "political heritage" of the years since 1974, has taken on a different and more complex form, given the new post-cold war geopolitical realities affecting Turkey's international position and its internal development, as well as the nature of the challenges the two countries face in their bilateral relations. For Athens, during the 1990s, Ankara remained the main focus of Greek security and foreign policy concerns. However, as Panayotis Tsakonas has rightly argued, Greek security policy *vis-à-vis* Turkey began reformulation in the mid-1990s due to Greece's new strategic needs and priorities—mainly its ability to fully integrate into the EU.[33] The core of the new approach has been the identification of the EU as the most effective alignment to be utilized in the quest for a highly sophisticated "external balancing" strategy *vis-à-vis* Turkey.[34] The EU Helsinki summit (December 1999) was the departure point for engaging Turkey in a context where Greece has enjoyed a comparative advantage, thus making the EU a major determinant in Greek-Turkish relations and thereby also somewhat diminishing US leverage. As Marios Evriviades has pointed out:

> Working with the well-founded assumption that since 1987 Turkey's pre-eminent strategic goal has been integration into the European Union, Greece has responded with sophisticated strategy. This strategy linked Turkish progress with Brussels and with Greece's bilateral problems with Ankara and with Cyprus. This strategy would end up "Europeanizing" Greece's problems with Turkey, but in effect "Europeanized" Greece's foreign policy and other policies as well ... "Europeanization" of Greece would yield important dividends such as the opening wide the EU door for Cyprus and facilitating, ultimately, a Greek-Turkish rapprochement.[35]

In principle, this strategy seeks to maintain and enhance relations with Turkey as much as possible in various policy realms by using three elements. Regarding economics and trade, engagement has meant seeking an expansion of relations and the growth of exchanges. Politically, engagement seeks to maximize bilateral contacts at every level, while pushing back(stage) traditional disputes. Under this approach, Athens has agreed to Turkish candidacy for EU membership, a major political risk for the Greek government. Militarily, Greece has agreed to an enhancement of military-to-military relations within the NATO framework, with the specific aim of increasing mutual confidence and reaching agreement on the "rules of the game." The overall approach rests on the hope that growing economic, political and military contacts and cooperation, as well as enmeshing Turkey in the European integration system, can socialize the powerful and skeptical part of the Turkish elites into European norms of behavior and increase their stake in a course of reform. The successful EU-Turkish engagement is a definite "relative-gain" project for Turkey (*vis-à-vis* Europe). As such, Turkish elites feel and public opinion indicates that the arduous course of reform and modernization will clearly pay off, which greatly contributes to the attractiveness and popularity of the European orientation in Turkey.[36]

At the same time, the "Helsinki strategy" has compelled Europe to pay closer attention to areas and issues of concern to Athens—the most important of which is Cyprus—and has increasingly "Europeanized" the question of Athens' Turkish policy, to a certain extent balancing out the overwhelming US security influence. Turkey's European aspirations are now directly tied to a resolution of its differences with Greece over the Aegean and Cyprus.[37]

Reflections on the "Troubled Triangle:" From Copenhagen to Baghdad

There can be little strategic rationale for premeditated conflict between Greece and Turkey. Open conflict would pose enormous political risks for both, quite apart from uncertainties at the operational level. Yet the risk of an accidental clash remains, given the continuing armed air and naval operations that occur in close proximity to each other and the highly charged atmosphere that surrounds their competing claims.[38] The Aegean and especially Cyprus are sensitive national questions *par excellence.* Moreover, with both countries modernizing their military capabilities, the potential for destructiveness and escalation is far greater today than in the past. A Greek-Turkish clash would have profound implications for Turkey and the West. Conflict would undermine stability across southeastern Europe, further complicate the settlement of disputes elsewhere in the region as well as the NATO and EU enlargement processes in the East, and introduce new and unpredictable variables in relations with Russia and the Muslim word. For the United States (and NATO) the risk of a clash and the likely strategic and operational consequences make risk reduction an imperative. The same is true for the EU.

The slow pace in the evolution of EU-Turkish relations has also contributed to a sense of disappointment and uncertainty, and has added to the Greek anxiety as well, since Greece perceives that Turkish behavior towards Greece has become more unpredictable and thus harder for the United States to control. If Turkey cannot strengthen its relationship with the EU—in the context of future membership—it cannot successfully pursue its legitimate foreign policy goals. For the EU, it would be a disaster to "lose" Turkey, but how to properly bind it to Europe seems unclear even after Helsinki. The policy implications for Greece are that the longer the relationship between Turkey and the EU remains overshadowed by uncertainties, the more the United States remains "the only and undisputed" arbiter in essentially a balance of power game. The (potential) deterioration of Turkey's ties with the EU would further increase the importance of its strong ties to Washington. Turkey generally sees the United States as being more supportive of Turkey's security concerns than Europe is. Washington has strongly backed Turkey's candidacy for EU membership and has lent strong political support to Ankara's security efforts.

From the Turkish perspective, being part of European integration after the decisions taken at Helsinki and Copenhagen has been a great symbolic achievement, and should be treated as such. The prediction that Turkey would need at least ten years in order to reach membership levels of economic, political and social development should not be viewed with suspicion and disappointment in Turkey. Spain and Portugal also required a decade to undergo needed changes, and this occurred at a time when the *acquis communautaire* was a few hundred pages (before the Single European Market, EMU, etc.), not several thousand as it is today.

The nature of the European integration process has all the systemic properties needed to fundamentally alter the exclusive geopolitical "zero-sum-game" quality of the Greek-Turkish conflicting relationship. Progress in this context would "anchor" Turkey ever more closely to the West and lend greater stability to Greek-Turkish relations. This "desire" is actually what links Greek and US foreign policy towards Turkey.

However, the challenge for Turkey is enormous. Previously, Turkish elites have not had to confront the dilemma posed by a strong nationalist tradition and a powerful attachment to state sovereignty with the prospect of integration in a sovereignty-diluting EU. Even short of full membership, candidacy implies great institutionalized scrutiny, convergence and compromise. From the least political issues (for example, food regulations) to high politics, a closer relationship with formal EU structures will put tremendous pressure on traditional Turkish concepts of sovereignty at many levels and will severely question (as it has already done) the role of the military in Turkish politics. It is a process that has been difficult for all member states of the EU, though surrendering sovereignty has also been one of the most fundamental elements of European integration success. For an EU member state, pursuing nationalist options outside the integration context has become extremely difficult and costly, if not impossible.

For Turkey, the accession process, however long, will almost certainly reinforce dynamics unleashed by the 1999 earthquake. Because of the state's failure to come to the rescue and to the relief of the victims for almost three days, the earthquake destroyed the old *modus vivendi* between Turkish society and the state. According to Soli Özel, the social contract between the state and the *status quo*-oriented middle classes was broken. "Thenceforth the drive toward an accountable, transparent, and efficient government ruled by law would go forward on a stronger social basis than ever before. EU membership became all the more prized as an aid to this cause; some even saw it as a panacea."[39] The EU accession process would be instrumental in attracting much-needed foreign direct investment, achieving better and more efficient government, securing the rule of law and realizing the prospects for vast modernization.[40]

If there is a "Helsinki spirit," after the Copenhagen decisions and as the 2004 deadline is closing, it is the need—for both countries—for a more "strategic" approach towards each other. Both countries have a longer-term strategic interest in seeing Turkey's EU vocation succeed. For more than 25 years, Greeks have perceived "the threat from the East" as dominant. Military and diplomatic deterrence was indispensable to the concept of Greek security. The collapse of the cold war did not affect those basic parameters as they have been consistently perceived and articulated by both Greek elites and Greek public opinion. This perception of Turkey has been one of the constants in Greek public opinion and security culture. Turkey's European success has the potential to change Greece's perception of this threat, and foster political and economic reform in a Turkey reassured regarding its place in Europe. The United States and Europe, furthermore, will benefit from a more effective and predictable strategic partnership with Turkey. A key task for US foreign policy elites will be to make sure that Greek-Turkish brinkmanship no longer threatens the broader interests of regional détente and integration. The stakes to bring about this strategy of reciprocal accommodation are extremely high. Lasting rapprochement would yield immense benefits for everybody involved.[41]

However, the rapprochement remains nascent and fragile for three main reasons. First, in the eyes of Greek public opinion, most of the changes have originated on the Greek side. Indeed, there has been no major shift in Turkish policy. Without a Turkish gesture to match Greece's lifting of its veto to Turkey's EU candidacy, it may prove difficult for Athens to maintain domestic support in the long run.[42] Indeed, the Greek government has a slim margin of error even within its own party confines. Second, rapprochement has so far been limited to less-controversial areas such as trade, the environment and tourism. The sensitive issues have yet to be addressed. As Nazmi Akiman has observed, it is apparent that progress in improving the climate of relations and agreements on a host of uncontroversial subjects cannot be a substitute for resolving the two major issues, the Aegean and Cyprus. Just as the failure of Davos in the late 1980s subsequently brought more trouble to Turkish-Greek relations, there is a major risk that the current détente may falter and cause further aggravation, or even worse, for the two neighbors.[43] The détente remains subject to interruption or even reversals. For example, on October 23, 2000, Greece angrily withdrew from NATO's Destined Glory 2000 exercise following tense mock dogfights between Turkish and Greek Fighter jets which led to a disagreement over allowing Greek planes to fly over the Greek islands of Lemnos and Ikaria.[44] In 2002 and 2003, tension in the Aegean sky resurfaced: Athens noted there were 3,200 violations of its airspace in 2002 and 1,530 by mid-May 2003. On the other hand, the Turkish General Staff has claimed that Greek fighters have been harassing Turkish jets in international airspace. Turkey recognizes six miles of Greek airspace, not the ten miles declared by Athens.[45] This is clear evidence of the fragility of relations, particularly in the military sphere.

There are, then, a number of challenges impeding the consolidation of Greek-Turkish détente. The current climate will prove its durability only when these issues are included in the reconciliation agenda. While Cyprus is technically not a bilateral dispute, it is an integral element of the broader fabric of the relationship and cannot be ignored. Although currently there is a politically costly effort to downplay the linkage by Athens, without progress regarding Cyprus the current rapprochement will be impossible to sustain.[46] To some, the Cyprus policy of the AKP government is difficult to understand, as they seem to have exhibited a profound lack of coordination. When a clear sign had to be sent following Kofi Annan's initiative, a barrage of contradictory statements was issued—an indecisiveness that resulted in the island being admitted to the EU in April 2003 without a solution to the problem. The confusion was exacerbated by apparent differences between the AKP government and the more traditional Turkish establishment. For Turkey's defense and foreign policy establishment, Cyprus is a central foreign policy and security issue, as well as a source of pride and prestige—and thus almost exclusively the responsibility of the Turkish General Staff and the Ministry of Foreign Affairs.[47] According to Jenkins:

> The Turkish military believes that the *de facto* Turkish protectorate in northern Cyprus is vital to Turkey's strategic interests, safeguarding both Turkey's Mediterranean coastline and shipping lanes to the ports of Mersin, Iskenderun and Ceyhan. As a result, it

has been reluctant to agree to any solution, which would reduce either its influence or its military presence in northern Cyprus.[48]

Moreover, the "failure" of Ankara to secure a more favorable outcome at Copenhagen, plus the invitation to Cyprus to become an EU member on May 1, 2004, resulted in Turkish foreign policymakers "falling back into default mode,"[49] adding to the frustration and revealing Tayyip Erdogan's "lack of international experience and diplomatic finesse."[50] In the days that followed, growing concern over the Iraq crisis relegated Cyprus to a lower place on the Turkish foreign policy agenda and allowed the Turkish Cypriot leader Rauf Denkta° to rally his supporters among the Kemalist establishment and effectively undermine the UN-sponsored peace process.[51]

To the extent that Turkish accession to the EU remains an open question for years to come, the Greek-US-Turkish entanglement becomes even more complex. A Turkey disillusioned or bitter in its relations with the EU will have fewer incentives to compromise on the Aegean and Cyprus. At the same time, there are many in Turkey who argue that unless this tension in Cyprus is kept alive, there may remain few incentives for the EU to approve Turkey's membership. Greece and Cyprus, especially after the final resolution of the issues, may choose to keep Turkey out of the EU umbrella for a whole host of new reasons. This could be one reason why the security and defense establishment in Ankara, in particular, choose to postpone the contended issues to the very last minute before Turkey's full membership.[52] Evriviades might not be far from truth when arguing that,

> The irony of the accession of Cyprus to the EU is that, on account of it being realized and in the process of its accession, Cyprus has been generating and accelerating the necessary conditions that make possible the accession of Turkey as well. On account of Cyprus, whose EU membership Ankara bitterly opposes, Turkey now stands its best and only realistic chance of becoming politically, and not merely militarily, integrated into European institutions.[53]

Failure to reach a settlement acceptable to all parties involved could mean a return to brinkmanship and a major strategic burden on both the EU and (especially) the United States.[54] For Washington, strategic resolution of the Cyprus problem was central during 1999–2002, but remained a means to an end. The prize has always been a lasting anchoring of Turkey to the West through its political integration with the EU.[55] In any case, the issue here remains the extent to which US strategy, as far as the management of the Greek-Turkish conflict is concerned, will remain the same.

We have already identified strong elements of continuity in US foreign policy in general. In the context of Greek-US relations, the analysis over the years was shaped predominantly by the Greek-Turkish debate. This was appropriate given Greece's pre-eminent perception of the Turkish threat since 1974, but the rhetoric of this debate continues to shape both Greek and American thinking and strategy. As a result, the issue of US leadership—whether Washington can continue to fulfill a balancing role or whether there should be a different American approach and subsequently a different Greek response—is given continuing prominence.

Of all the issues, however, what has added the most to the complexity of the triangular arena has been the impact on US-Turkish relations of the American military intervention in Iraq in the spring of 2003. For the United States, the Middle East remains an area of vital importance. Turkey's strategic significance is powerfully defined by its centrality to a region of major instability and conflagration. The Second Gulf War has so far proven to be a watershed. Although Turkey will remain a key country for the United States for the foreseeable future, it is widely held that the partnership between Washington and Ankara will inevitably necessitate the shaping of a new agenda that would reflect the reality of the regime change and the large US military presence in Iraq and in the wider region.

Washington's unilateral and "military" approach to the Iraqi regime issue was certain to be viewed with uneasiness in Ankara. The severe economic recession and the adverse effect that the crisis was expected to have on Turkey's security further exacerbated Ankara's discomfort. As early as July 2002, the United States had made clear that, in the event of war, US plans would involve launching attacks from southeastern Turkey. Visiting Turkey on December 3, 2002, US Deputy Secretary of Defense Paul Wolfowitz laid out the ground attack plans and asked Turkey to allow the following: the use of its joint air bases; the stationing of 80,000 or more US troops in Turkey; and the transit of these troops to northern Iraq in order to establish a second front. Developments in Iraqi Kurdistan following the 1990–91 Gulf War and the potential ramifications of the Kurdish issue in the US war with Iraq constituted a great headache for Ankara.[56] Tension between Turkey and the Iraqi Kurds was particularly high concerning the fate of the Kirkuk and Mosul oil fields, as well as the possibility of the United States arming Kurdish fighters.[57] This was the fundamental security concern that prevented Ankara from following Washington's war plans and strategic agenda.

It was, therefore, almost natural that the AKP government policy towards US war preparations and the prospect of a post-Saddam, "federal" Iraq would come under tremendous pressure. Nevertheless, it was widely assumed that at the critical moment, Ankara would have no choice but to support Washington logistically and, probably, militarily.[58] However, by mid-December 2002, the mood of the Turkish elites was changing. The level of distrust of the West further increased following the disappointing outcome at Copenhagen. As Philip Robins posited, "the old ghosts of the early 1920s also began to stir, notably the so-called Sèvres Syndrome, a Turkish preoccupation with renewed attempts by the great powers to remake the Middle East to Turkey's great disadvantage."[59] The Turkish General Staff finally submitted detailed plans for potential Turkish support for a US military campaign to the National Security Council meeting of January 31, 2003, although it stipulated that any decision would have to be approved by the Turkish parliament. On March 1, 2003, the Turkish parliament rejected the resolution and with it Washington's war requests by a margin of just three votes. Tied to American war requests was a massive US aid package—including 6 billion USD in grants convertible to up to 24 billion USD in low-interest, long-term loans. In an extremely belated and watered-down version, parliament voted on March 20 to grant the US military overflight privileges, making Turkey the last NATO ally to grant such rights to the United States.[60]

While September 11 had served to strengthen the US-Turkish strategic partnership by once more elevating Turkey's value to the war against terrorism, the cleavage over Iraq meant that anxieties resurfaced and questions were raised about Turkey's geopolitical destiny. According to Morton Abramowitz, "Turkey has endangered the whole westward edifice of its policies. It has taken positions that have left it, at least momentarily, without the strong support of major western allies."[61] Following these events, the American press criticized Ankara sharply. Turkish-US relations experienced a quick and dramatic deterioration, at least temporarily. The incorporation of a 1 billion USD supplement for Turkey into the US war budget and an early April 2003 fence-mending visit to Ankara by US Secretary of State Colin Powell indicated that Turkey remains a strategically located NATO ally. It should be noted, however, that the Pentagon, hitherto Ankara's most ardent advocate in Washington, has been reported to be the most frustrated. As Park noted:

> There will be many in the Pentagon who will remain conscious of the consequences of Turkish non-cooperation. For America's military planners, what good is Turkey's strategic location if it is unavailable to US troops? Furthermore, should a stable and pro-western regime emerge in Baghdad, Iraq could offer Washington an oil-rich, grateful and still more strategically located regional alternative to Turkey. In

the foreseeable future, it is less likely that the Pentagon will be quite so willing to lobby on Turkey's behalf ... The United States is now more indebted to Iraqi Kurds, and Ankara is less well placed to have a say in post-Saddam arrangements in Iraq, as a consequence of Turkey's failure to cooperate.[62]

All of the above indicates that the relationship between Turkey and the United States faces some pressures to change. As Operation Iraqi Freedom demonstrates, US involvement and its growing military presence in the wider Middle East can pose dilemmas for Turkey, and that interpretations of security concerns do not always coincide. At a fundamental level, Turkish and American interests are broadly convergent, and the bilateral relationship remains heavily focused on security. This is not going to change given the character of the regional environment and the continuing involvement of the United States. Consequently, vital Turkish national interests remain subject to Washington's pivotal role as security arbiter in the adjacent regions. In the context of this fundamental rationale, critical Greek stakes turn on external variables, such as Turkey's relationship with Washington (and Brussels), and the impact on the Greek-Turkish bilateral agenda can be enormous—however narrowly (or widely) this agenda is defined.

CONCLUSION

A full discussion of the history and points of contention in Greek-Turkish relations is beyond the scope of this contribution. What is important here is that the overall American strategic interest in the area has almost inevitably drawn the United States into the dispute. The discussion aimed at evaluating the significance and the policy impact of the US grand strategic presence in the Greek-Turkish subregional system. The focus has been on the course of relations between Washington, Athens and Ankara in the post-September 11 and post-Iraq international environment. The emphasis has been on the evolution of the foreign policy priorities and preferences as well as dynamic domestic political arenas, which are shaped by an aggregation of different internal and external influences—the most important being the EU (in the case of Greece and, increasingly, Turkey). The analysis underlined the impact of the systematic change on the international and regional role, power position and behavior of the three actors.

Washington's approach has always been a pragmatic one, since no American initiative has succeeded in achieving the normalization of Greek-Turkish relations. The primary objective of US foreign policy has been to control Greek-Turkish tensions and to manage the implications of the problem in order to allow NATO to function. Since 1980, the two countries have been entangled in a low-intensity conflict interrupted by shorter or longer détente breaks. It is, however, a situation that has the disturbing potential to escalate to a more serious crisis with alarming destabilizing effects at the regional level.

This essay has identified some underlying issues that have been dictating the conduct of the trilateral interactions: wider US geostrategic interests, regional turmoil and domestic uncertainties. Unprepared for the end of the cold war, Greek, as well as American, leaders have been slow to devise a comprehensive strategy to cope with the plethora of social, political, economic and security problems deriving from the collapse of the old European state system. Similarly, Turkey also found itself overburdened after the cold war: being a pillar of stability in an ocean of troubles, on the one hand, and seeking to project its concepts of stability, cooperation and order onto an enormous land mass, on the other.

Although there is guarded optimism, the prospects for Greek-Turkish relations remain uncertain. The Aegean and Cyprus will remain potential flashpoints and pose a continuous crisis-prevention situation for the United States (and Europe). The rapprochement is intimately linked to the positive development of the relationship between Ankara and Brussels. The start of accession negotiations could be instrumental. Stagnation or deterioration of the EU-Turkey relationship would almost certainly complicate and perhaps threaten the Greek-Turkish rapprochement. A stable and positive development of EU-Turkish relations would also simplify and enhance US-Turkish relations. For Ankara and Washington, the bilateral relationship is increasingly difficult to assess and conduct in isolation: the American campaign against terrorism and the EU are critical backdrops. The EU, especially, is becoming an increasingly important factor, and it heavily influences relations between Greece and Turkey.

The course of EU-Turkish relations after Helsinki has changed the context of Greek-US-Turkish as well as EU-US-Turkish relations. With Ankara's candidacy confirmed, Turkish-EU relations have become less uncertain, but they "have moved into a more highly structured and legalistic pattern, with fixed criteria and fewer opportunities for arguments on strategic grounds."[63] The EU increasingly emerges as Turkey's best strategic option. In both the security and modernization (political, economic and social) realms, the EU's influence is great—as has been the case with the other southern, eastern and central European states.

However, prospects for Turkey to ascend to the EU will now depend far more on the reform process and its substance in Turkey. Effective US lobbying is now more likely to take place in Ankara than in Brussels, Helsinki or Copenhagen. The prospects for a lasting détente will also be influenced by the longer-term evolution of the foreign and security policy priorities on all sides, and the dynamics of EU integration and NATO strategic adjustment, as well as more stability in southeastern Europe, the eastern Mediterranean and the Middle East. Turkey's (and Greece's) strategic environment will be strongly influenced by the evolution of US regional, security and defense policies beyond the Gulf, and especially the global campaign against terrorism.[64] The role of the United States is nothing less than vital for making and sustaining more positive regional security settings. Any credible assessment of the future course of the trilateral relationship will need to reflect a changing Turkey, a changing Greece and a quickly evolving strategic environment, and will need to take into account the evolving global security debate—especially as regards the United States.

NOTES

1. John O. Iatrides, "The United States, Greece and the Balkans," in Van Coufoudakis, Harry J. Psomiades and Andre Gerolymatos (eds.), *Greece and the New Balkans: Challenges and Opportunities* (New York: Pella, 1999), pp.273–4. See also Bruce R. Kuniholm, *The Origins of the Cold War in the Near East: Great Power Conflict and Diplomacy in Iran, Turkey and Greece* (Princeton, NJ: Princeton University Press, 1994), pp.383–425.
2. Iatrides (1999), p.274.
3. Theodore A. Couloumbis, *The United States, Greece and Turkey: The Troubled Triangle* (New York: Praeger, 1983), especially chapters 2, 3 and 7.
4. Theodore A. Couloumbis, "Greek-US Relations in the 1990s: Back into the Future," in Harry J. Psomiades and Stavros B. Thomadakis (eds.), *Greece, the New Europe and the Changing International Order* (New York: Pella, 1993), p.381.
5. On this, see especially Theodore A. Couloumbis and John O. Iatrides, *Greek American Relations: A Critical Review* (New York: Pella, 1980).
6. Couloumbis (1993), p.381.
7. James Brown, *Delicately Poised Allies: Greece and Turkey. Problems, Policy Choices and Mediterranean Security* (London: Brassey's, 1991), p.62.
8. David A. Rustow, *Turkey: America's Forgotten Ally* (New York: Council on Foreign Relations, 1987), p.84.
9. See the excellent study by Ekavi Athanasopoulou, *Turkey: Anglo-American Security Interests 1945–1952* (London and Portland, OR: Frank Cass, 1999).
10. Bruce R. Kuniholm, "Turkey and the West since World War II," in Vojtech Mastny and R. Craig Nation (eds.), *Turkey between East and West: New Challenges for a Rising Regional Power* (Boulder, CO: Westview, 1996), p.55.
11. Ibid., p.57.
12. Ibid., p.58.
13. Nasuh Uslu, "The Cooperation Amid Problems: Turkish-American Relations in the 1980s," *The Turkish Yearbook of International Relations*, No.27 (1997), p.17.
14. Ibid., p.19.
15. Sean M. Lynn-Jones, "Preface," in Michael E. Brown, Owen R. Cote, Jr., Sean M. Lynn-Jones and Steven E. Miller (eds.), *America's Strategic Choices* (Cambridge, MA: The MIT Press, 1997), p.ix.

16. Julian Lindley-French, *Terms of Engagement: The Paradox of American Power and the Transatlantic Dilemma post-11 September*, Chaillot Papers, No.52 (Paris: The European Union Institute for Security Studies, 2002), pp.10–11.
17. Kenneth N. Waltz, "The Continuity of International Politics," in Ken Booth and Tim Dunne (eds.), *Worlds in Collision: Terror and the Future of Global Order* (Basingstoke: Palgrave, 2002), pp.348–9.
18. Ibid., p.350.
19. Nicole Gnesotto, "Reacting to America," *Survival*, Vol.44, No.4 (Winter 2002–3), p.99.
20. Ibid.
21. Ibid., p.100.
22. Ibid., p.101.
23. Duygu B. Sezer, "Turkey in the New Security Environment in the Balkan and Black Sea Region," in Mastny and Nation (1996), p.74.
24. Ibid.
25. Ibid., pp.74–5.
26. Coufoudakis (1993), p.394.
27. Robert Chase, Emily Hill and Paul Kennedy, "Pivotal States and US Strategy," *Foreign Affairs*, Vol.75, No.1 (Jan.–Feb. 1996), pp.33–51.
28. Ibid., p.28.
29. During 2001, the Turkish economy contracted by 9.4 percent, resulting in over 1 million redundancies and forcing the government to agree to a painful IMF-sponsored economic stabilization program.
30. The three parties in the coalition government saw their total vote fall to 14.7 percent from 53.4 percent in 1999. Additionally, the opposition leaders were voted out. Tansu Ciller's True Path Party (*Doğru Yol Partisi*—DYP) won just 9.6 percent of the vote as compared to 12 percent in 1999. See Gareth Jenkins, "Muslim Democrats in Turkey?" *Survival*, Vol.45, No.1 (Spring 2003), pp.54–5. For further details, see Ali Çarkoğlu, "The Rise of the New Generation Pro-Islamists in Turkey: The Justice and Development Party Phenomenon in the November 2002 Elections in Turkey," *South European Society & Politics*, Vol.7, No.1 (2003), pp.123–56.
31. Panayotis J. Tsakonas, "Turkey's Post-Helsinki Turbulence: Implications for Greece and the Cyprus Issue," *Turkish Studies*, Vol.2, No.2 (Autumn 2001), pp.10–11.
32. See Ian O. Lesser, *NATO Looks South: New Challenges and New Strategies in the Mediterranean* (Santa Monica, CA: Rand, 2000), pp.27–8.
33. See Panayotis Tsakonas, "Post-Cold War Security Dilemmas: Greece in Search of the Right Balancing Recipe," in Christodoulos P. Yallourides and Panayotis J. Tsakonas (eds.), *Greece and Turkey After the End of the Cold War* (New York: Caratzas, 2001).
34. At the same time, the "internal balancing" needs were catered to through a series of decisions in favor of rapid change and improvement of the Greek security and defense planning system. The focus has been on overall strategic planning and reshaping defense doctrine, the restructuring of the armed forces, military spending and military diplomacy. Regarding the Defense Doctrine, the solution to the strategic dilemma that Greece faced was the adoption of a "flexible response," meaning the creation of additional choices in crisis management. The theoretical elaboration of the new doctrine is still in process, since it is a multifaceted matter of major political and strategic significance with multiple parameters and consequences. Concerning armaments, the defense doctrine revision required the intensification of defense efforts, that is, an increase in the amount of resources devoted to defense. In 1996, an armaments program worth almost €15 billion was agreed upon and implemented in the following five years. In 2000, a second five-year (2001–5) program was agreed upon, which, if implemented in full, will amount to more than €20 billion. Throughout this period, Greek military procurement put exclusive emphasis on the acquisition of modern weaponry and the development of high quality defense capabilities (C4, force multipliers, etc.). See Kostas Ifantis, "The New Role of Greece in the Regional System: Trends, Challenges and Capabilities," in Panayotis C. Ioakimidis (ed.), *Greece in the European Union: The New Role and the New Agenda* (Athens: MPMM, 2002), p.258.

35. Marios L. Evriviades, "Europe in Cyprus: The Broader Security Implications," *The Brown Journal of World Affairs*, Vol.10, No.1 (Summer/Fall 2003), pp.246–7.
36. There is, of course, another—extremely hawkish—school of thought. Some have suggested that a containment strategy would be a more realistic way to deal with Turkey. The goal of such a policy would be to avoid an increase in Turkey's political, economic and diplomatic power relative to that of Greece. This would include efforts to slow down the development of Turkey's relations with the EU, thus limiting the expansion of its influence. Containment assumes that allowing Turkey to expand its relations with Europe will not change its behavior but rather will embolden its leadership, making an eventual clash with Greece even more likely. Thus, even modest progress in EU-Turkish relations should be resisted. Under containment, all elements of Turkish-Greek relations would be subordinate to the goal of preventing the growth of Turkey's European (and international) standing. See Kostas Ifantis, "Perception and Rapprochement: Debating a Greek Strategy Towards Turkey," in Mustafa Aydin and Kostas Ifantis (eds.), *Greek-Turkish Relations: Overcoming the Security Dilemma in the Aegean* (London and Portland, OR: Frank Cass, forthcoming).
37. F. Stephen Larrabee and Ian O. Lesser, *Turkish Foreign Policy in an Age of Uncertainty* (Santa Monica, CA: Rand, 2003), p.72.
38. Lesser (2000), p.32.
39. Soli Özel, "After the Tsunami," *Journal of Democracy*, Vol.14, No.2 (2003), p.90.
40. Ibid., p.91.
41. Charles A. Kupchan, "Greek-Turkish Rapprochement: Strategic Interests and High Stakes," *The Strategic Regional Report*, Vol.5, No.2 (Feb. 2000), p.9.
42. See Charles A. Kupchan, *The End of the American Era: US Foreign Policy and the Geopolitics of the Twenty-First Century* (New York: Knopf, 2003), p.271.
43. Nazmi Akiman, "Turkish-Greek Relations: From Uneasy Coexistence to Better Relations? A Retired Ambassador Takes Stock," *Mediterranean Quarterly*, Vol.13, No.3 (Summer 2002), p.30.
44. See Bahar Rumelili, "Liminality and Perpetuation of Conflicts: Turkish-Greek Relations in the Context of Community-Building by the EU," *European Journal of International Relations*, Vol.9, No.2 (June 2003), p.240.
45. See "Anger Over Air Space," *Kathimerini*, May 16, 2003 (English Edition).
46. F. Stephen Larrabee, "Greek-Turkish Rapprochement: Is it Durable?" *The Strategic Regional Report*, Vol.5, No.4 (May/June 2000), p.15.
47. Philip Robins, "Confusion at Home, Confusion Abroad: Turkey between Copenhagen and Iraq," *International Affairs*, Vol.79, No.3 (May 2003), p.557.
48. Jenkins (2003), p.58.
49. Robins (2003), p.558.
50. Jenkins (2003), p.57.
51. Robins (2003), p.559.
52. I would like to thank Ali Çarkoğlu for highlighting this point.
53. Evriviades (2003), p.241.
54. Larrabee and Lesser (2003), p.191.
55. Evriviades (2003), p.243.
56. See the excellent account in Bill Park, "Strategic Location, Political Dislocation: Turkey, The United States, and Northern Iraq," *Middle East Review of International Affairs (MERIA)*, Vol.7, No.2 (June 2003), pp.1–12.
57. Ibid., p.6.
58. Robins (2003), p.560.
59. Ibid., p.561.
60. Park (2003), p.8.
61. Quoted in Frank Bruni, "For Turkey, Uncertainty Over Which Road to Take," *International Herald Tribune*, April 1, 2003, p.3.
62. Park (2003), p.9.
63. Larrabee and Lesser (2003), p.174.
64. Ibid., p.7.

4

Greece and Turkey in the Balkans:
Cooperation or Rivalry?

OTHON ANASTASAKIS

Most studies of Greek-Turkish relations have concentrated on the rivalry between the two countries; the issues that divide rather than unite. As such, the Aegean and the Cyprus issues stand out as the current main manifestations of a longstanding zero-sum antagonistic relationship. Although relations have improved since 1999, the issues that give rise to discord remain unresolved, and a new confrontation resulting from an incident in the sea or the airspace in the Aegean is always a possibility. That said, what the post-1999 rapprochement has shown is that relations between the two countries are not necessarily one-sided, black and white, or exclusively zero-sum. There can also be a policy of constructive engagement as envisaged by foreign ministers İsmail Cem and George Papandreou in the fields of low politics (trade, investment, infrastructure, environment or tourism), which can bring the elites and civil societies together and have a beneficial spillover on other, more contentious, questions of high politics.

The following essay bypasses the antagonistic bilateral relationship between Turkey and Greece by concentrating on their multilateral interactions at the regional level. It compares Greek and Turkish foreign policy considerations in the Balkan context as an arena for common action and/or rivalry between the two countries. This essay examines the nature of their bilateral and multilateral presence in the region by asking the following main questions: Why are Greece and Turkey involved in the post-Communist Balkans? How are they involved? What has been the impact of their involvement? And, finally, has their presence in the Balkans been a mere reflection of their bilateral behavior, or has it generated a more positive dynamic?

During the catastrophic 1990s in the Balkans, the West feared that Greece and Turkey would become part of the Balkan problem and that any new war in the region might ignite a conflict between these two countries as well. Moreover, incidents such as the Imia/Kardak crisis in

1996, although not related to the Yugoslav differences, added to the negative view of a wider region in turmoil. Yet, as this contribution argues, both countries tried to avoid entanglement in the Balkan conflicts and even explored constructive multilateral engagements in the region.

WHY INVOLVEMENT?

Developments in the Balkans have affected both Greece and Turkey in one way or another as a result of a common geography and a long historical involvement in the region: Turkey as the former imperial power in the Balkans and Greece as one of its subjects with a dominant administrative or economic presence in many parts of the region. Consequently, the countries of the Balkan region, including Greece and Turkey, share many common historical, diplomatic, economic and cultural links, as well as a certain regional affinity and a sense of a common collective identity. This shared historical experience has left an ambivalent legacy in the Balkan countries' perceptions towards each other: on the one hand, a similar political culture and a higher level of knowledge and appreciation of the realities in the region; on the other hand, a sense of competition and a certain skepticism concerning each other's motives.

Competition was largely generated during the disintegration of the Ottoman Empire in the nineteenth and early twentieth century and the subsequent course towards statehood and nation-building in the Balkans. During the twentieth century, Greece remained engaged through coalitions as well as rivalries with the other Balkan countries, while Turkey largely withdrew from the Balkans after the Balkan wars and focused on its own domestic nation-building. Select instances of cooperation did occur, however, during the interwar period, such as when Greece and Turkey both participated in the Balkan Pact in 1934 against Italian and Bulgarian revisionism.[1]

After the end of the Second World War, Greece and Turkey focused on the North Atlantic Treaty Organization (NATO) and Western Europe and kept up limited relations with Yugoslavia, the friendliest of the Communist countries to the west. The Balkans were not high on Turkey's cold war foreign policy agenda; post-1974 Greek foreign policy, on the other hand, pursued bilateral and multilateral cooperation, mostly in the field of low politics (economic, scientific, cultural, technical) and some failed attempts in the field of high politics.[2] Greece also maintained good relations with Bulgaria, Romania and, at a later stage, Albania (the state of war was terminated between the two in 1987).

The end of the cold war had a significant impact on Greek and Turkish domestic and external developments. Post-Communist changes in the wider Eastern bloc dramatically affected the two countries' strategic roles, their sense of security and their societies, as well as their economies. Post-Communist developments added more military threats as a result of the disintegration of Yugoslavia and the Soviet Union, the modification of borders and the creation of new states in their vicinity. Moreover, they widened the security agenda to include new problems of a cross-border and transnational nature (illegal immigration, refugee flows, cross-border crime, environmental threats, illegal trafficking). In the economic field, the opening up of new markets in the East brought about new opportunities and possibilities for trade, investment, banking and infrastructure. At a societal level, both countries became destinations for refugees and immigrants from former Communist territories. One of the main effects of the new situation was their transformation into countries with potential influence in their unstable neighborhoods.

In principle, the regional power of a country rests on its ability to influence its external environment through the use of positive (economic, diplomatic or other support) and/or negative measures (sanctions, military threat or action). The influence capability of a country rests,[3] *ceteris paribus*, on 1) its economic potential—a more advanced economy is able to have a regional impact through investment, financial aid or trade; 2) its political power—a consolidated democracy tends to avoid conflicts and tends to act as a stabilizing point of reference for less stable neighboring countries; 3) its military power—a country with an organized army and military potential is able not only to deter through the threat or the use of force but also to have a presence through participation in peacekeeping forces abroad; and 4) its international status—derived from membership in powerful organizations and providing a country with a potent political, economic or military superiority *vis-à-vis* neighboring non-member states.

Yet the regional influence and dominant status of a country is also balanced by the country's vulnerability to internal and/or external difficulties, such as weak domestic governments and/or unstable regional surroundings. The more advanced—economically, politically and militarily—a country is, the better prepared it is to offset the shortcomings of its internal and external vulnerabilities and increase its regional influence, and vice versa. It is therefore able not only to influence its neighboring environment but in many cases can act as a positive model for emulation for less advanced neighboring countries.

The post-Communist European experience presents some indicative examples of countries with influence capability over their neighboring regions. Germany and Austria have contributed significantly to the economic development of the central European region and have been pivotal in pursuing and sustaining the enlargement agenda of the central European countries. Similarly, Scandinavian countries have supported the development of the Baltic region and have kept up the European Union's (EU) interest in the three small Baltic republics.[4] These EU countries have been able to exert a strong influence on their respective regions and have acted as stabilizing forces in the initial, uncertain stages of post-Communist transition, as well as subsequent stages of democratic consolidation and economic development.

Based on the above, both Turkey and Greece have the potential to influence the Balkans. In addition, with the changing Yugoslav and Soviet borders and the problematic nature of transition in those regions, both countries became surrounded by new states that are more vulnerable economically, diplomatically and militarily. In the economic field, Greece and Turkey developed an interest in investment and trade opportunities; through their more experienced market economies and more advanced business sectors both were poised to explore the post-Communist markets. From the start, Greece has been oriented towards the Balkan markets as its natural geographical expansion and its only land link with the EU. Greece's influence has also been strengthened by its Gross Domestic Product (GDP), which is bigger than that of all the Balkan countries put together.[5] Turkey had a similar interest and advantage in fostering economic ties. For Turkey, the Balkans was one of a number of new regional markets, along with neighboring former Soviet territories and cooperation in the Black Sea region. Although of a less stable nature, the Turkish economy has been characterized as a very large, dynamic and ever-growing market with a significant potential for domestic and external expansion.[6]

Politically, during the postwar period both countries had democratic experiences, which in both cases were interrupted by authoritarian regimes and the intervention of the military in politics. Yet for Greece, the post-1974 period was a gradual consolidation of democratic processes in the sense that democracy became "the only game in town."[7] Together with Spain and Portugal, Greece has undergone a democratization and Europeanization process greatly assisted by its membership in the EC/EU.[8] On the other hand, Turkish democracy has not been a strong point of regional influence in the Balkans; rather, it has been a secular democratic state with flaws regarding such issues as the protection of human rights and the role of the military in politics, and difficulties such as an internal war against the Kurdistan Workers' Party

(*Partiya Karkeren Kurdistan*—PKK) and weak governmental coalitions (no single party won an overall majority in parliament in any of the three general elections held in 1991, 1995 and 1999). These political features took their toll on the country's foreign relations and its potential for regional influence.[9]

In the military field, both countries have been dedicating a significant portion of their GDP to military spending, largely due to competition with each other. Greece's military expenditures have been higher than all other EU countries, ranging from 5.5 to seven percent of its GDP. Turkey has the second-biggest army in NATO and a defense budget of around 11 percent of its national budget. It is, therefore, bigger and stronger than Greece's army with a more advanced and larger military power structure; the military also plays a more significant role in domestic politics. Both countries are also vulnerable to external threats and the instabilities of their neighboring regions: Greece feels the threats from the Balkans and Turkey; Turkey sees threats emanating from the Aegean, the Caucasus region and the Middle East. These feelings propel their propensity for military expenditure and preparedness.

Diplomatically, both countries are in a good position by virtue of their participation in influential Western international organizations and enjoy advanced links with the United States and Western Europe. Greece's membership in the EU has made it a more influential partner for its Balkan neighbors as it has the ability to promote their cause for integration into the EU. Turkey, on the other hand, has been a more reliable NATO ally by virtue of the country's Atlanticist orientation and its special relationship with the United States. Since the end of the cold war, Turkey has been considered increasingly important for the West and the United States in the unstable Middle Eastern and post-Soviet contexts. Yet, its complex relationship with the EU has been its main weakness as a regional interlocutor in the Balkans: it eventually became a more problematic candidate country than certain Balkan countries—even more so than Bulgaria and Romania.

Finally, the fact that both countries have been historically involved in the Balkans has given them a comparative advantage over other Western countries in terms of better knowledge and access to the new markets and societies. However, Turkey's imperial past has also been its weakness,[10] occasionally making Turkey a player with suspicious revisionist motives in the eyes of some Balkan countries. The relationship between Greece and the Balkan countries has been more balanced in that respect, although Greece has, at times, been perceived as pursuing an arrogant policy towards its Balkan neighbors.[11]

By and large, both countries have been better positioned to influence developments in the Balkan region since the beginning of the post-Communist transition. For Greece, the end of the cold war restored its lost Balkan identity in the sense that it re-entered the region. For Turkey, an area of significant historical importance and European value was redis-covered. Moreover, both countries exhibited an interest in their respective populations living in the Balkans (Turks living in Bosnia-Herzegovina, FYR Macedonia, Kosovo and Bulgaria; Greeks living in Albania). Thus Greece and Turkey have become involved in the Balkans because both countries were affected in numerous ways by developments there and both countries became regional players with the potential to influence and benefit. Yet, both countries also displayed vulnerabilities that diminished their potential to influence. Greece is the weakest link in the 15 member states of the EU, with a less advanced economy, and is geographically isolated from the rest of the EU. Turkey, on the other hand, has an ambiva-lent and contested European identity, and a bad reputation concerning human rights and its intransigence on the Cyprus issue. It also has unstable domestic politics, an unstable economy and an uphill struggle for EU membership, and is surrounded by additional areas of instability.

HOW HAVE TURKEY AND GREECE BEEN INVOLVED IN THE BALKANS?

The absence of systemic bipolarity led to the deterioration of bilateral relations between Greece and Turkey on a range of issues and a series of crises and disputes during the 1990s (for example, the Turkish parliament's declaration in 1994 that extension of Greek territorial waters in the Aegean to the 12-mile limit would be a *casus belli*, the Imia/Kardak near-war in 1996, the S-300 crisis in Cyprus in 1998 and the Öcalan affair in 1999). In this competitive bilateral climate, both countries displayed reinforced skepticism towards each other's intentions in the Balkans. Greek and Turkish Balkan policies and reactions to events were often contradictory—expressing their elites' antagonistic feelings as well as differences in the ways they perceived their respective national interests: Greeks supported the Serbs, Turks blamed the Serbs for the problems in former Yugoslavia; Greeks sided with Orthodox populations, Turks with Muslims; Turkey profited from Greece's weakness in FYR Macedonia and Albania by strengthening bilateral ties when Greece's bilateral relations were strained.[12] Greece tried to win over Bulgaria and Romania and was very negative towards international interventions in Bosnia-Herzegovina and Kosovo, while Turkey enthusiastically supported international action.

Turkey adopted an Atlanticist, NATO-oriented conception of European security, Greece adopted a Europeanist, EU-centered approach—and their views differed markedly on the issue of European Security and Defense Identity (ESDI).

From the onset of the post-Communist transition, two main issues preoccupied the minds of the Greek political elites concerning the Balkans: the creation of the new state of Macedonia and the status of the Greek minority in Albania.[13] The first issue caused considerable anxiety for the Greek government and society as the country had been supporting the territorial *status quo* in the Balkans and viewed the creation of new states in Yugoslavia with skepticism. Moreover, its reaction was more pronounced in the case of Macedonia, an issue that dominated Greek foreign policy from 1991 until 1995 (frequently referred to as the "Skopjanisation" of Greek politics). During that time, Greece focused on the non-recognition of a state by the name of Macedonia, adopting maximalist demands from the new state (non-use of the term Macedonia, disavowal of all territorial claims on Greece from the new Macedonian constitution, refusal to acknowledge that there is a "Macedonian" minority in Greece). The Greek political elites and public feared that the recognition of a country as "the Republic of Macedonia" would legitimize the latter's irredentist claims. The Macedonian question caused vast public anxiety because of the territorial implications that the adoption of the name "Macedonia" entailed.[14] Both governing parties (New Democracy and PASOK) adopted a rather nationalist and aggressive policy on the issue, culminating in a trade embargo in 1994 on FYR Macedonia—which lasted for a year and a half and negatively affected the latter's transition and economy.

Relations with Albania were also complicated by the substantial Greek minority in the south and the initial relaxation of border restrictions, which brought many illegal Albanian immigrants to Greece. At various points during the first part of the 1990s, relations soured when, for instance, the Greek government vetoed EU aid to Albania and expelled 50,000 illegal immigrants in retaliation for the internment of five ethnic Greeks in Albania on espionage charges.[15] On the eastern Balkan front, relations with Bulgaria and Romania were more promising, although there had been some initial sensitivity concerning the former related to the Bulgarian government's recognition of Macedonia and the Bulgarian-Turkish post-1989 rapprochement.

In the first part of the 1990s, Greek foreign policy was strongly influenced by a neo-realist, nationalistic and populist approach with a propensity for pressure and bilateral action. This traditionalist conception of the national interest—to be found in influential political as well as social circles such as the Church and the media—generates a "threat syndrome," according to which the country is vulnerable to external threats from Turkey or other irredentist nations in the Balkans. The Greek affinity with Serbia is seen *inter alia* as a counterbalance to such perceived threats from other countries in the region. Drawing on common historical and Orthodox ties, Greece became the most vociferous ally of Serbian interests in the region, even at a time when the international community blamed Serbia for most of the tragedy in the former Yugoslavia. As a result, Greece often found itself isolated on the international front with little sympathy—even from its EU allies.

Turkey pursued a more balanced and measured regional policy in the Balkans. Its main preoccupations involved identity questions of the Turkish and Muslim populations in Bosnia-Herzegovina, Sandjak, Kosovo, FYR Macedonia and Bulgaria, as well as the inflow of refugees from the Balkans to Turkey. Initially Turkey, like Greece, was against the disintegration of Yugoslavia, but following the EC recognition of Slovenia and Croatia, Turkey immediately recognized all four breakaway republics (including Bosnia-Herzegovina and Macedonia). Within the disintegrating Yugoslav territory, Bosnia-Herzegovina became the primary concern of Turkish foreign policy as well as the Turkish public's concern, not least because a large number of Turks of Bosnian origin were living in Turkey. This is, of course, also the case today: the number is estimated to be between 2 and 4 million. Additionally, Turkey identified with Bosnia-Herzegovina as a fellow secular government with a predominantly Muslim country.[16] It therefore intervened actively, advocating an end to the war through multilateral—rather than bilateral—actions (NATO, UN or Islamic Conference Organization). Arguing in defense of Bosnia, Turkey blamed Serbian aggression and criticized the international organizations for indecision and for acting like a Christian club. Turkish policymakers maintained that the UN arms embargo was punishing the Bosnian government by denying Bosnia-Herzegovina the ability to defend its own territory and called for stern multilateral action as well as the territorial integrity of the country.[17] Eventually, Turkey acted as a broker between the Bosnians and the Croats in November 1993, contributing to the American-led Washington Agreement of March 1994, and participated in the subsequent monitoring of the ceasefire in Zenica. Following the Dayton accords, Turkey assumed a major role in training the Bosnian-Croatian Federation army.

Apart from its activist policy in Bosnia-Herzegovina, Turkey established close bilateral relations with Albania, FYR Macedonia, Croatia, Bulgaria and Romania. Bulgaria, in particular, Turkey's only neighboring Balkan country (not counting Greece), has been very important for Turkey due to its sizable Turkish population (around 800,000) and a traumatic recent history of bilateral relations. Despite Todor Zivkov's policy of "Bulgarification" (a vigorous assimilation campaign carried out between 1984 and 1989 that resulted in a massive exodus of Turks from Bulgaria to Turkey), Ankara chose to establish close links with the post-Communist Bulgarian regime. Turkey settled the identity, representation and repatriation issues concerning the Turks in Bulgaria and signed the Treaty of Friendship, Good Neighborliness, Cooperation and Security in 1992. Moreover, Turkey invited Bulgaria, Romania (and Greece) into its Black Sea Economic Cooperation regional scheme, a Turkish initiative of the late 1980s that was formally constituted in 1992.[18]

Overall, in the initial stages of post-Communist transition, Greek foreign policy appeared to be not so confident and less in tune with the international community, as opposed to Turkey's—which was more balanced and synchronized with the international community's policy. Greece's bilateral relations with the individual Balkan countries, as well as its relationship with its EU partners, suffered from serious setbacks. Meanwhile, Turkey managed to capitalize on Greece's weaknesses by building bilateral relations with those countries and pursuing an activist policy in Bosnia-Herzegovina, which was eventually justified. Turkey pursued a policy geared towards the protection of the Muslim and Turkish populations in the Balkans, supporting multilateral actions in the region. However, Turkey did not feel the same imminent threat that Greece felt from the disintegration of Yugoslavia and was preoccupied with other sources of regional instabilities, such as from neighboring Abkhazia, Chechnya and northern Iraq. Greece, for its part, viewed Ankara's bilateral relationships in the Balkans with suspicion and feared that Turkey was attempting to create a Turkish/Muslim "arc" and trying to restore its Ottoman legacy in the region in an alternate form.

The antagonistic climate between the two countries also extended into the economic sphere. Greece was suspicious of the Black Sea Economic Cooperation Initiative (BSEC initiative) and chose to participate in order to keep an eye on Turkey's regional intentions. Furthermore, while Turkey supported the West-East motorway through Durres, Skopje, Sofia and Istanbul, Greece supported its own "Egnatia" national highway, and while Ankara promoted the overland pipeline from Baku terminating on its own Mediterranean port of Ceyhan, Athens supported the funneling of Caspian oil from the Russian port of Novorossiysk by tanker to the Bulgarian port of Burgas and thence by pipeline to the Greek Aegean port of Alexandroupolis—thereby circumventing the Turkish Straits.

In the post-Dayton era, Greece gradually developed a more balanced, multilateral and technocratic approach to the Balkans and focused on the intensification of economic links with most of its Balkan neighbors. The end of the Greek embargo and the signing of an interim agreement brought considerable relaxation to relations with FYR Macedonia, whereby—while the issue of the name was not resolved—economic and diplomatic relations were normalized, and have improved substantially since then. Similarly, relations with Albania have been steadily improving since joint bilateral committees were set up, agreements allowing Greek schools and consulates to open in Albania were signed, Albanian immigrants gained legal status in Greece and direct financial assistance for various projects in Albania was provided. Greece, together with Italy, assumed a leading position in the restoration of order following the collapse of the Albanian pyramid schemes in 1997.

The Crete Balkan summit in 1997—the follow-up to the Balkan Conference on Stability, Security and Cooperation in Southeastern Europe that was launched in Sofia the previous year—was seen as a way to promote multilateral cooperation in political, cultural, economic, security and human rights issues in the midst of a tense and very critical period for the Balkans. Even during the 1999 NATO bombing of Yugoslavia, the Greek government managed to maintain a fine balance between its obligations as a NATO member and particularly reluctant Greek public opinion. Thereafter, Greece tried on several occasions to act as an intermediary between Serbian interests and the EU by arguing against the international isolation of the Serbian people and trying to keep the channels of communication open. In the post-Milosevic context, Greece has been supporting the European orientation of all the countries in the Balkans (including Turkey) and, while holding the EU Presidency during the first half of 2003, sought to fight against the West's "Balkan fatigue" by advocating a more committed approach towards EU membership for the Balkans.

With the end of the war in Bosnia-Herzegovina, Turkey lost part of its active interest in the Balkans and even sought to re-establish working relations with Belgrade. However, Serbian actions in Kosovo, which has a Turkish population of 30–40,000, reminded Turks that Serbian aggression was the main reason for the situation in former Yugoslavia. Therefore, the Turkish leadership advocated the intervention of an international peace force in Kosovo to prevent a repetition of the Bosnian war and the suffering of fellow Muslims and declared its readiness to take part in such a force. It also strongly supported NATO intervention by providing bases and aircraft and accepted some Albanian refugees. However, Turkey made clear that this should not lead to Kosovo's declaration of independence from the Federal Republic of Yugoslavia (FRY) but to the full restoration of its autonomy within the FRY.[19]

In Kosovo, and later in FYR Macedonia, Greece and Turkey expressed their common concern that Balkan conflict might spill over and even sought to cooperate on matters of security concerning the southern Balkans. As a result, Greece joined Turkey in providing troops for the NATO-led force in Kosovo (KFOR) and cooperated in providing humanitarian relief to Kosovar refugees. Since then, both have been advocating the current *status quo*: the non-changeability of Balkan borders and the solution of ethnic problems within these borders.

GREEK AND TURKISH REGIONAL INFLUENCES COMPARED

In retrospect, both Greece and Turkey have been able to significantly influence developments in the Balkans. Greece, for instance, had an immediate economic impact on the region when Greek entrepreneurs entered the Balkan markets sooner than other European partners. On the other hand, Greece's embargo on FYR Macedonia had a negative impact on the latter's development, as mentioned above. Through its membership in the EU, Greece was also able to exert some influence (mainly through its veto power) regarding aid to Albania and the recognition of FYR Macedonia.

Eventually, the notion of "soft power" as a means of external influence gained increasing favor in Greece.[20] Some have attributed this dramatic change in Greek foreign policy to the role of political personalities. As the "modernizers" gained momentum and influence in politics from 1996 onwards (through the transition from Andreas Papandreou to Kostas Simitis at the Premiership and the Presidency of PASOK), conditions looked more propitious for a more cooperative and open strategy in the region. Indeed, it is difficult to perceive this change without acknowledging the reformed political profiles of the new leaders and the predominance of the "modernizing" PASOK fraction of Kostas Simitis. Andreas Papandreou's successor has been a pragmatic reformer committed to multilateralism and functional cooperation, while his foreign minister, George Papandreou, has been a vociferous supporter of Greek-Turkish reconciliation.[21]

But apart from political personalities, economic factors have had a powerful—and perhaps more durable—influence on Greece's external behavior. In many ways, the argument for economic opportunities held more weight than the strictly speaking political argument concerning security and national dangers. In fact, one of the main reasons the country's foreign policy towards FYR Macedonia was relaxed was because of economic interest and the realization that Greece could benefit more from economic interaction and investment than from coercion and sanctions. Strong economic and commercial interests, particularly in Northern Greece, had suffered losses and missed opportunities through the embargo and were critical of any barriers to regional trade and free economic cooperation in the Balkans.

Even in periods of tension with its northern neighbors, Greek entrepreneurs sought to expand, export and invest in the Balkans and the Black Sea. Greek export performance in the region rose and diversified substantially and gradually became predominant compared to that of other EU members in FYR Macedonia and Albania and significant in Bulgaria and Romania, and included items such as industrial goods and raw materials, food, consumption goods and fuel. Physical proximity, historical links and the legacy of the Greek diaspora in those territories enabled the development of partnerships and business transactions between Greek businesses and their northern counterparts as well as Greek involvement in privatization and acquisition schemes.[22]

On the other hand, the economic impact of immigrants on the Greek economy has been equally substantial. Greece's agriculture, service and construction industries have benefited greatly from Bulgarian, Albanian and Romanian workers. The influx of these immigrants has proved beneficial to the Greek economy, providing cheap labor and keeping the rural and abandoned areas alive. With the help of this influx of labor, Greece—following its entry into the euro zone—has been able to project itself as an equal member state of the EU and a more confident market in the Balkans.

For its part, Turkey as a large and militarily powerful country has been able to exert an influence on the Balkans through its contribution towards ending Bosnian-Croat hostility, the Washington Agreement, its involvement in peacekeeping operations and police forces in Bosnia-Herzegovina, its participation in Operation Alba in Albania and its involvement in KFOR in Kosovo. Turkey's participation in international forces in the region has increased its military credibility as a regional player. Furthermore, economic diplomacy, initiated during the Turgut Özal era, has been gaining momentum on the Turkish foreign policy agenda concerning issues such as energy investment, Caspian oil routes, water sharing, environmental issues and Balkan reconstruction. Private NGOs, such as TÜSİAD (*Türk Sanayicileri ve İşadamları Derneği*—Turkish Industrialists' and Businessmen's Association), present Turkey's more technocratic, entrepreneurial face abroad. Turkey has concentrated on the Bulgarian and Romanian markets with numerous small and medium joint ventures and growing trade. Yet, as Mehmet Öğütçü argues, a more coherent institutionalized framework for economic diplomacy has yet to be developed and, according to most of the foreign trade and investment statistics in southeastern Europe and the ex-Soviet area, Turkey trails behind many OECD countries.[23]

In Turkey, the notion of security is still a predominant consideration in foreign policy matters. The September 11 events increased the geostrategic significance of Turkey in the fight against terrorism. Moreover, Turkey's geography makes it difficult for policymakers to disentangle its policy from serious security concerns. Turkish political elites are obsessed with the lack of security in their vicinity and the potential or actual dangers surrounding the country. At the center of this security preoccupation is the armed forces, the foreign ministry bureaucracy and a number of intelligence and security services that have an opinion on external matters. Foreign policymaking in Turkey still remains the domain of the Turkish political elites (who control diplomatic and military bureaucracy) and political considerations overrule purely economic considerations. Moreover, the recent years of economic and financial crises have exacerbated the power of economic diplomacy by projecting a Turkish economy with diminishing confidence abroad.

In the eyes of the Balkan countries, Greece and Turkey have different potentials for influence. Turkey, through its Atlanticist orientation, is able to promote the integration of the Balkan countries into NATO mechanisms more effectively. Greece, through its EU membership and its Europeanist orientation, is able to promote their integration into the EU. In Kagan's terminology, Turkey—in many respects—lives in a "Hobbesian" anarchical regional environment, surrounded by conflicts and hard security choices.[24] Its struggle to be part of the EU is also a struggle to be part of the "Kantian paradise" where functional cooperation, perpetual peace and soft security issues are the name of the game. This is where Greece derives much of its influence, not just in its relationship with the Balkans but, more significantly, towards Turkey.

CONCLUSION: ZERO- OR POSITIVE-SUM RELATIONSHIP?

The Balkan experience demonstrates that the relationship between Turkey and Greece need not necessarily be zero-sum and antagonistic. National interests may vary and foreign policy priorities may be different but, by and large, the two countries share similar assumptions and have identified some common areas of cooperation.

Greece and Turkey are both in favor of the *status quo* in the Balkans. Both of them initially supported the unity of Yugoslavia but were forced to accept reality. They both believe that further conflicts in FYR Macedonia, Kosovo or Albania could lead to dangerous situations in the southern Balkans and could bring the conflict closer to them. They have tried to avoid being entangled in the Balkan conflicts, thus favoring multilateral actions through big international entities such as the EU, the UN, NATO, the Council of Europe and OSCE initiative (Organization for Security and Cooperation in Europe). They are both members of a series of regional initiatives, including the Stability Pact, the South East European Cooperation Process and the BSEC initiative. Finally, they both recognize the value of the new regionalist context, which prescribes functional cooperation, interdependence and networking.

Following the recent rapprochement, both countries chose to identify areas of common interest in the fields of economy, trade, tourism, environment, culture, multilateral cooperation and combating crime. They have progressed by signing a series of joint agreements at the governmental level and have also developed civil society links. Business and other activities have extended beyond the strictly bilateral area to include joint activities and ventures in Eastern Europe, the Eastern Mediterranean and Central Asia. From a technocratic point of view, both can benefit from the fact that Greek businesses are more developed in the Balkans and Turkish companies are more influential in Central Asia and the Middle East.

Despite bilateral antagonisms, the Balkans has proved to be a common area for action—and one which has had a spillover effect into the bilateral relations of the two countries. Paradoxically, the Balkan "neutral" common ground has generated healthy competition between the two countries and allowed for more active involvement. Yet the Balkans has also been the dependent, rather than the independent, variable in the Greek-Turkish relationship. Thus, while common action in the Balkans can generate a more positive dynamic between the two countries, it is mostly conditioned upon the state of Greek and Turkish bilateral relations.

NOTES

I would like to thank Ali Çarkoğlu for his contribution to this volume, as well as his comments on my essay. I benefited enormously from the workshop that he organized in Istanbul in June 2003. I would also like to thank Ioannis N. Grigoriadis for his assistance with this essay.

1. The "Balkan Agreement Pact" of February 1934 between Greece, Romania, Yugoslavia and Turkey was one of the great instances of Balkan cooperation, and was turned down by Bulgaria and Albania. The latter two countries refused to accept the territorial *status quo* in the Balkans and moved closer to Italy and Hungary. See Duško Lopandiæ, *Regional Initiatives in South Eastern Europe* (Belgrade: European Movement in Serbia, 2001), p.45.
2. Andreas Papandreou's idea for a Balkan Nuclear Free Zone in 1984 was resisted by NATO members who insisted that the Balkan region should not be separated from the rest of Europe for the purposes of arms control and disarmament. See Thanos Veremis, *Greece's Balkan Entanglement* (Athens: ELIAMEP, 1995), p.39.
3. Nikolaj Petersen, "National Perspectives in the Integration Dilemma: An Adaptation Approach," *Journal of Common Market Studies*, Vol.36, No.1 (March 1998), pp.33–54.
4. Othon Anastasakis and Vesna Bojicic-Dzelilovic, *Balkan Regional Cooperation and European Integration* (London: The Hellenic Observatory, 2002); see <http://www.lse.ac.uk/collections/hellenicObservatory/pdf/brie.pdf>.
5. Loukas Tsoukalis, "Greece: Like Any Other Country?" *The National Interest*, No.55 (Spring 1999); <http://www.nationalinterest.org/ME2/default.asp>.
6. Mehmet Oğütçü, "Turkey's New Economic Diplomacy: Balancing Commercial Interests with Geopolitical Goals," paper presented at a conference entitled "La Turquie dans les Politiques Europeène et Americaine," organized by CERI, Paris, Dec. 10–11, 2001, pp.4–5.
7. Juan Linz and Alfred Stepan, *Problems of Democratic Transition and Consolidation: Southern Europe, South America, Post-Communist Europe* (Baltimore, MD and London: The Johns Hopkins University Press, 1996), p.5.
8. Kevin Featherstone and George Kazamias (eds.), *Europeanization and the Southern Periphery* (London and Portland, OR: Frank Cass, 2001).
9. William Hale, "Economic Issues in Turkish Foreign Policy," in Alan Makovsky and Sabri Sayari (eds.), *Turkey's New World: Changing Dynamics in Turkish Foreign Policy* (Washington DC: The Washington Institute for Near East Policy, 2000), pp.20–38.
10. Philip Robins, *Suits and Uniforms: Turkish Foreign Policy since the Cold War* (London: Hurst, 2003), p.101.
11. As Misha Glenny points out, during Samaras' tenure at the Greek Foreign Ministry, Greece attempted to portray itself as "the godfather of Balkan diplomacy" and "instead of exploiting the possibilities offered by the opening of the Balkans," it alienated pro-Greek elements in Albania, FYR Macedonia and even Bulgaria. Misha Glenny, "The Temptation of the Purgatory," in Graham Allison and Kalypso Nicolaidis (eds.), *The Greek Paradox: Promise vs. Performance* (Cambridge, MA and London: MIT Press, 1997), pp.73–82.
12. Tozun Bahçeli, "Turkish Policy Towards Greece," in Alan Makovsky and Sabri Sayari (eds.), *Turkey's New World: Changing Dynamics in Turkish Foreign Policy* (Washington DC: The Washington Institute for Near East Policy, 2000), pp.131–52.
13. Sotiris Wallden, "La Politique Balkanique Grecque de 1990 a 1995," *CSS Survey*, Nos.7–8 (July–Aug. 1996); see <http://www.geocities.com/CapitolHill/2890/css-s6.html>.
14. Evangelos Kofos, "Greece's Macedonian Adventure: The Controversy over FYROM's Independence and Recognition," *Macedonian Heritage* (an On-line Review of Macedonian Affairs, History and Culture); <http://www.macedonian-heritage.gr/Contributions/contr Kofos19990705.html>.
15. Richard Crampton, *The Balkans since the Second World War* (London: Pearson Education, 2002), p.338.
16. Robins (2003), p.351.
17. Sule Kut, "Turkish Policy Towards the Balkans," in Makovsky and Sayari (2000), pp.74–91.
18. For more information on the Black Sea Economic Cooperation, see <http://www.bsec.gov.tr>.

19. Heinz Kramer, *A Changing Turkey: The Challenge to Europe and the United States* (Washington DC: Brookings Institution, 2000), p.153.
20. According to Joseph Nye Jr., soft power is the ability to get what you want by attracting and persuading others to adopt your goals rather than forcing them to do what you want them to do. Greece's soft power relies on its political integration with Western Europe and its economic integration into the global marketplace. Joseph S. Nye Jr., "Greece and the Balkans: A Moment of Opportunity," in Allison and Nicolaidis (1997), pp.145–50.
21. A. George Papandreou, "Principles of Greek Foreign Policy," *Mediterranean Quarterly*, Vol.12, No.1 (Winter 2001), pp.1–10.
22. Companies like 3E, DELTA, CHIPITA, Hellenic Petroleum, Titan Cement, OTE, and large financial institutions like the National Bank of Greece or Alpha Bank and smaller banks like Xios Bank and Ionian Bank, established units in Bulgaria, Romania and elsewhere. Antonis Kamaras, *A Capitalist Diaspora: The Greeks in the Balkans*, Discussion Paper No.4 (London: The Hellenic Observatory, 2001); <http://www.lse.ac.uk/collections/hellenicObservatory/pdf/KamarasDiscussionPaper4.pdf>.
23. Oğütçü (2001), p.6.
24. Robert Kagan, *Paradise and Power: America and Europe in the New World Order* (London: Atlantic Books, 2003), *passim*.

5

A Model of Power-Sharing in Cyprus: From the 1959 London-Zurich Agreements to the Annan Plan

AHMET SÖZEN

The Cyprus conflict has been on the international community's agenda, awaiting resolution, for half a century. The conflict has cost the two Cypriot communities—Greek and Turkish—dearly in terms of property and lives lost and years of uncertainty regarding the future. The two communities in Cyprus have been deeply divided in many respects, most notably politically and economically. Today, the *status quo* on the island has become almost unbearable for the two communities, though more so for the Turkish Cypriots—who have been isolated from the rest of the world for almost four decades. The conflict has also poisoned relations between the two North Atlantic Treaty Organization (NATO) allies and neighbors, Turkey and Greece. Instead of realizing the great potential for cooperation on many issues in accordance with their mutual interests, the two countries have been spending billions of dollars each year on military expenditures to counter the perceived threats from one another. Furthermore, the non-resolution of the Cyprus problem poses a significant challenge for the next wave of enlargement of the European Union (EU) in May 2004, when the Republic of Cyprus—together with nine other countries—is scheduled to become a full member of the EU. It is this background that makes the resolution of the Cyprus conflict critical and urgent and makes relevant current research on the Cyprus conflict.

It is clear from the principles adopted by the international community in many United Nations (UN) Security Council resolutions and many UN Secretary General reports and statements that any durable solution to the Cyprus conflict should include an innovative design to accommodate the needs and interests of the two deeply divided Cypriot communities and their respective motherlands, Greece and Turkey, as well as in accordance with both the realities on the ground in Cyprus and the widely agreed upon principles and norms of international law. Thus, a durable solution should be based on a design of "governance in multi-ethnic societies" where the two Cypriot communities are required to operate through a true power-sharing mechanism and resolve their problems through relevant conflict-resolution mechanisms.

Since 1968, the two sides have been negotiating under UN auspices to find a comprehensive solution to the Cyprus problem. In 2002, after the most recent set of negotiations, the UN Secretary General Kofi Annan presented a comprehensive overall agreement to the two sides, known as the "Annan Plan."

This contribution begins by depicting the history of the Cyprus conflict, and then follows with a discussion of the evolution of the concept of governance in multi-ethnic societies. Next, it describes the fundamental elements of the Annan Plan and evaluates the plan as a new hybrid model of confederation and federation, and whether this model would satisfy the needs and interests of the disputed sides, and concludes by asking whether it is a durable solution for the two ethnically distinct communities.

A BRIEF HISTORICAL BACKGROUND OF THE CYPRUS CONFLICT

The Republic of Cyprus was created after long and arduous negotiations, mostly between the two "motherlands"—Greece and Turkey, in order to reach a compromise between the two ethnic communities in Cyprus in the wake of British colonial rule. The 1959 London and Zurich Agreements were the international treaties that led to the creation of the Republic of Cyprus. This republic was a consociational democracy,[1] also known as a functional federation.[2] The structure of the republic reflected a delicate system of power-sharing between the two communities of the island, which manifested itself in all three branches of the republic: the executive, the legislative and the judiciary.

By the end of 1963, the republic had collapsed because of the inability of the two ethnic communities, the Greek and Turkish Cypriots, to work together.[3] The ethnic clashes had actually begun in the 1950s in the wake of debates over the future political form of the island after the end of British colonial rule and the withdrawal of the British from the island. These clashes erupted frequently, with major flare-ups in 1963 and 1967, and finally culminated in 1974 when a military *coup d'état* engineered by the then military regime of Greece tried to overthrow the Greek Cypriot government and annex the whole island to Greece. In order to prevent the Greek coup from actualizing *enosis* (union with Greece), Turkey deployed troops in Cyprus.

Today, the two communities—the Greek and Turkish Cypriot communities—that co-founded the 1960 Republic of Cyprus live separately, each community in its own geographically separate territory. What is known as the Republic of Cyprus (RoC) has been under total Greek Cypriot administration since the end of 1963, and is recognized internationally and maintains a seat in the UN General Assembly as a sovereign state. The other co-founder of the 1960 Republic, the Turkish Cypriot community, has been living under a separate Turkish Cypriot administration since 1963.[4] Since 1983, the Turkish Cypriots have been living under the banner of their self-declared Turkish Republic of Northern Cyprus (TRNC), which has all the characteristics and the organs of a small nation state in accordance with the modern state system since the Peace of Westphalia (1648). Yet, it is recognized internationally only by Turkey.

Therefore, in reality, there have been two nation states in Cyprus since 1963. Only one (RoC) is recognized as the *de jure* state of the whole island. Although it claims sovereignty over the entire island, it has *de facto* sovereignty over two-thirds of the island—the southern part of Cyprus. On the other hand, there is also a *de facto* republic, the TRNC, which, like Taiwan, is not recognized internationally, but has *de facto* sovereignty over one-third of the island, the northern part, with the help of some 30,000 Turkish troops.

While the two communities developed their respective separate governing institutions, the leaderships of the two communities have continued to negotiate—on and off—since 1968 under UN auspices in order to devise a comprehensive solution to the Cyprus problem. All the proposals for a comprehensive solution to the Cyprus problem have called for some degree of cooperation, power-sharing and integration of the two communities and their respective governing bodies.[5] The most recent UN proposal is the Annan Plan, which was first proposed to the two sides on November 11, 2002, after intensive face-to-face talks between the relevant leaders in 2002. The plan was revised twice, based on feedback from the leaderships of the two communities, and presented to them again on December 10, 2002, and on February 26, 2002. According to the UN, the plan offers a balanced solution where the needs and interests of the two ethnic communities are accommodated in a true power-sharing and conflict resolution mechanism. The UN also claims that the plan is compatible with a new idea of governance in multi-ethnic societies, which the international community has been trying to promote.

GOVERNANCE IN MULTI-ETHNIC SOCIETIES

Since the Peace of Westphalia (1648), the international political system can be characterized as a modern "state" system based on the notion of territorially sovereign states. After the French Revolution, the emergence and subsequent spread of nationalism in almost all areas of the world created a new actor in the international political system—the nation state. As opposed to states being defined by their territory, nationalism champions the idea that a *nation* has the right to possess its own *state*. The end of the First World War and the collapse of the Austro-Hungarian and the Ottoman empires paved the way for the creation of dozens of new nation states from the remnants of the collapsed multi-ethnic empires. It was during this period that *self-determination*—the right of a *people* (nation) to govern itself and decide on the legal and political status of the territory it occupies—became a widely accepted principle of international law and customary practices.

Until the 1970s, self-determination had been interpreted as the right of a *people* to establish its own state. This is a *secessionist* explanation. However, who decides what a *people* consists of and whether it has the right to a separate statehood? Is rebellion or revolution or secession justified as the means a people use to establish its own state? In that regard, how feasible or just is the claim of many ethnic groups to self-determination? It was these questions that led the international community to rethink and redefine the concept of self-determination after the 1970s. The end of the cold war and the collapse of the multi-ethnic states such as the former Soviet Union and the former Yugoslavia brought the issue of self-determination into the international limelight. The international community is now faced with a dilemma: to allow secession of ethnic groups, political fragmentation and divorce, or to find political solutions for multi-ethnic coexistence and multi-ethnic governance.

In general, the international community has chosen to solve this dilemma by redefining the concept of self-determination and attempting to avoid further fragmentation of the international system. Hence, today self-determination is interpreted as the right of a people to participate in the democratic governance of the state in which it resides. In that sense, the secessionist interpretation applies only if it is impossible for a certain people to participate in the democratic governance of their state.

The dissolution of existing multi-ethnic states into new ethnically homogeneous states contains many problems for the international political system. Hence, today, the international community, as Timothy Sisk claims, has adopted an alternative approach, namely an all-inclusive participatory democratic governance and power-sharing mechanism in multi-ethnic states:

Given increasing emphasis on democratic governance as a fundamental human right, ethnic group claims for self-determination should ideally be accommodated in a democratic framework *within* existing states. Although not all ethnic conflicts begin as a quest for territorial sovereignty and self-determination, they often result in such maximalist claims unless they are addressed early and effectively. Power-sharing, defined as practices and institutions that result in broad-based governing coalitions generally inclusive of all major ethnic groups in society, can reconcile principles of self-determination and democracy in multiethnic states, principles that are often perceived to be at odds.[6]

It is known that power-sharing usually evolves as a result of an internal process. However, as an external dynamic, the international community has often attempted to promote power-sharing as means to prevent, manage and resolve ethnic conflicts in multi-ethnic states. In that regard, the international community has encouraged the state to stand above the ethnic conflicts and to impartially mediate them. It is no secret that the Annan Plan exemplifies this spirit.

THE ANNAN PLAN:
A HYBRID SYSTEM OF FEDERATION AND CONFEDERATION

According to the Main Articles (MA) of the Foundation Agreement of the second revision, or the third Annan Plan (hereafter simply called the Annan Plan), the Treaty of Guarantee and the Treaty of Alliance of the London and Zurich Agreements will remain in force and will apply *mutatis mutandis* to a new "state of affairs" (MA, Article 1).

In the new state of affairs there will be a federal/confederal state, the United Cyprus Republic, and two constituent states—the Greek Cypriot State and the Turkish Cypriot State. According to the Annan Plan, the status of the relationship of the United Cyprus Republic, its federal government and its two constituent states is modeled on the status of the relationship of Switzerland, its federal government and its Cantons (MA, Article 2.1 and 2.1.a). According to MA, Article 2.1.a:

> Cyprus is a member of the United Nations and has a single international legal personality and sovereignty. The United Cyprus Republic is organised under its Constitution in accordance with the basic principles of rule of law, democracy, representative republican government, political equality, bi-zonality, and the equal status of the constituent states.

The federal government sovereignly exercises the powers specified in the Constitution. According to the Constitution of the United Cyprus Republic (Article 14), the federal government shall sovereignly exercise legislative and executive competences and functions in the following matters:

a. External relations, including conclusion of international treaties and defence policy;
b. Relations with the European Union;
c. Central Bank functions, including issuance of currency, monetary policy and banking regulations;
d. Federal finances, including budget and all indirect taxation (including customs and excise), and federal economic and trade policy;
e. Natural resources, including water resources;
f. Meteorology, aviation, international navigation and the continental shelf and territorial waters of the United Cyprus Republic;
g. Communications (including postal, electronic and telecommunications);
h. Cypriot citizenship (including issuance of passports) and immigration (including asylum, deportation and extradition of aliens);
i. Combating terrorism, drug trafficking, money laundering and organized crime;
j. Pardons and amnesties (other than for crimes concerning only one constituent state)
k. Intellectual property and weights and measures; and
l. Antiquities.

The constituent states, moreover, will be of equal status. They will be able to "sovereignly exercise all powers not vested by the Constitution in the federal government." Furthermore, they will be able to freely organize themselves under their own Constitutions (MA, Article 2.1.c). According to MA, Article 2.2,[7] the relationship between the federal government and the constituent states, and between the constituent states themselves, regarding external relations and the EU has been modeled on the Belgian system.

The United Cyprus Republic will have a special type of presidential system. The executive power will be vested in a Presidential Council composed of six members—at least two (one-third) from each constituent state. There will be a President and a Vice President, each from a different constituent state, who will serve for ten months. No more than two consecutive presidents may come from the same constituent state. The members of the Presidential Council will be elected on a single list by special majority in the Senate and approved by majority in the Chamber of Deputies. Decisions in the Presidential Council will be reached by consensus. In the event of a lack of consensus, the Presidential Council will, unless otherwise specified, make decisions by a simple majority. However, this majority requires at least one member from each constituent state. The members of the Council will be equal and each member will be the head of a department. The heads of the Departments of Foreign Affairs and European Union Affairs will not come from the same constituent state.[8]

The federal Parliament will be composed of two chambers—the Senate and the Chamber of Deputies. Together they will exercise the legislative power. According to MA, Article 5.1.a, each chamber will have 48 members. While the Senate will be composed of an equal number of senators from each constituent state, the Chamber of Deputies will be composed proportionally of persons holding internal constituent state citizenship status of each constituent state. In the Chamber of Deputies, each constituent state shall be attributed no less than one-quarter of the seats.[9] According to MA, Article 5.1.b, the decisions of the bicameral Parliament will require the approval of both Chambers by simple majority, which must include at least one-quarter of voting senators from each constituent state. For specific issues, two-fifths of sitting senators from each constituent state shall be required.

Each constituent state will have its own courts. They will be responsible for judicial issues within the boundaries of the constituent state. The judiciary power of the federal State will be the Supreme Court. It shall uphold the Constitution and ensure its full respect. The Supreme Court will have an equal number of judges (three) from each constituent state and three non-Cypriot judges until otherwise provided by law. The Court will be responsible for resolving disputes between the constituent states, or between one or both of them and the federal government, and resolving, on an interim basis, deadlocks within federal institutions if this is absolutely crucial to the efficient functioning of the federal government (MA, Article 6).

According to Article 30 of the proposed Constitution of the United Cyprus Republic, the composition of the public service will be proportional to the populations of the constituent states. However, at least one-third of the public servants at every level of the administration must hail from each constituent state.

The updated Treaty of Guarantee will cover, in addition to the independence, territorial integrity, security and constitutional order of the United Cyprus Republic, the territorial integrity, security and constitutional order of the constituent states (MA, Article 8.1.a).

According to the updated Treaty of Alliance, there will be one Greek and one Turkish military contingent stationed on the island, which is not to exceed 6,000 (all ranks) each. They will be stationed in both the Greek Cypriot State and the Turkish Cypriot State. In addition, upon accession of Turkey to the EU, all Greek and Turkish troops shall be withdrawn from Cyprus unless it shall be otherwise agreed between the United Cyprus Republic, Greece and Turkey (MA, Article 8.1.b).

MA, Article 8.1.f clearly states that a Monitoring Committee, which will be composed of representatives of the guarantor powers, the federal government and the constituent states, and chaired by the United Nations, will monitor the implementation of this Agreement. In addition, Cyprus will be demilitarized. All Greek Cypriot and Turkish Cypriot forces, including reserve units, will be dissolved, and their arms removed from the island in specific phases as stated in the Agreement.

In accordance with the demilitarization of the island, there will be no paramilitary or reserve forces or military or paramilitary training of citizens. All weapons, except licensed sporting guns, will be prohibited on the island. Until the full accession of Turkey to the EU, the United Cyprus Republic will not put its territory at the disposal of international military operations without the consent of both constituent states and the consent of Greece and Turkey.

Upon a comprehensive solution to the Cyprus problem, each constituent state will have a fixed territory and there will be a clearly defined boundary between the two constituent states. Special arrangements will be implemented in order to safeguard the rights and interests of the current inhabitants of areas subject to territorial adjustment. The arrangements will provide for orderly relocation of these persons to adequate alternative accommodation in appropriate locations.

According to MA, Article 10 on property, the property claims of the displaced persons due to the 1963 and 1974 events will be resolved in a comprehensive manner in accordance with international law, respect for the individual rights of dispossessed owners and current users, and the principle of bi-zonality. In the areas subject to territorial adjustment, properties will be reinstated to the dispossessed owners of that specific constituent state.[10] The property claims of the dispossessed persons will be received and administered by an independent, impartial Property Board. The Property Board will be composed of an equal number of members from each constituent state, as well as non-Cypriot members. Hence, there will be no direct dealings between the dispossessed individuals of the two communities.

Last but not least, there will be an independent, impartial Reconciliation Commission, which will promote understanding, tolerance and mutual respect between Greek Cypriots and Turkish Cypriots. The Reconciliation Commission will include men and women, in equal numbers, from each constituent state, as well as at least one non-Cypriot member, which the Secretary-General of the United Nations will appoint in consultation with the federal government and the constituent states.

The Annan Plan is a 192-page document with substantial details and it is beyond the scope of this article to discuss more than the fundamental elements of the plan. The critical question to be asked, though, is whether the Annan Plan can provide a stable, durable democratic and multi-ethnic solution to the Cyprus conflict in light of the reality of life on the island and in accordance with the widely agreed upon norms and principles of international law.

THE ANNAN PLAN: AN EVALUATION THROUGH GOVERNANCE IN MULTI-ETHNIC SOCIETIES

According to the literature on governance of multi-ethnic societies, one can detect two broad approaches in designing democratic institutions, especially where there are deep divisions between ethnic groups and where power-sharing is the central locus. One approach is *consociational* power-sharing, which is regarded as a successful conflict-management model for deeply divided societies. Lijphart presents this model better than anyone else.[11] The other approach is *integrative* power-sharing, which is widely associated with Horowitz.[12] While the former approach emphasizes a power-sharing model based on the protection of the rights and representation of various ethnic groups within the state machinery, the latter approach stresses the creation of incentives for inter-ethnic cooperation and inter-ethnic coalitions in multi-ethnic societies. Sisk provides an excellent summary of these two approaches,[13] as set out in Table 1.

In the consociational model, according to Sisk, in power-sharing matters the elites cooperate only after elections and the ethnic groups are autonomous. Group rights are protected by veto rights and proportionality in government representation, civil services and the allocation of funds and resources. The main weakness of this model is the possibility that the elites may resort to conflict to further their opportunistic interests. However, it is widely agreed that this is a better model for multi-ethnic governance where territorial division exists between the different ethnic groups.

TABLE 1
APPROACHES TO POWER-SHARING

Approach	Consociational	Integrative
Characteristics	Elites cooperate after elections to form multi-ethnic coalitions and manage conflicts; groups are autonomous, minorities are protected.	Parties encouraged to create coalitions before elections creating broadly inclusive but majoritarian governments
Principles	Broad-based or "grand" coalitions; minority veto; proportionality in allocation of civil service positions and public funds; group autonomy.	Dispersion and devolution of power; promotion of intra-ethnic competition; inducements for inter-ethnic cooperation; policies to encourage alternative social alignments; managed distribution of resources.
Institutions and practices to promote these principles and effects	Parliamentary government; proportional reservation of seats; proportional representation electoral system.	Federalism; vote-pooling; electoral systems; president elected by "supermajority".
Strengths of the approach	Provides groups firm guarantees for the protection of their interests.	Provides politicians with incentives for moderation— "coalitions of commitment."
Weaknesses	"Coalitions of convenience." Elites may pursue conflict rather than try to reduce it; communal groups may not defer to their leaders; system relies on constraints against immoderate politics.	Lack of whole-country empirical examples of working systems; assumptions that politicians respond to incentives and citizens will vote for parties not based on their own groups.

Source: Timothy D. Sisk, *Power Sharing and International Mediation in Ethnic Conflicts* (Washington DC: United States Institute of Peace, 1996), p.35.

For multi-ethnic governance where territorial division does not exist between the ethnic groups, the integrative model is considered more appropriate. Here, elites are encouraged to cooperate and form coalitions before elections. The integrative system is designed to provide continuous incentives for moderation in order to encourage smooth governance.

Which of the two approaches should be chosen depends on the nature of the case at hand. The Cyprus conflict is an excellent example of two deeply divided ethnic groups. The division has been deepened by many violent clashes, as illustrated above. In addition, the *de facto* physical separation of and the limited contacts between the two communities since

1974 has created additional negative myths and images of the "other," which, in turn, has intensified the deep division between the two communities. Unsurprisingly, in 1993, UN Secretary General Boutros Ghali called for the implementation of a series of confidence building measures (CBMs) before an overall solution could be brought forward. His suggestion was based on his timely and correct diagnosis that the root of the Cyprus conflict was the growing mistrust between the two communities. In that regard, the consociational model offers a more realistic model than the integrative model for a united Cyprus. Does the Annan Plan provide such a model?

The Annan Plan clearly took into consideration the basic principles of international law, human rights and the realities of the island, as well as the necessary characteristics of good governance in a multi-ethnic society. The Annan Plan offers a consociational model where the two deeply divided and territorially separated ethnic communities of the island will have a second attempt (the 1959 London and Zurich Agreements was the first) to create a new state based on power-sharing.

In terms of its characteristics, the Annan Plan is influenced by and has adopted elements characteristic of Belgium and Switzerland, which are regarded in the literature as successful consociational democracies.[14] In these two countries, the ethnic communities are highly autonomous and are required to cooperate only after their separate elections in a central government. According to the Annan Plan, the two constituent states will have competences that they will sovereignly exercise in all areas outside the competencies of the federal government as stated in the Constitution. Besides the election of the Presidential Council from a single list—which carries an integrative element—both constituent states will hold their own separate elections in all areas. They are expected to cooperate only after their separate elections in accordance with the consociational model.

In accordance with the principles of the consociational model, the Annan Plan provides proportional representation for the two ethnic communities in all political offices and in the allocation of civil service positions and public funds. In addition, the decisionmaking on the federal government level is consensus based, requiring at least the minimum participation of both communities. Hence, it is a hidden veto for the two communities respectively. For example, in the Presidential Council, although decisions requiring votes will be decided based on a simple majority, at least one vote from each constituent state will be required.

The institutions that will be created in the United Cyprus Republic support the principles of consociationalism by means of proportional reservation of seats and proportional representation of the two constituent

TABLE 2
CONFLICT-REGULATION PRACTICES

Approach	Consociational	Integrative
Territorial divisions of power	Granting autonomy and creating confederal arrangements; creating a poly-communal federation.	Creating a mixed or non-communal federal structure; establishing a single inclusive unitary state.
Decision rules	Adopting proportional representation and consensus rules in executive, legislative, and administrative decision-making; adopting a highly proportional electoral system.	Adopting majoritarian but integrated executive, legislative, and administrative decision making; adopting a semi-majoritarian or semi-proportional electoral system.
State-ethnic relations	Acknowledging group rights or corporate federalism.	Adopting ethnically blind public policies.

Source: Timothy D. Sisk, *Power Sharing and International Mediation in Ethnic Conflicts* (Washington DC: United States Institute of Peace, 1996), p.70.

states. In addition, the Annan Plan provides firm guarantees for the protection of communal interests (such as the Treaty of Guarantee), which will assure the territorial integrity and the constitutional order of not only the United Cyprus republic but also of the two constituent states.

Of equal—if not greater—importance than the power-sharing elements of governance in a multi-ethnic society are the conflict-regulation practices. Conflict-regulation practices ensure the smooth operation of the institutions in a multi-ethnic state. As depicted in Table 2, Sisk provides a summary of conflict-regulation practices for both the consociational and integrative approaches.[15]

In the consociational model, conflicts are avoided or resolved by granting autonomy and acknowledging separate group rights within federations or confederations of different ethnic groups that are territorially separated. In such an arrangement, proportionality and consensus are required in all branches of the state. In the integrative model, however, since no territorial division between the ethnic groups exists, the system tries to avoid or resolve conflicts by creating non-communal federal structures or a unitary state where ethnically blind public policies are designed in the majoritarian-but-integrated branches of the state.

The Annan Plan allows for good conflict-regulation practices. The Plan grants a high degree of autonomy to each constituent state by creating confederal arrangements within a bi-communal federation which will be based on a territorial division of power. As for state-ethnic community relations, the federal government is not superior to the constituent states and the relations between the constituent states are based on political equality.

In terms of decision rules, the Annan Plan provides proportional representation and consensus rule in two of the branches of power—executive and legislative—as well as for administrative decisionmaking. In addition, the two constituent states elect their own separate personnel for all of the political posts of the United Cyprus Republic except the joint list for the Presidential Council.

As the above evaluation shows, the Annan Plan provides the basic elements of power-sharing and the conflict-regulation practices of a consociational model, which is more suitable for the Cyprus conflict than the integrative model.

CONCLUSION

The 1959 London and Zurich Agreements established a consociational democracy in Cyprus. However, the 1960 Republic of Cyprus failed to last more than three years. Since then, the two conflicting sides have been unable to resolve the conflict. Most recently, the Annan Plan proposed the creation of a consociational federation/confederation in accordance with the most popular interpretation of the concept of self-determination: participation of different ethnic groups in democratic governance within the same federal state.

At present, however, neither Greece nor Turkey accepts the Annan Plan as the basis for a solution to the Cyprus conflict. Meanwhile, the leaderships of the two Cypriot sides continue to follow their traditional maximalist strategies in their efforts to solve the Cyprus conflict. The Greek Cypriots would like to achieve a solution based on a *unitary state*, which means that the 1960 Republic of Cyprus would continue to exist and the Turkish Cypriot community would be absorbed into it as a protected minority. On the other hand, the Turkish Cypriots advocate a confederal solution in which the TRNC would continue to exist and be acknowledged as a separate sovereign state but would cooperate as little as possible with the Greek Cypriot state.

By and large, the two motherlands have so far supported the maximalist strategies of their respective Cypriot communities. However, the EU factor—the accession of Cyprus to the EU in May 2004 and Turkey's struggle to start accession talks with the EU in 2004—has changed the dynamics of the Cyprus conflict. On the one hand, Turkey and the Turkish Cypriots realize that if a solution to the Cyprus conflict is not found by

May 2004 it will be almost impossible to persuade the Greek Cypriot side, which will become an EU member on behalf of the whole island, to accept the Annan Plan as a solution. After May 2004, Turkey and the Turkish Cypriots will be forced to accept a far less favorable solution than the Annan Plan. Moreover, the current Justice and Development Party (*Adalet ve Kalkınma Partisi*—AKP) government of Turkey has also realized that the EU will not begin accession talks with Turkey until the Cyprus conflict is resolved. The issue has also become much more complicated and difficult for Turkey because of the widespread belief among the nationalist and some of the Kemalist elites in Turkey that the EU will never allow Muslim Turkey to be a full member of the Union. If that becomes the case, such elites advocate that Turkey should not be flexible (some even say "Turkey should not give up") regarding Cyprus until Turkey (if ever) becomes a full member of the EU. Meanwhile, the Greek Cypriot leadership supports the Annan Plan, while the Turkish Cypriot leader Rauf R. Denktaş publicly denounces it. The Greek Cypriot rationale for supporting the Annan Plan is to avoid any major problems that could jeopardize the full EU membership of Cyprus. Recently, the current PASOK government of Greece has begun to show less open support for the Annan Plan compared to its earlier positive stance. This is most likely because PASOK is afraid of being labeled as the "party who sold the national cause to the Turks," which could easily jeopardize PASOK's position in the upcoming parliamentary elections. These factors are why the Annan Plan has so far failed to be endorsed and implemented by the two sides.

As the evaluation of the Annan Plan in the previous section shows, the Plan is designed to accommodate the two ethnically distinct communities in a governance structure where power-sharing and conflict-regulation practices are carefully crafted in a truly consociational manner. In this case, what factors would help the new consociational United Cyprus Republic to flourish and be stable, in contrast to the consociational Republic of Cyprus—which in the literature has become an example of the failure of the consociational model?

The Annan Plan provides a territorial federation/confederation as opposed to the non-territorial functional federation structure of the 1959 London and Zurich Agreements. Since the two communities have been governing themselves through their respective administrations and in their own geographic areas since 1963, it is more practical to ensure that the two political bodies continue to administer their separate zones and cooperate under a common umbrella—the federal government.

The Annan Plan grants each community a very high degree of autonomy (even semi-sovereignty) within their respective constituent states as opposed to the 1959 London and Zurich Agreements, where each community had autonomy only in purely communal affairs. This is also compatible with the separate experiences of the two communities since 1963.

The opening of several borders and the easing of restrictions on the freedom of movement between the two sides on April 23, 2003 yielded no significant incidents of violence between the two communities. An optimistic interpretation of the latest peaceful developments could be that the two communities have learned their lesson from their history of violent ethnic conflict and have matured. Both communities now know that their best choice is to reach a compromise and cooperate under a common umbrella. They understand that the alternative is the current *status quo*, which mostly hurt the Turkish Cypriot community but nonetheless has affected both sides negatively.

If a solution based on the Annan Plan is reached before the accession of Cyprus to the EU in May 2004—that is, the Treaty of Accession is to be ratified in May 2004 and the United Cyprus Republic will become an EU member—the EU itself, together with its institutions and norms, will provide another umbrella under which the two Cypriot communities can cooperate peacefully. Such an arrangement within the EU will also foster integration between the two deeply divided Cypriot communities.

The peaceful resolution of the Cyprus conflict will contribute positively not only to Turkey-Greece relations but also to EU-Turkey relations. The resolution of the Cyprus conflict will create a suitable environment of trust in which Turkey and Greece can attempt to resolve their Aegean conflict. The resolution of the Cyprus conflict will also greatly assist the beginning of Turkey's accession negotiations with the EU. However, the opposite is also true: the EU can play an instrumental role in resolving the Cyprus conflict in line with the Annan Plan through linkage politics. If the EU gives a clear signal to Turkey that it will start the accession talks if the Turkish side endorses the Annan Plan, then it is probable that the Turkish side would accept the Annan Plan as a solution to the Cyprus conflict. In the same vein, if the EU signals to the Greek Cypriot leadership that it should accept the Plan or face difficulties in attaining EU membership, it would be very difficult for the Greek side to spoil the Plan.

NOTES

1. The term "consociational democracy" is used by Arend Lijphart to describe the "politics of accommodation," where different ethnic groups are represented in the government and their rights and interests are protected (*Democracy in Plural Societies: A Comparative Exploration* [New Haven, CT: Yale University Press, 1977], pp.25–44). According to Donald Horowitz, Belgium, the Netherlands and Canada are regarded as successful examples of consociational systems, while Cyprus and Lebanon are seen as the two failures of consociational systems (*Ethnic Groups in Conflict* [Berkeley, CA: University of California Press, 1985], pp.568–71).
2. Zenon Stavrinides, *The Cyprus Conflict: National Identity and Statehood* (Nicosia: Stavrinides, 1976), p.76.
3. For an in-depth analysis, see Ahmet Sözen, *The Cyprus Conflict and the Negotiations: A Political and International Law Perspective* (Ankara: Can Reklam, 1998); Ahmet Sözen, "Cyprus Conflict: Continuing Challenge and Prospects for Resolution in the Post-Cold War Era" (unpublished Ph.D. thesis, University of Missouri-Columbia, 1999); and Stavrinides (1976). The literature on Cyprus is mostly partisan writing. For an analysis of the Turkish thesis, see Rauf R. Denktaş, *The Cyprus Triangle* (London, Boston, MA and Sydney: K. Rüstem and George Allen & Unwin, 1982); Rauf R. Denktaş, *The Cyprus Problem and The Remedy* (Nicosia: Turkish Republic of Northern Cyprus Press Office, 1992); Necati Münir Ertekün, *Inter-Communal Talks and The Cyprus Problem* (Nicosia: Turkish Federated State of Cyprus Press Office, 1977); and M. Zaim Necatigil, *The Cyprus Question and the Turkish Position in International Law* (New York: Oxford University Press, 2nd Edn. 1993). For an in-depth analysis of the Greek thesis, see Glafkos Clerides, *Cyprus: My Deposition Vol.1* (Nicosia: Alithia, 1989); Glafkos Clerides, *Cyprus: My Deposition Vol.2* (Nicosia: Alithia, 1989); Glafkos Clerides, *Cyprus: My Deposition Vol.3* (Nicosia: Alithia, 1990); Glafkos Clerides, *Cyprus: My Deposition Vol.4* (Nicosia: Alithia, 1992); Kyriacos C. Markides, *The Rise and Fall of the Cyprus Republic* (New Haven, CT and London: Yale University Press, 1977); and Polyvios G. Polyviou, *Cyprus: The Tragedy and the Challenge* (Washington DC: American Hellenic Institute, 1975).
4. After the 1963 ethnic clashes, the Turkish Cypriot community established different governing structures in order to maintain its communal existence: The Provisional Turkish Cypriot Administration (1967), The Autonomous Turkish Cypriot Administration (1974) and The Turkish Federated State of Cyprus (1975).
5. The Draft Framework Agreement (1985) proposed by Secretary General Perez De Cuellar, and the Set of Ideas (1992) proposed by Secretary General Boutros Ghali, were comprehensive agreement plans that called for the creation of a bi-zonal and a bi-communal federation between the two communities. Each of these proposals called for a high degree of cooperation, power-sharing and at least some degree of integration between the two communities.
6. Timothy D. Sisk, *Power Sharing and International Mediation in Ethnic Conflicts* (Washington DC: United States Institute of Peace, 1996), p.vii.
7. "The constituent states shall cooperate and coordinate with each other and with the federal government, including through Cooperation Agreements, as well as through Constitutional Laws approved by the federal Parliament and both constituent state legislatures. In particular, the constituent states shall participate in the formulation and implementation of policy in external relations and European Union affairs on matters within their sphere of competence, in accordance with Cooperation Agreements modeled on the Belgian example. The constituent states may have commercial and cultural relations with the outside world in conformity with the Constitution." The third Annan Plan (26 Feb. 2003) is available at <http://www.trncpresidency.org/press/news/26_2_03_new_plan.doc>.
8. MA, Article 5.2.b.
9. There will be 24 senators from the Greek Cypriot Constituent State and 24 senators from the Turkish Cypriot State in the Senate. There will be no less than 12 deputies in the Chamber of Deputies who will come from the Turkish Cypriot Constituent State.
10. MA, Article 10.3: 3. "In areas not subject to territorial adjustment, the arrangements for the exercise of property rights, by way of reinstatement or compensation, shall have the following

A Model of Power-Sharing in Cyprus 77

basic features: a. Dispossessed owners who opt for compensation or whose properties are not reinstated under the property arrangements shall receive full and effective compensation on the basis of value at the time of dispossession adjusted to reflect appreciation of property values in comparable locations; b. Current users, being persons who have possession of properties of dispossessed owners as a result of an administrative decision, may apply for and shall receive title if they agree in exchange to renounce their title to a property, of similar value and in the other constituent state, of which they were dispossessed; c. Persons who own significant improvements to properties may apply for and shall receive title to such properties provided they pay for the value of the property in its original state; d. There shall be incentives for owners to sell, lease or exchange properties to current users or other persons from the constituent state in which a property is located; e. Properties not covered by the above shall be reinstated five years after entry into force of this Agreement (three years for vacant properties), provided that no more than 10% of the area and residences in either constituent state and 20% in any given municipality or village (other than villages specifically designated in this Agreement) shall be reinstated to owners from the other constituent state; and f. Current users who are Cypriot citizens and are required to vacate property to be reinstated shall not be required to do so until adequate alternative accommodation has been made available."

11. Lijphart (1968); Arend Lijphart, "Consociational Democracy," *World Politics*, Vol.4, No.2 (Jan. 1969), pp.207–25; Lijphart (1977); Arend Lijphart, "Majority Rule versus Consociationalism in Deeply Divided Societies," *Politikon*, Vol.4, No.2 (Dec. 1977), pp.113–26; Arend Lijphart, *Power-Sharing in South Africa* (Berkeley, CA: University of California Press, 1985).
12. Donald Horowitz, "Comparing Democratic Systems," *Journal of Democracy*, Vol.1, No.4 (1990); Donald Horowitz, "Making Moderation Pay," in Joseph Montville (ed.), *Conflict and Peacemaking in Multiethnic Societies* (Lexington, MA: Lexington Books, 1990); Donald Horowitz, *A Democratic South Africa? Constitutional Engineering in a Divided Society* (Berkeley, CA: University of California Press, 1991); Donald Horowitz, "Democracy in Divided Societies," *Journal of Democracy*, Vol.4, No.4 (1993).
13. Sisk (1996), p.35.
14. Ibid., p.34.
15. Ibid., p.70.

6

An Analysis of the Action-Reaction Behavior in the Defense Expenditures of Turkey and Greece

GÜLAY GÜNLÜK-ŞENESEN

The economic and political relations between Turkey and Greece in recent years, especially since 2000, diverge from the past both in terms of the coverage of issues and the nature of the relations. The wide range of bilateral agreements signed in order to cooperate in economic, business and legal domains in a genial climate might be taken as indicators of mutual preference for prospective convergence rather than conflict. Despite these recent developments, and moments of irregularly peaceful times in the past notwithstanding, bilateral relations in the post-Second World War era have been generally characterized by conflict.

One major response of parties in conflict would be to improve their security capabilities. Assuming symmetry, one area reflecting threat perceptions would be increases in stocks of arms. This issue has been dealt with widely in the defense economics literature within the context of an arms race between Turkey and Greece. However, measurement problems have led to the analysis of trends in military or defense expenditures rather than the level and composition of the armaments actually acquired.

This contribution attempts to find out whether Turkish and Greek defense expenditures in the post-1980 era have responded to conflicts in bilateral relations. The period of analysis was chosen on the basis of the data availability for various indicators. The rather short time span restricts the analysis to descriptive tools. In this respect, the present study deviates from the established literature.

The essay is organized as follows: the following section discusses the recent literature concerning an arms race between Turkey and Greece; observations regarding the ups and downs in Greek-Turkish relations are outlined in the next section; this is followed by observations about the arming indicators for both countries with respect to their bilateral relations; the subsequent section explores whether there is any support for reactionary behavior on the basis of nonparametric statistical tests; the final section summarizes the findings and presents challenges for future research.

RECENT RESEARCH FINDINGS IN THE DEFENSE ECONOMICS LITERATURE

Brauer's survey of the literature on arms race models estimated for the Greek-Turkish case in the post-1980 era provides an overview of both the methodology and the findings.[1] Therefore, for the sake of parsimony, this study will not attempt to review individual works unless some specific points demand it. A common feature of previous studies is their methodology: namely, advanced econometric estimation of arms race models in the Richardson tradition. Among determinants, threat variables as well as economic variables are included in these models. Though there are variations in the structures of the estimated models, a large observation set is a prerequisite. This leads to another commonality of these contributions: their analyses are based on long time spans. Coverage varies, but is roughly between 30 to 50 years. The starting point in these related studies postulates the existence of an arms race. Thus, the main motive has been verification of the presence of an "average" bilateral behavior in recent history, in this case an arms race.[2]

Despite the logical and/or political justification for an arms race based on a variety of issues of conflict between the two countries, empirical findings lack coherence. Interestingly, the issue becomes inconclusive when attempting to identify such a long-term relationship when one single year, 1974, is left out.[3] On the other hand, Smith *et al.* find that there is no mutual dependence regarding military expenditures, and therefore internal—rather than external—political or bureaucratic inertia might be shaping decisions.[4] This point or "noise" is elaborated further by Kollias, who discusses possible non-bilateral determinants of military spending for both Greece and Turkey.[5] Furthermore, it is possible that there might be bilateral but asymmetric causality, in the sense that the effect of Turkey's military expenditure is stronger on Greece than Greece's military expenditure is on Turkey.[6] Finally, Brauer concludes that there is no support for an arms race between Greece and Turkey in the 1990s.[7]

Both the conceptual and related measurement issues regarding arms races are very problematic indeed, as has been generally recognized in the literature.[8] This alone could be identified as the main factor behind the disparity of findings in the Turkey-Greece case. Furthermore, structural changes in the internal and external political and economic environments in the last 60 years and the arming decisions that have occurred in response have been major changes and therefore might be posing additional challenges to the quantitative analysis of the long-term behaviors of both Turkey and Greece. Aside from that, as Brauer puts it, we know little about the trends in the 1990s.[9]

Obviously, the above-mentioned "noise" variables may be contributing more to the inconclusive state of the analyses than merely bilateral relations. In this sense, military expenditures may not be an ideal indicator. A better indicator might be spending on military equipment, which might reflect the capacity of one country to attack the other and/or to defend itself against the attack of the other. This theory would be improved by a comparative analysis of the types of armaments accumulated by both parties. Better still, analyzing the trends in "threat-specific arming" might actually provide more insight. In a geographical sense, for example, the cost, level and composition of military equipment—in short, arms—in the Greek islands of the Aegean Sea and on the Aegean coast of Turkey may be related more to bilateral threat perceptions when compared to the overall defense expenditures. Similarly, dismantling with respect to threat-specific spending (such as on the air force and/or the navy) would be more relevant.[10] The significance of these aspects notwithstanding, they fall outside the scope of this essay.

The alternate route adopted in this essay concerns responses in the defense spending of both Turkey and Greece to the nature of their bilateral relations in the post-1980 period. The purpose is to complement the findings of an earlier essay, in which it was sought to relate such responses to bilateral relations on the Turkish side by using national data.[11] Taking the trends in bilateral relations as the main frame of reference, this study incorporates both the Turkish and the Greek sides, mostly through the use of international data. The expectation is that defense expenditures reflect reactions to bilateral tensions: increase during (and following) tense years, decrease or stagnate during (and following) lenient years.

TURNING POINTS IN TURKEY-GREECE RELATIONS
IN THE POST-1980 ERA

As Ifantis points out, "Since 1980 Greece and Turkey have been in a relationship of low intensity conflict 'disrupted' by shorter or longer détentes."[12] The list of turning points in bilateral relations is presented in Table 1, which obviously is not comprehensive and might not be in perfect chronological order within a given year.[13] We denote those events which

TABLE 1
ANNUAL CHRONOLOGY OF MAJOR RELATIONS BETWEEN
TURKEY AND GREECE

1980	−	Turkey (TR) and Greece (GR) lifted Notices to Airmen (NOTAM); military government in TR until 1983
1981	−	Andreou Papandreou's call to NATO for protection against TR
1982	−	Conflict in the Aegean over seismic exploration by GR (Jan.)
	+	Agreement by GR & TR to refrain from provocations (June)
1983	−	Independence of the Turkish Republic of Northern Cyprus (TRNC) declared
1984	−	Conflict over NATO military operations in the Aegean
	−	Conflict over arming of Lemnos by GR
1985	−	TR initiated modernization program for the TR Armed Forces
	−	GR officially declared new defense doctrine: principal threat from TR; moved forces to TR borders
1986	−	Frontier incident between border patrols
1987	−	Conflict over oil exploration in the Aegean
1988	+	GR and TR presidents meet in Davos; business meeting, tension reduction
1992	−	Bosnian war—GR supports Belgrade, TR supports Sarajevo
	+	The Black Sea Economic Cooperation launched
1993	−	GR declared Greek Republic of Cyprus (RoC) Joint Defense Doctrine
1994	−	Extension of territorial waters to 12 miles: United Nations Convention of the Law of the Sea (UNCLOS) in effect
1995	−	GR parliament approved UNCLOS
	−	TR parliament declared warning on TR rights in the Aegean
	−	GR decided to populate remote Aegean islands
	−	GR initiated "strategic partnership" with Syria
	+	GR lifted its veto against TR's accession to the Customs Union
1996	−	Imia/Kardak crisis
	−	GR-Armenia defense cooperation
	−	TR-Israel military cooperation agreement
	−	GR announced modernization program for the GR Armed Forces
	−	Clashes on the Greenline between TRNC and RoC
1997	−	GR vetoed TR's bid for eligibility for EU membership
	−	Conflict over intended procurement of S-300 missiles in RoC
1998	−	Conflict over intended procurement of S-300 missiles in RoC
	−	EU began accession talks with the RoC
	+	US ended foreign aid program to both GR and TR (end of 7 to 10 disputes).
	+	Madrid Declaration on peaceful solutions for UNCLOS issues
1999	−	Öcalan sheltered in GR embassy in Kenya (Jan.–Feb.)
	+	Simitis affirmed GR's opposition to terrorism (March)
	+	GR ended official restrictions on assertions of Turkish ethnicity in western Thrace (July)
	+	Earthquakes in TR (Aug.) and GR (Sept.): earthquake diplomacy
	+	GR lifted veto on Turkey's candidacy for EU membership
	+	S-300 project cancelled (transferred to Crete)
	+	GR, TR and Balkan states signed agreement on regional peacekeeping
2000	+	GR and TR signed 9 (economic, social, legal) cooperation agreements (Jan.–Feb.)
	+	GR and TR agreed on cooperation in NATO exercises (Dec.)
2001	+	GR and TR signed 5 (cultural, social, legal) cooperation agreements (June)
	+	GR and TR agreed on cooperation in education, sports and environment (Nov.)
2002	+	Busy agenda of bilateral meetings (foreign affairs and business)

Note: Tense years are indicated by −, harmonious years by +.

improved relations or reduced tensions by a + sign and therefore expect reverse effects on Turkish and Greek defense expenditures in that year and/or in subsequent years. On the other hand, deterioration of relations, indicated by a − sign, is expected to induce increases in the defense expenditures of both sides.

Obviously, all the events listed do not have equal weight in increasing/decreasing the defense spending of both sides. In fact, there are only five events that can be associated with risk of war: 1986, 1987, 1994, and 1996–97. Still, we expanded our context to include major climate changes in search of possible reactions on both sides.

Several features arise from Table 1. First, tension and relief can be observed in the same year, such as in 1982, 1992, 1995 and 1998, which, in a way, cancel each other out. The best example for this occurrence is 1999, where the large "negative" was cancelled out by even bigger "pluses," which is when the positive trend began and has continued to the present day. Second, there are periods when no significant incident is observed, such as 1989–91, although that period did succeed 1987—a troubled year; the Davos meeting in 1988 must have served to cool tensions. Finally, the 1980–81, 1983–87 and 1993–97 sub-periods (except for 1995) are clearly ones of trouble (− signs); the rest, all recently (1999–2002), are not characterized by much tension, with more weight on improvements (+ signs) in relations—except for the Öcalan issue in 1999, which quickly faded.

In short, of the past 23 years of bilateral relations, 11 years can be characterized as tense (− sign), some being more severe than others, four years as harmonious (+ sign) and eight as either neutral or both tense and harmonious; the latter can be termed slack years. An assessment of whether this pattern is reflected on the defense budgeting behavior of Turkey and Greece is made in the next section, based on data for 1980–2001.

IS THERE A REACTION TO TENSION? OBSERVATIONS

The obvious expectation is that in response to tensions between Greece and Turkey, both would have increased their defense expenditures over the last two decades. In the case of a long-term concept like defense, it would not be realistic to expect a contraction when the waters are still. However, there would be less significant increases, as other priorities in the budget are expected to overtake defense concerns. On the other hand, this approach overlooks the process of threat perception on both sides, and hence their defense budgeting behavior in response. The justification for this approach is that incurred defense spending in general, and acquired arms in particular, is a composite indicator of perceived threats—internal, bilateral and external. A search for the bilateral component is attempted here. This endeavor, however, faces challenges from the data, which will be mentioned for each case. We will be elaborating on three indicators: military expenditure, military equipment expenditure and conventional arms transfer from abroad. Rather than discussing the annual behaviors with reference to bilateral relations, we will, for the purposes of illustration, refer only to cases of the most severe tension, whereby it is most likely to observe reactionary behaviors, if any.

We begin with observations on the military spending (which here equates to spending on personnel, maintenance and equipment) of both Turkey and Greece, using the Stockholm International Peace Research Institute (SIPRI) data in 1990 constant USD prices.[14] These are plotted in Figure 1.

FIGURE 1
MILITARY EXPENDITURES OF TURKEY AND GREECE,
MILLION USD, 1990

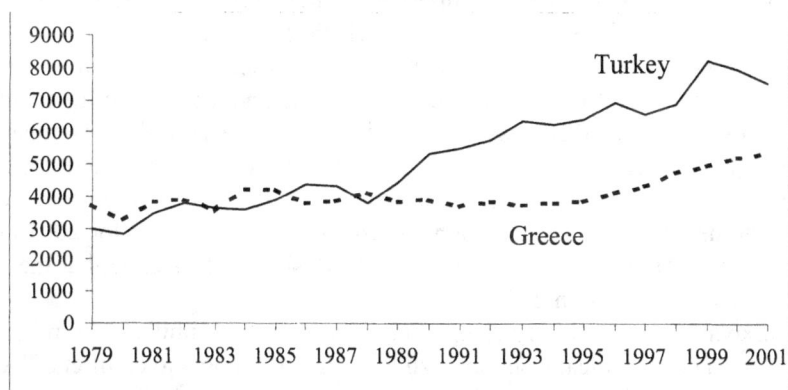

Despite the differences between the two sides in scale, comparatively, regarding the size of the army and the land, the level of Greek defense spending was close to, or more than, that of Turkish defense spending in the 1980s. The significant increase in Turkish military expenditures, starting in 1989, begins the 1990s with a remarkably huge divergence from the Greek expenditure, as the latter only started increasing, and even then at a milder pace, in 1994. On average, Turkish defense spending is about 60 percent higher than that of Greece during the period 1990–2001.

With reference to serious tensions, we note that the 1986 incident corresponds to an increase (decrease) for Turkey (Greece). The subsequent 1987 incident is marked with a decrease (increase) for Turkey (Greece), while in the following year, 1988, a decrease (increase) for Turkey (Greece) is once again obvious. The cool phase until 1993 is interesting due to a continuous increase in spending by Turkey but a slight decrease in spending by Greece. The 1993–94 incidents seem to have provoked the increasing trend in Greek spending in the subsequent phase, within which the 1996 and 1997 incidents took place. Turkey decreased such spending in 1997.[15] This leads to the conclusion that there is a lack of a consistent response to severe tensions. Whether responses are detectable with respect to conflict/harmony years in the entire period will be elaborated later.

Since SIPRI military expenditure data, even in national currencies, deviate from the national data series, cross-checking with national data for both Turkey and Greece would have improved clarity.[16] The main sources for the incoherence are coverage, USD exchange rates, USD price deflator and national price deflators. However, national data for Greek expenditures was not available. *SIPRI Yearbooks* publish military expenditure data in national currencies. These series for Greece were deflated by the GDP deflator to see whether the trend, especially the turning points, in constant drachmas differ from those in Figure 1. National data for Turkish spending is available and a similarity of trend prevails for the Turkish case. Since the above analysis remains intact with these alternative series, the details will not be presented here. Nevertheless, one point deserves attention: Turkish data is very sensitive to high devaluations and although a sharp decline is observed for 2001 in constant USD, national data in constant Turkish lira (TL) show that there is in fact an increase in 2001.

Expenditure on military equipment, armaments and similar items might even be a better indicator for analyzing reaction behaviors to conflicts. The data, however, is more problematic. First, national data for Greece is unavailable. National data for Turkey, though, is available for 1981–99. The 1990s, based on this data, were characterized with a much higher level of spending on military equipment: the amount spent in 1999 is 5.7 (3.6) times that which was spent in 1987 in USD (in constant TL).[17]

Resorting to data on military equipment spending published in the *SIPRI Yearbooks* far from resolves the comparability matter. Base years for constant USD data are changed periodically, complicating the task of forming long series for both countries. Since monetary values cannot be compared for the whole period, derivations of coherent price indices might be a solution. However, as illustrated in Table 2, this might also be

TABLE 2
RATIO OF EXPENDITURES: TURKEY TO GREECE

Price	Military Equipment Expenditures					Military Expenditures
	1998 $	1995 $	1990 $	1991 $	1988 $	1990 $
1981					0.31	0.9
1982					0.46	1.0
1983				0.65	0.48	1.0
1984				0.72	0.53	0.8
1985			0.83	0.84	0.63	0.9
1986			1.33	1.34	1.00	1.2
1987			1.37	1.47	1.03	1.1
1988		0.71	0.90	0.90	0.76	0.9
1989		0.72	0.90	0.90	0.78	1.2
1990		1.02	1.29	1.28	1.11	1.4
1991	1.53	1.32	1.67	1.66	1.01	1.5
1992	1.47	1.26	1.60	1.80		1.5
1993	1.45	1.25	1.58			1.7
1994	1.81	1.56	1.97			1.6
1995	2.27	1.96	2.42			1.7
1996	2.34	2.02		2.58		1.7
1997	2.18	1.88				1.5
1998	1.51	1.30				1.5
1999	2.09	2.24				1.6
2000	2.31					1.5
2001	3.29					1.4

Source: *SIPRI Yearbooks.*

misleading as there are serious discrepancies observed among different series between the ratios of Turkish expenditure to Greek expenditure values for the same year.[18]

With reservations concerning the SIPRI data, one feature is obvious: with the exception of 1986–87, Turkish military equipment expenditure lagged significantly behind that of Greece until 1990. However, from 1990 on, it began overtaking the latter in earnest, eventually becoming more than twice as much in 1995 and more than three times as much in 2001. The final column of Table 2 shows the ratios of Turkish military expenditure to Greek expenditure, based on the data for Figure 1. The trends in military equipment spending, based on three different base years, are plotted in Figure 2.[19]

The severe tension during 1986 and 1987 corresponds to a sub-period when Greek spending on military equipment fell behind Turkey's, but also when Greece entered an increased spending phase. Similar to the trend observed in Figure 1 with overall spending, the 1986 incident corresponds

FIGURE 2
MILITARY EQUIPMENT EXPENDITURES, TURKEY AND GREECE,
CONSTANT PR, MILLUSED USD

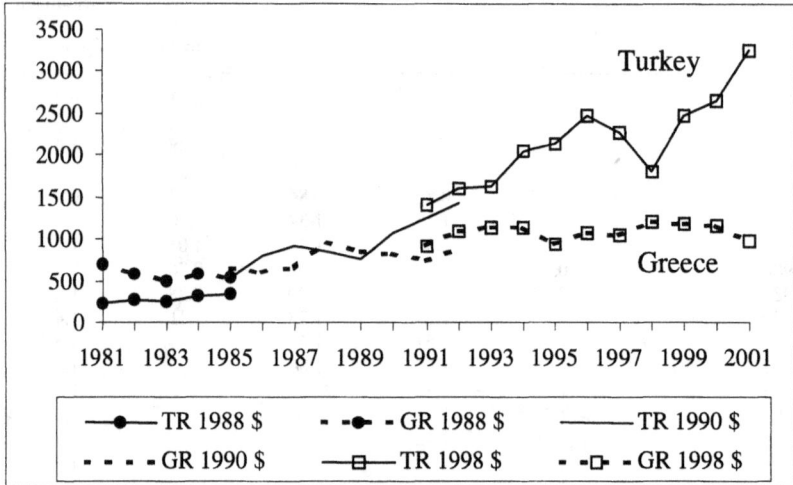

to an increase (decrease) for Turkey (Greece). In contrast, the subsequent 1987 incident is marked with increases for both Turkey and Greece, while in the following year, 1988, a decrease (increase) for Turkey (Greece) is obvious. Finally, during 1988–89, Greece's military equipment expenditure exceeds Turkey's.

The next year of severe tension, 1994, corresponds to an increase by both Turkey and Greece, although less significantly for Greece. The level of spending for Greece during 1995–97 is lower than the levels in the pre- and post-sub-periods. This is in contrast to the observations in Figure 1, which cover equipment and non-equipment military spending. Both sides increased spending in equipment in 1996, but decreased in 1997. Immediately after these final years of severe tension, in 1998, Turkey severely decreased spending on military equipment, but Greece—though not significantly—increased spending. The trends observed concerning military equipment expenditure for years of severe tension again do not provide convincing support for reactionary behavior as the cause on both sides.

Finally, acquisition of foreign arms by both Greece and Turkey might reveal reactionary behavior to bilateral conflicts, as both countries are net importers of arms due to weak military industrial bases and due to their similar positions with respect to the Conventional Armed Forces in Europe (CFE) Treaty. These transfers include cash paid and/or committed imports as well as cost-free relocation. It is a known fact that Turkey has been among the leaders in this trend, especially from the 1990s on, with Greece slightly lagging behind.[20]

There are no national data for such transfers available for both countries. However, there are two alternatives regarding international sources: the *SIPRI Yearbooks* and the *US World Military Expenditure and Arms Trade (WMEAT) Yearbooks*.[21] SIPRI data is available for 1980–2001 in constant 1990 USD prices; WMEAT data is available for 1980–99 for Turkey and 1984–99 for Greece in current USD prices. Time patterns in the two sources for each country are not expected to overlap because of this evaluation difference—aside from additional possible variations in coverage, the discussion of which is beyond the scope of this essay. However, reflections on this issue of coverage can best be described and tested with the data for 1990 for both Turkey and Greece in both sources.

Greece was delivered *arms transfers* worth 725 million USD (WMEAT) and *major conventional weapons* worth 1,221 million USD (SIPRI) in 1990; the respective values for Turkey are 1,381 million USD (WMEAT) and 804 million USD (SIPRI). It is clear that the scope of both databases is quite different; otherwise they should be equal for each country in 1990. What is more striking is that for 1990, according to WMEAT, the volume of transfers to Turkey is 1.9 times that of the volume of transfers to Greece, but according to SIPRI this ratio is 0.66. Therefore, it is equally justified to conclude that Turkey is transferred either 90 percent more than Greece or 34 percent less than Greece, depending on the database. Figures 3 and 4 should be studied with these and related drawbacks in mind.

According to Figure 3, where WMEAT data in current prices are plotted, the volume of transfers to Turkey is well above Greece for the period for which data is available. Although both data sources revise data backwards, this is much more the case for WMEAT data. For example, Turkey's arms imports in current prices in 1994 is 950 million USD in the 1995 *Yearbook*, but it is 2,000 million USD in the 1998 *Yearbook*. Therefore, we will not elaborate further using this data-set with respect to severe tensions between Turkey and Greece.

SIPRI data in constant prices are plotted in Figure 4, which certainly displays a different time pattern.[22] In the severe tension year 1986, arms transfers to both Greece and Turkey decreased. The decrease continued in 1987 for Greece, but the data shows arms transfers to Turkey increased. In 1994, there is a decrease (increase) by Turkey (Greece). The 1996 tension took place following decreases in arms transfers to both countries. And

FIGURE 3
ARMS TRANSFERS, MILLION USD, WMEAT

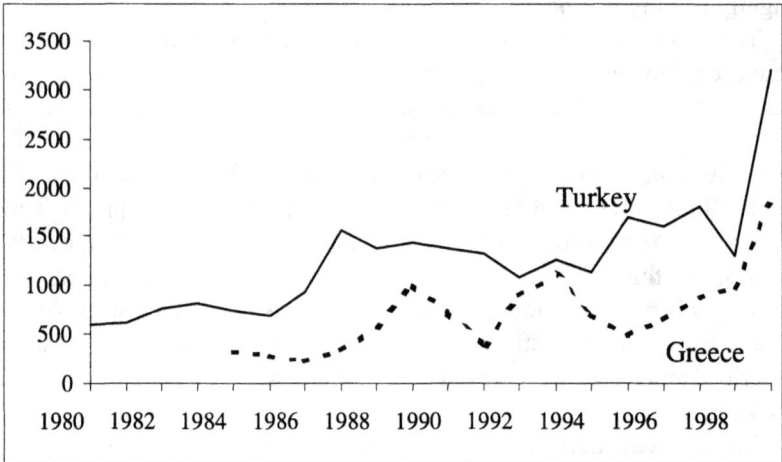

FIGURE 4
ARMS TRANSFERS, MILLION USD, 1990, SIPRI

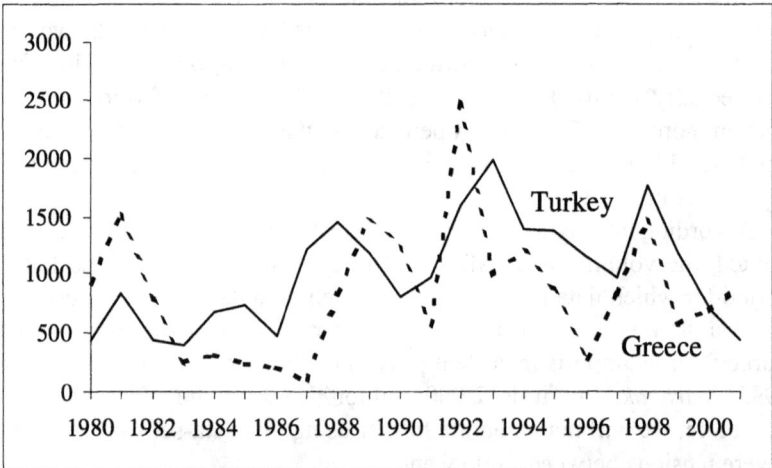

finally, transfers to Turkey declined but those to Greece increased in 1997, the following year. Apparently, severe tensions do not prevent arms transfers from the international markets/community. The outcomes of the foregoing analysis are summarized in Table 3.

TABLE 3
SUMMARY OF OBSERVATIONS WITH RESPECT TO SEVERE TENSION YEARS
BETWEEN TURKEY AND GREECE

	1986		1987		1994		1996		1997	
	TR	GR	TR	GR	TR	GR	TR	GR	TR	GR
Military Expenditures	↑	↓	↓	↑	↑	↑	↑	↑	↓	↑
Military Equipment Expenditures	↑	↓	↑	↑	↑	↑	↑	↑	↓	↓
Arms Transfers (SIPRI)	↓	↓	↑		↓	↑	↓	↓	↓	↑

This rather rough descriptive analysis leads to the conclusion that indicators for action/reaction can be very problematic, posing serious challenges to validity and reliability. Although these issues are depicted with alternative indicators here, consistent action-reaction behaviors to severe tensions are not observed for both countries. However, a further check might supply better grounds for generalizations, since fund allocation to defense involves decisions over longer periods, rather than spontaneous reactions. In addition, the next section could provide better clarification, as the magnitude of the changes throughout the period will also be taken into account.

IS THERE A REACTION TO TENSION? STATISTICAL ANALYSIS

Although the above analysis does not provide support for the theory that both countries responded similarly to severe bilateral conflicts, one might expect to see similarities in behavior (in terms of conflict and harmony) in the long run, or—in our case—two decades. The indicators we use are military expenditures, changes in the military expenditures, arms imports (transfers), changes in military equipment expenditures and changes in arms imports. All changes are expressed in percentages. Tables 4 and 5 summarize the values for the simple and rank correlation coefficients between the indicators, both concurrent and lagged, for Turkey and Greece respectively. Since simple correlation coefficients have statistical restrictions (for example, normality) and can suffer from spuriousness caused by time trends, the rank correlation coefficient is used as a compensating measure.

Simple correlations between Turkey's military expenditures in year t are highly significant compared to Greece's military expenditures in year t, t-1 and t-2, as Table 4 demonstrates. However, correlation fades away for further lags. Correlation regarding the ranking fades sooner, and is significant only for year t and t-1. This might lead to a tentative conclusion that Turkey plans its military spending level in reaction to Greece's spending levels of the last two–three years, but only to a certain extent, as correlation is not very high. This is a rather short time pattern. Naturally, it would be misleading to infer causality from this limited data. On the other hand, none of the correlations with other indicators, except concurrent arms imports, are significant. This lack of significance might lead to the conclusion that there is an absence of any reaction on the Turkish side. The lesson to be drawn is that conclusions are very sensitive to the indicators used, so caution must be used when making general statements.

A similar analysis on the Greek side yields slightly different results. By definition, the first columns (concurrent correlations of Greece and Turkey in the same t year) of Tables 4 and 5 are identical. Both simple and rank correlations between Greece's military expenditures in year t and Turkey's military expenditures are significant for a longer period, as shown in Table 5. Although not shown in the table, Greece's military expenditure in year t is also highly correlated with Turkey's five years before. Furthermore, simple correlations exceed 0.8 and rank correlations exceed 0.6 for six, seven and eight years back. The tentative conclusion would be that the Turkish military spending level acts as a reference for the Greek side. This can be identified as a long-term behavior. However, there is not much support for such a reaction from findings based on the other indicators. There are two exceptions: the change in Greek military equipment expenditures has significant correlations with respect to Turkish behavior two years back, yet the change in Greek arms imports has a significant simple correlation with respect to Turkish behavior in the previous year. In the light of the rest of Table 5, it would be too forceful a conclusion to state that Greece takes into account Turkey's behavior of two year ago for its present equipment expenditures. The lower, but significant, simple correlation between concurrent arms transfers to both countries might be interpreted as a matching of their procurement in light of their past (length unknown) perceptions. Yet again, change in arms imports does not reveal symmetry. Since this correlation does not coincide with the correlations for military equipment discussed above, overstatements should be avoided. Besides, these transfers are not solely determined by choices made at the national level.

TABLE 4
TURKEY'S REACTION (AT TIME T) TO GREECE

Indicator	Correlations	GR_t	GR_{t-1}	GR_{t-2}	GR_{t-3}	GR_{t-4}	n
Military Expenditures	Simple r	** 0.70	** 0.63	** 0.55	0.41	0.27	18–22
Military Expenditures	Rank ρ	** 0.56	** 0.56	0.41	0.29	0.23	18–22
Change in Military Expenditures	Simple r	0.11	-0.06	-0.06	-0.22	-0.23	18–22
Change in Military Expenditures	Rank ρ	-0.07	-0.01	0.01	-0.20	-0.17	18–22
Arms Imports	Simple r	* 0.44	0.31	-0.08	0.11	0.20	18–22
Arms Imports	Rank ρ	0.40	0.12	-0.20	0.02	0.16	18–22
Change in Military Equipment Expenditures	Simple r	-0.17	-0.34	0.32	0.20	-0.23	16–20
Change in Military Equipment Expenditures	Rank ρ	-0.04	-0.32	0.20	0.25	-0.30	16–20
Change in Arms Imports	Simple r	0.14	-0.04	-0.36	0.05	0.17	17–21
Change in Arms Imports	Rank ρ	0.16	-0.05	-0.44	0.28	0.20	17–21

Notes:
* Significant at 0.05 level.
** Significant at 0.01 level.

TABLE 5
GREECE'S REACTION (AT TIME T) TO TURKEY

Indicator	Correlations	GR_t	GR_{t-1}	GR_{t-2}	GR_{t-3}	GR_{t-4}	n
Military Expenditures	Simple r	0.70**	0.72**	0.71**	0.71**	0.72**	18–22
Military Expenditures	Rank ρ	0.56**	0.51*	0.51*	0.57**	0.54*	18–22
Change in Military Expenditures	Simple r	0.11	-0.31	-0.009	0.43	-0.35	18–22
Change in Military Expenditures	Rank ρ	-0.07	-0.39	0.08	0.25	-0.41	18–22
Arms Imports	Simple r	0.44*	0.25	0.23	0.19	0.27	18–22
Arms Imports	Rank ρ	0.40	0.36	0.41	0.35	0.28	18–22
Change in Military Equipment Expenditures	Simple r	-0.17	-0.17	0.59*	-0.07	0.08	16–20
Change in Military Equipment Expenditures	Rank ρ	-0.04	-0.27	0.47*	0.005	0.06	16–20
Change in Arms Imports	Simple r	0.14	0.49*	-0.26	-0.18	0.19	17–21
Change in Arms Imports	Rank ρ	0.16	0.12	-0.24	-0.16	0.01	17–21

Notes:
 * Significant at 0.05 level.
** Significant at 0.01 level.

The statistical tests with correlations above did not discriminate between the annual characteristics of the bilateral relations outlined in Table 1 but served as examples for sources of disparities in judgments. The responses of both Turkey and Greece to each other for the entire period might be explored on the basis of the following general hypothesis: Turkey's (Greece's) military expenditure indicators during the harmony years are in general lower than those during conflict years. This requires splitting the data-set with respect to bilateral relations: 1980–81, 1983–87, 1993–94 and 1996–97 are identified as conflict years; the rest are identified as harmony years, though it is clear that of these, harmony is strongest only after 1999. The very recent harmony year 2002 is excluded due to data unavailability. Hence, of the 22 years in our data-set, we identify 11 with conflict (Case 1) and the remaining 11 with harmony (lenient and/or slack) (Case 2).

The statistical tests for this purpose are chosen on the basis of their underlying assumptions. Since we have limited observations, a selection of nonparametric tests was made: the Median test (to compare the medians of two cases with a common median for the whole period), the Mann-Whitney test (to compare the medians of two cases with each other) and the Kolmogorov-Smirnov test (to compare the distributions of the two cases with each other). Results of two parametric tests regarding the comparisons of the variances and means are also provided.

Table 6 presents the significance levels of these tests for Turkey. As the highly insignificant values imply, Turkish military spending indicators do not vary between Case 1 and 2. Stated differently, Turkish indicators do not support the above stated hypothesis. On the Turkish side, behavior is similar in harmony and conflict years as well as in subsequent years, as one- and two-year lagged responses are also insignificant. This outcome is in conformity with our earlier findings based on the national data-sets for indicators.[23]

On the Greek side, the general picture is identical, as shown in Table 7. Reactionary behavior to bilateral relations is not observed. The only exception is the variance test: dispersions in the harmony and conflict years are significantly different. However, note that variation for the harmony years is found to be greater than for conflict years.

Statistical analysis in this section provides no contradictory results to the former analysis. Based on available data taken from international sources, one does not detect a Turkish (Greek) reaction of defense-spending indicators to relations with Greece (Turkey). The justification is that findings with various indicators do not support each other on the one hand, and on the other, the bilateral factor is not significant for either of the countries.

TABLE 6
TURKEY'S REACTION TO BILATERAL RELATIONS WITH GREECE
(SIGNIFICANCE LEVELS)

Indicator Statistical Test	Military Expenditures	Change in Military Expenditures	Arms Imports	Change in Military Equipment Expenditures	Change in Arms Imports
Median	0.40	~1.0	~1.0	~1.0	~1.0
Mann-Whitney	0.08	0.70	0.40	0.94	0.22
Kolmogorov-Smirnov	0.21	0.81	0.81	~1.0	0.53
Variance	0.99	0.93	0.95	0.73	0.29
Means (t-test)	0.08	0.76	0.46	0.86	0.29

Note: Lagged responses (1 and 2) have also high insignificance levels.

TABLE 7
GREECE'S REACTION TO BILATERAL RELATIONS WITH TURKEY
(SIGNIFICANCE LEVELS)

Indicator Statistical Test	Military Expenditures	Change in Military Expenditures	Arms Imports	Change in Military Equipment Expenditures	Change in Arms Imports
Median	0.40	0.40	~1.0	~1.0	0.67
Mann-Whitney	0.13	0.56	0.12	0.55	0.25
Kolmogorov-Smirnov	0.46	0.46	0.08	0.60	0.70
Variance	0.003**	0.06	0.99	0.14	0.24
Means (t-test)	0.06	0.84	0.06	0.93	0.09

Note: Lagged responses (1 and 2) have also high insignificance levels.
 ** Significant at 0.01 level.

CONCLUDING REMARKS

This essay has focused on whether the nature of bilateral relations between Turkey and Greece is reflected in their defense-spending behaviors. Generally speaking, arming (or spending on defense, where practical data problems are encountered) behaviors obviously involve threat perceptions (bilateral and other), economic capabilities and/or opportunity costs as well as historical factors. Previous empirical work has taken these aspects into account in varied forms. This essay has introduced the variations in bilateral relations in the post-1980 era in an attempt to search for the bilateral component. Nonbilateral external and internal security and policy issues as well economic factors in the post-1980 era are deliberately left out of the analysis, since previous research indicates that their importance emerges to overrule that of the bilateral component.

Both previous econometric work on the long-term bidirectional arms race between Turkey and Greece and our defense-spending indicators analysis on the shorter-term bidirectional reactions deduce that the issue remains inconclusive. Two dimensions of this outcome need to be considered. The first is related to the essence and the second is related to its reflections—in other words, data.

The essence of the issue is the history of bilateral relations, which are widely characterized by conflict. This has been the motivation for the search to find an arms race and/or an action-reaction behavior pattern. However, asymmetry in threat perceptions and/or deviation of action from rhetoric might lead in different directions, depending on the choices made. To cite a few possibilities, one can argue with equally logical justification that Turkey's ambitious arming is the driving force behind Greece's or that Greece has given up following Turkey, resorting to the EU for an alternative means of protection. Similarly, one could argue that relations with Greece occupy a major place in Turkish security considerations, or Turkey's confidence in its much larger scale might allow for not making its plans specific to Greece.

To what extent these and many other "verbal" arguments are justified empirically can be judged on the basis of their reflections. We identify these reflections as the values of indicators for arming. As discussed in the first parts of this essay, the indicators used in the literature so far are those for which data is readily available. However, the indicators are limited and the data is problematic, and so we have serious reliability and validity problems. This could partly be compensated for if related national data of equal standard were available. This is, of course, a universal problem. Still, lack of transparency in national data on military expenditures and its monetary and physical components for both Turkey and Greece pose serious limitations for comparative analysis. Acknowledgement of this, however, brings no solution, as both "verbal" and "empirical" analyses seem to be lacking the indispensable support of each other.

APPENDIX

FIGURE A1
CHANGES IN MILITARY EXPENDITURES OF TURKEY AND GREECE
(FOR FIGURE 1), %

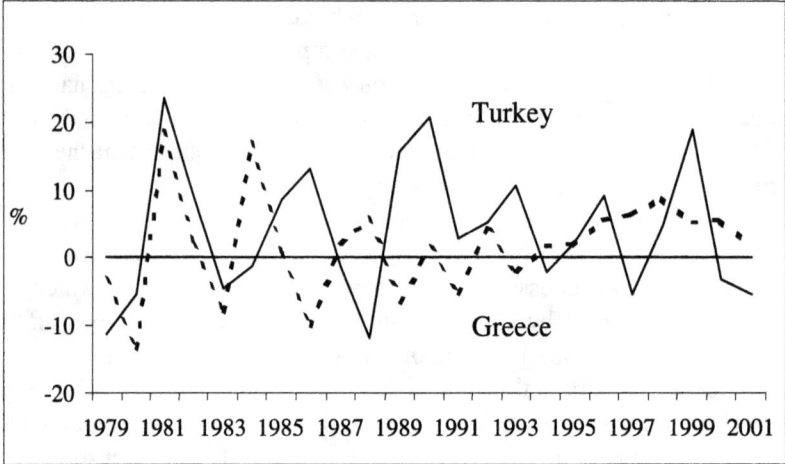

FIGURE A2
CHANGES IN MILITARY EXPENDITURES OF TURKEY AND GREECE
(FOR FIGURE 2), %

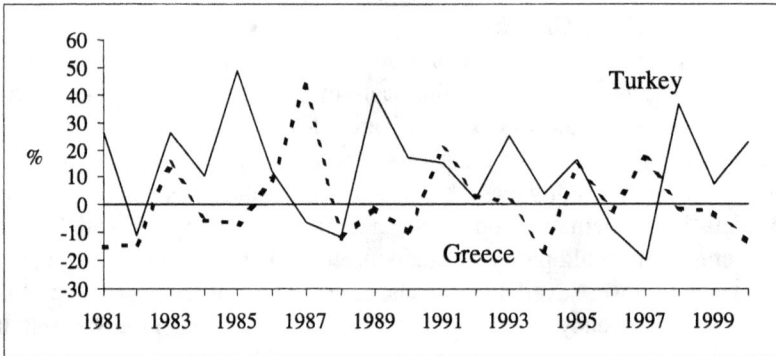

NOTES

1. Jurgen Brauer, "Survey and Review of the Defense Economics Literature on Greece and Turkey: What Have We Learned?" *Defence and Peace Economics*, Vol.13, No.2 (April 2002), pp.85–107; Jurgen Brauer, "Greece and Turkey: A Comprehensive, Critical Review of the Defense Economics Literature," in Christos Kollias and Gülay Günlük-Şenesen (eds.), *Greece and Turkey in the 21st Century: Conflict or Cooperation? The Political Economy Perspective* (New York: Nova Science, forthcoming).

2. Perhaps the strongest statements are attributed to Andreou *et al.*: "The existence of an arms race between Greece and Turkey is a well established fact" (p.330), and "This is a finding that confirms the leading role of Turkey in this arms race" (p.340). A.S. Andreou, K.E. Parsopoulos, M.N. Vrahatis and G.A. Zombanakis, "Optimal versus Required Defence Expenditure: The Case of the Greek-Turkish Arms Race," *Defence and Peace Economics*, Vol.13, No.4 (Aug. 2002), pp.329–47.

3. Paul Dunne, Eftychia Nikolaidou and Ron Smith, "An Econometric Analysis of the Arms Race between Greece and Turkey," paper presented at the "Fifth Annual Middlesex Conference on Economics and Security" (ECAAR-UK and MUBS, London, June 15–16, 2001); Ron P. Smith, J. Paul Dunne and Eftychia Nikolaidou, "The Econometrics of Arms Races," *Defence and Peace Economics*, Vol.11, No.1 (2000), pp.31–43.

4. Ron P. Smith, Martin Sola and Fabio Spagnolo, "The Prisoner's Dilemma and Regime-Switching in the Greek-Turkish Arms Race," *Journal of Peace Research*, Vol.37, No.6 (2000), pp.737–50.

5. Christos Kollias, "A Look at the Methodological Issues Involved in the Greek-Turkish Arms Race Hypothesis," *Hellenic Studies*, Vol.9, No.2 (Autumn 2001), pp.91–114. See also Brauer (2002), pp.85–107, and Brauer (2003).

6. Christos Kollias and Suzanna-Maria Paleologou, "Is There a Greek-Turkish Arms Race? Some Further Empirical Results From Causality Tests," *Defence and Peace Economics*, Vol.13, No.4 (Aug. 2002), pp.321–8; Nadir Öcal, "Asymmetric Effects of Military Expenditure Between Turkey and Greece," *Defence and Peace Economics*, Vol.13, No.5 (Oct. 2002), pp.405–16.

7. Brauer (2002), p.91.

8. For detailed discussion of these issues see, for example, Brauer (2002), pp.85–107; Brauer (2003); Dunne *et al.* (2001); and Kollias (2001), pp.91–114. See also Michael Intriligator and Dagobert L. Brito, "Arms Races," *Defence and Peace Economics*, Vol.11, No.1 (2000), pp.45–54.

9. Brauer (2002), p.103.

10. Thanks are due to Erhan Keleşoğlu, Hakan Kurunç and the participants—in particular, Ersin Kalaycıoğlu—of the workshop on Greek and Turkish Relations (Sabancı University, Istanbul, June 13–14, 2003) for raising these points.

11. Gülay Günlük-Şenesen, "Turkish Defense Expenditures in View of Ups and Downs in Turkish-Greek Relations: Is There A Reaction?" *Hellenic Studies*, Vol.9, No.2 (Autumn 2001), pp.73–89.

12. Kostas Ifantis, "Power Politics, Security Dilemma, and Crisis Behaviour: The Case of Imia," *Hellenic Studies*, Vol.9, No.2 (Autumn 2001), pp.29–48.

13. This table is a revised version of Table 1 in Günlük-Şenesen (2001). Thanks are due to Gülden Ayman and Faruk Sönmezoğlu for guidance. Updating was based on information provided by Faruk Sönmezoğlu, to whom I am especially indebted for his patience and support. All errors are mine. The table was compiled from the following sources: Emmanuel Athanassiou and Christos Kollias, "Military Tension and Foreign Direct Investment: Evidence from the Greek-Turkish Rivalry," in Jurgen Brauer and Keith Hartley (eds.), *The Economics of Regional Security* (Singapore: Harwood, 2000), pp.97–112; Emmanuel Athanassiou and Christos Kollias, "Modeling the Effects of Military Tension on Foreign Trade: Some Preliminary Empirical Findings from the Greek-Turkish Rivalry," *Defence and Peace Economics*, Vol.13, No.5 (Oct. 2002), pp.417–27; Tozun Bahcheli, "Turkish Policy Toward Greece," in Alan Makovsky and Sabri Sayari (eds.), *Turkey's New World: Changing Dynamics in Turkish Foreign Policy* (Washington DC: The Washington Institute for Near

East Policy, 2000), pp.131–52; Christos Kollias and Stelios Makrydakis, "Is there a Greek-Turkish Arms Race? Evidence from Cointegration and Causality Tests," *Defence and Peace Economics*, Vol.8, No.4 (1997), pp.355–79; Christos Kollias, "The Greek-Turkish Conflict and Greek Military Expenditure 1960–92," *Journal of Peace Research*, Vol.33, No.2 (1996), pp.217–28; and Faruk Sönmezoğlu, *Türkiye ve Yunanistan İlişkileri & Büyük Güçler* [Turkish Greek Relations and Great Powers] (Istanbul: Der, 2000). Consequent diplomatic contacts (such as the Davos meetings, with the exception of the one in 1998 which was important for tension reduction) are left out of the list due to their high frequency and less significant outcomes.

14. The data for Figure 1 was provided by Christos Kollias. Thanks are due to him for sharing his data-set.

15. Percentage changes in military expenditures are plotted in Figure A1 in the Appendix to complement the present analysis for the whole period.

16. These deviations regarding Turkey are discussed in Gülay Günlük-Şenesen, *Türkiye'de Savunma Harcamaları ve Ekonomik Etkileri 1980–2001* [Defense Spending in Turkey and Its Economic Effects] (Istanbul: TESEV, 2002), pp.82–5.

17. Günlük-Şenesen (2002), pp.73–83.

18. Although *SIPRI Yearbooks* are prepared with utmost care, they occasionally suffer from typos: for example, Turkish military equipment spending for 1985 (in 1988 USD prices) is given as 3,336, both in the 1991 and 1992 yearbooks. This value is 11 times the value of 1984, which is implausible (see *SIPRI Yearbook 1991* [OUP, 1991], p.133, and *SIPRI Yearbook 1992* [OUP, 1992], p.229). This flaw is not observed for 1985 in later publications. It is presumed in Table 2 that the value for Turkey is 336 (in 1988 USD prices) for 1985, which appears consistent with the remaining series.

19. Interestingly, values for percentage changes in military equipment spending as published in *SIPRI Yearbooks* are consistent for all base years. These values are plotted in Figure A2 in the Appendix. By applying these percentage changes to 1998 USD data, we also estimated a complete series for both countries for the whole period. While the time pattern is the same, however, relative ratios are not reliable. We chose to present original data here.

20. In terms of aggregate volume of transfers of major conventional weapons for 1997–2001, Turkey ranks forth following Taiwan, China and Saudi Arabia; Greece ranks sixth following India. The total for Turkey is 5,028 and for Greece is 4,436 (both in 1990 USD prices). *SIPRI Yearbook 2002* (OUP, 2002), p.229.

21. For example, US Department of State, Bureau of Verification and Compliance, *World Military Expenditures and Arms Transfers 1999–2000* (Washington, 2002).

22. Note, for example, that for 1999, very steep *increases* are observed for both countries with WMEAT data, but very steep *decreases* are observed for both countries with SIPRI data. The magnitudes of percentage changes in the data for Figure 4 vary in a very wide range, as would be expected; these, therefore, are not presented in the Appendix.

23. Günlük-Şenesen (2001), pp.73–89.

7

The Greek-Turkish Rapprochement, the Underlying Military Tension and Greek Defense Spending

CHRISTOS KOLLIAS

Greece is a member of both the North Atlantic Treaty Organization (NATO) and the European Union (EU), having joined in 1952 and 1981 respectively. In the pursuit of national security, it has, over the years, allocated substantial human and material resources to defense.[1] The Greek defense burden, that is, military expenditure as a share of Gross Domestic Product (GDP), has invariably been appreciably higher than the EU and NATO averages. It is not surprising to note, therefore, that Greece has attracted considerable attention in defense economics literature.[2]

In defense economics literature, several factors are used as explanatory determinants of military expenditure.[3] Econometric models of the demand for military expenditure typically assume that such expenditure is determined by GDP, threat(s), aid from allies and other variables that allow for the effects of the domestic political agenda on such expenditures.[4] Not surprisingly in the case of Greece, defense economics studies have concentrated on external security determinants stemming from the ongoing Greek-Turkish conflict over several issues important to both countries. This being the case, the recent improvements in Greek-Turkish bilateral relations have not as yet resulted in any reductions in defense expenditures. In fact, Greek defense spending has continued to grow in real terms.

GREEK DEFENSE EXPENDITURE: COMPARATIVE FACTS AND FIGURES

As already implied, in comparative terms Greece is one of the most militarized countries in NATO and the EU. Expressed as a share of GDP, Greek military spending has invariably been higher than the Organization for Economic Cooperation and Development (OECD), EU and NATO averages, as seen in Figure 1. For example, during 1988–2000, the average yearly defense burden in the 15 countries of the EU was 2.1 percent of

FIGURE 1

MILITARY EXPENDITURE AS A PERCENTAGE OF GDP

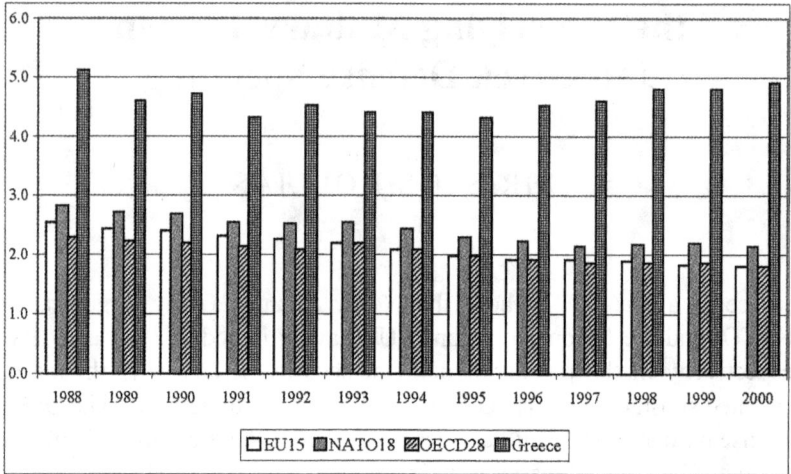

FIGURE 2

MILITARY EXPENDITURE 1988–2001 (IN CONSTANT PRICES)

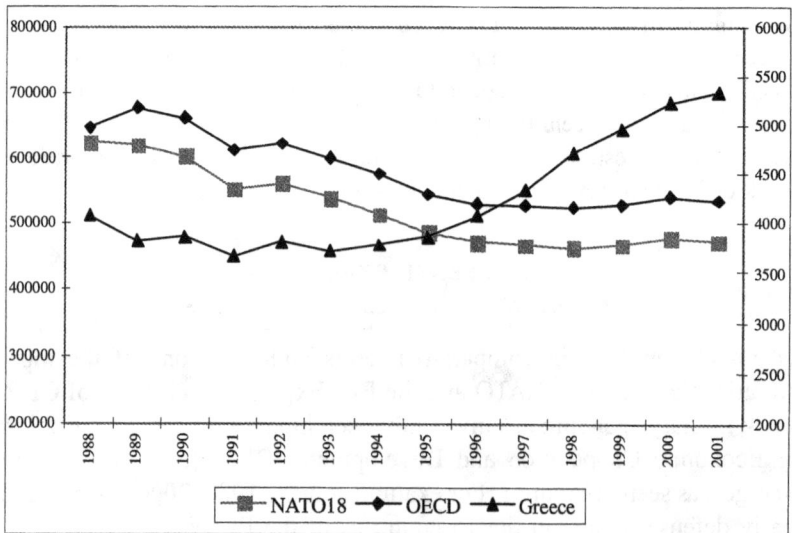

GDP, for the 18 members of NATO 2.4 percent of GDP and in the case of the OECD countries two percent of GDP. In comparison, for the same period Greece—on average—allocated 4.6 percent of its GDP to defense.

Furthermore, while the defense budgets of most countries shrank during the post-bipolar period, Greek defense spending grew in real terms—as seen in Figure 2. For example, according to Stockholm International Peace Research Institute (SIPRI) data, during 1988–2001 total NATO and OECD military spending fell in real terms by 24.3 percent and 17.4 percent respectively. Similarly, the EU 15 total defense expenditure declined by 14.3 percent for the same period. In comparison, military spending by Greece grew by as much as 30.9 percent in real terms.

The Greek defense effort, as reflected by the various indices, cannot be explained solely in terms of the broader Western security priorities as they have evolved during the bipolar and post-bipolar eras. In Greek defense policy, Turkey has invariably ranked as the main military threat to its national interests.[5] High defense spending is thus justified in terms of the perceived military threat that Turkey poses. Empirical findings by econometric studies that have estimated military expenditure demand functions suggest that Greek defense allocations are in fact strongly influenced by external security considerations, and Turkish military spending is used as the threat variable in the relevant estimations.[6] In fact, a visual inspection of the long-term trend of the Greek and Turkish military expenditure graphs reveals very strong similarities, which suggest at least some degree of interdependence. However, this interdependence may be asymmetric, as some of the reported findings suggest.[7] As Figure 3 illustrates, the two series appear to follow a common pattern up to the late 1980s, where they start to diverge. From then onwards, Turkish defense expenditure increases at a faster rate than Greek defense expenditure, which nevertheless also exhibits an upward trend—albeit less pronounced.[8] The observed long-term common pattern and trend of the two expenditure graphs is further verified if we estimate the correlation coefficient of the two. Although strong correlation does not imply the presence of a causal relation and hence an armaments race, it is nevertheless a useful tool to explore the presence of common trends between two variables—in this case Greek and Turkish defense spending. Not surprisingly, the value of the estimated correlation coefficient for the whole postwar period (1950–2001) is quite high—a value of 0.914— suggesting strong correlation between the two defense expenditure series.

The correlation between the two variables, although by no means evidence of a causal relation, nonetheless points to the presence of a long-term relation. This relation however, could, for shorter time periods, be

FIGURE 3
GREEK AND TURKISH DEFENCE SPENDING 1950–2001
(IN CONSTANT PRICES)

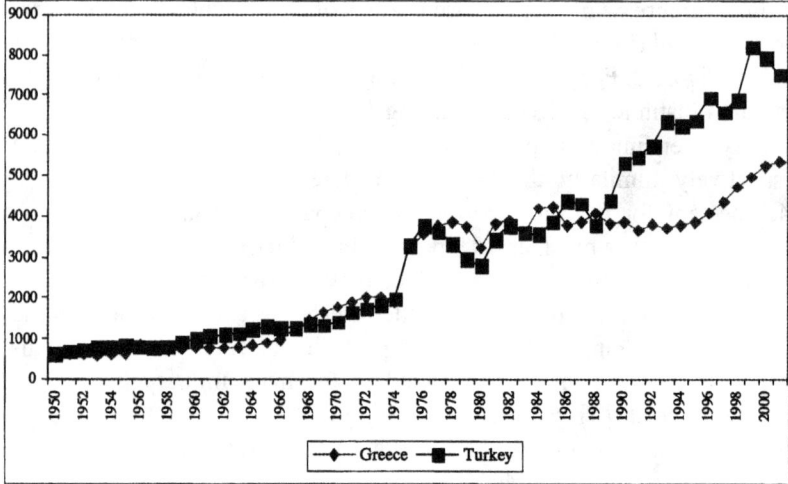

FIGURE 4
DETERMINANTS OF GREEK AND TURKISH MILITARY SPENDING

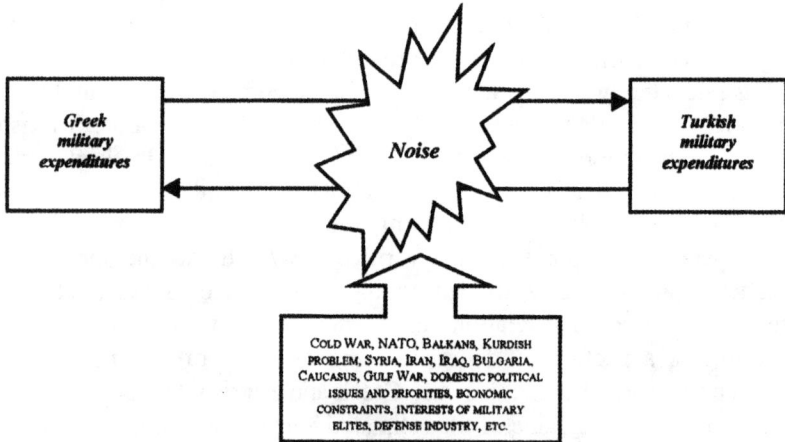

affected by other factors of both external and internal nature such as economic and fiscal constraints as well as other domestic or external security concerns and issues.[9]

As demonstrated in Figure 4, the empirical investigation attempting to uncover a relationship between the two military expenditure variables is hindered by the presence of what could be termed "external noise." External noise includes the effects that other determinants have on the two variables, thus hindering any empirical investigation of their relation. Of course, the significance and impact of such effects varies through time. For example, factors such as fiscal constraints undoubtedly influence defense-spending decisions in both countries. The observed decline in real Turkish defense expenditure over the past couple of years may be at least partially attributed to the economic crisis and the devaluation of the Turkish lira (Figure 3). Similar fiscal problems may also be cited in the case of Greece in order to explain the military spending trend in the late 1980s and early 1990s (Figures 2 and 3). The war against the PKK guerillas certainly influenced Turkish military expenditure from the late 1980s until the recent resolution of the problem (from a military perspective). Likewise, NATO commitments by both countries may be cited as partial explanations for the modernization and upgrade programs of armed forces' capital equipment that both have undertaken in recent years. Consequently, given the presence of such external noise, it is not surprising to observe that the correlation coefficient between the two variables—that is, Greek and Turkish military spending—varies for different sub-periods, taking values of 0.91 for 1950–73; 0.74 for 1974–2001; 0.69 for 1980–2001; 0.87 for 1990–2001; 0.66 for 1985–2001; and a low 0.59 for the period 1980–90. For example, in the case of Greek defense spending, it has been demonstrated that it is strongly influenced by domestic political factors and in particular by the "political color" of the incumbent party—that is, its ideological and political position.[10]

Other external noise to the underlying relation between the two variables in question may be due to structural changes in the international strategic environment, such as the end of the cold war, with the concomitant changes in the geopolitical scene of the region. Alternatively, noise may be due to short-term changes in security and defense priorities caused by the appearance of events such as the Gulf War, the Kurdish-PKK problem in Turkey or the recent war in Iraq. The presence of such external noise, graphically represented by Figure 4, partly explains the difficulties in unequivocally establishing an action-reaction regime between the two defense expenditure series that would otherwise point to an armaments race between the two countries.[11]

Yet, despite such effects from external noise, the important issues that divide the two countries, such as Cyprus and the Aegean, form a fertile ground on which mutual suspicion over long-term intentions and threat perceptions flourish. In fact, the two countries have come close to war on more than one occasion, narrowly averting a military engagement only after stern external intervention. Hence, given this context in which their bilateral relations have—until recently at least—oscillated, it is plausible to argue that in their respective security agendas and defense planning, mutual concerns regarding the other are an important long-term determinant of military spending. With a time varying weight, each country's military strength and preparations have—to different extents—influenced their respective defense expenditures. This has perhaps fueled an armaments race, which may, nonetheless, be difficult to trace empirically. For example, a recent study found that the evidence is inconclusive either in favor of or against the presence of such an action-reaction regime between the two time series that would point to an armaments race or at least to the conclusion that the two countries are not arming in a totally independent manner.[12] Equally inconclusive findings have been reported by studies that set out to address the question of whether the hypothesis of a Greek-Turkish arms race can find a modicum of empirical verification.[13] The findings reported by these studies vary depending on the time period covered and the methodology employed. Unidirectional, bidirectional and no causality between Greek and Turkish military expenditures have all been reported. Clearly, apart from the external noise pointed out earlier, a number of data reliability problems hinder the investigation of an action-reaction regime, whilst important methodological questions should also be raised.[14]

THE RAPPROCHEMENT, THE UNDERLYING TENSION AND GREEK DEFENSE SPENDING

As pointed out in the previous section, Greek military spending continued to grow in real terms throughout the post-bipolar period, despite the reverse trends observed in almost all members of NATO, the OECD and the EU. Greece, however, was not the only marked exception to this predominant post-bipolar trend of shrinking defense budgets. A similarly sharp upward trend was also exhibited by Turkish military expenditure, which increased in real terms by approximately 97 percent from 1988–2001 (Figure 5). The upward trend in their respective military spending is clearly depicted by the linear trend of the two time series in Figure 5. This offers further evidence in favor of the argument that the two

FIGURE 5
GREEK AND TURKISH MILITARY SPENDING EXPENDITURE 1988–2001
(IN CONSTANT PRICES)

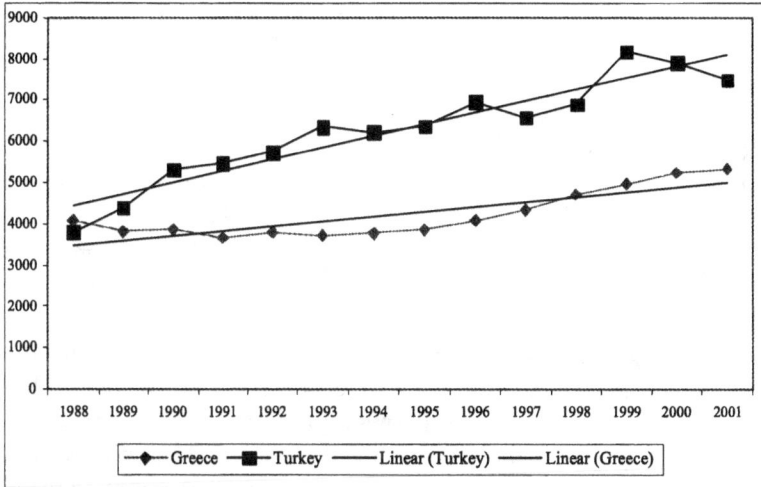

countries are not arming totally independent of each other and that the large and extensive modernization programs of their respective armed forces undertaken in recent years are, at least to some extent, interdependent. However, having said this, it is also necessary to stress that the exhibited trends of their respective military spending should by no means be wholly attributed to an armaments race between the two, as mentioned above.

In the post-bipolar period, Greek-Turkish bilateral relations have gone through a tension-negotiation-tension cycle.[15] As has been pointed out elsewhere,[16] some major events during this period mark downturns in the Greek-Turkish bilateral relations cycle, such as the Imia/Kardak crisis in 1996, the proposed deployment of the S-300 missiles in Cyprus in 1997–98, the declaration of the joint defense area by Greece and Cyprus in 1993, the issue of the extension of territorial waters to 12 miles and the Öcalan affair in 1999. Other events, such as the lifting of the Greek veto in 1995 to Turkey's accession to the Customs Union and in 1999 the lifting of the veto to Turkey's EU candidacy, the Madrid Declaration in 1998, the recent advancements and improvements spurred by "earthquake diplomacy" and the signing of a number of bilateral treaties during the same period mark upward turns in the cycle.[17] In fact, ever since the rapprochement prompted by the earthquakes, Greek-Turkish bilateral relations improved in an unprecedented manner. Yet, at least on the basis of the data available thus far, this has not filtered through to Greek military spending, which has continued to rise—by 7.5 percent in real terms between 1999–2001—as observed in Figure 5. On the other hand, Turkish military spending during the corresponding period has decreased by around 8.4 percent, which is probably at least a partial result of the deep economic crisis that Turkey faced. Thus, it is too early to conclude whether the recent Turkish downturn in spending signals a long-term downward trend or is nothing more than a mere short-term downward fluctuation— attributed to acute short term fiscal problems—of a long-term upward trend. Certainly, this upward trend could be strengthened by new security developments in the aftermath of the 2003 Iraqi War that presents Turkey with new concerns independent of the Greek-Turkish conflict over the Aegean and Cyprus. One could argue, though, that the recent rapprochement will eventually trickle down to the defense budgets after a certain time lag before any appreciable effect is observed on defense expenditures. In any case, even if small reductions in such expenditures are observed in the future, they could be interpreted as the result of improved efficiency or fiscal constraints (such as the impact of the EU Stability Pact in the case of Greece that imposes restrictions on fiscal deficits and public debt), rather than the result of the improvements in Greek-Turkish bilateral relations.

It has been demonstrated that the marked progress in bilateral relations since 1999 essentially changed the climate between the two countries,[18] and has led to bilateral agreements on issues that fall into the sphere of "low politics," while both countries have not changed their firm positions on issues of "high politics." Little (or no) real progress has been achieved, despite the good will and the concomitant rhetoric, on issues that fall within the "strategic core" of Greek-Turkish bilateral relations. Such issues include the size of Greek airspace over the Aegean, territorial waters and the continental shelf, and Cyprus.

In fact, if a graphical representation of Greek-Turkish bilateral relations is attempted, it would be made up of different layers (Figure 6). Issues that can be placed in the sphere of low politics would form the upper layer(s) of bilateral relations. Such "soft issues" could, for example, include Aegean Sea ecological issues or arrangements to facilitate ferrying foreign tourists daily to and from the Greek islands and the coast of Anatolia and vice versa. As one progresses through the layers of bilateral relations, issues such as combating international crime and drug trafficking or bilateral trade also appear as soft issues; these are issues on which it is comparatively easy to reach bilateral agreements and work out mutually accepted solutions and even policies. Thus, it is of no surprise that the

FIGURE 6
THE LAYERS OF GREEK-TURKISH BILATERAL RELATIONS

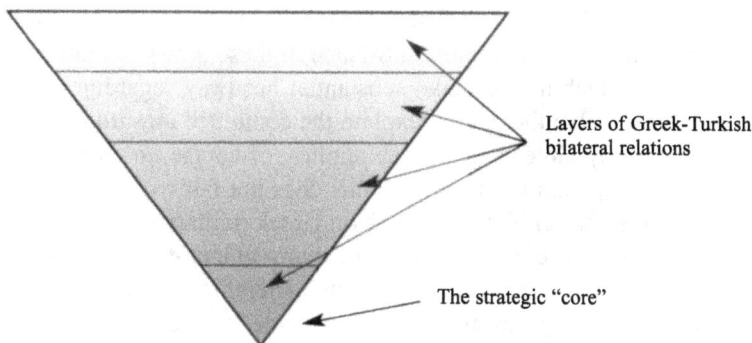

Layers of Greek-Turkish
bilateral relations

The strategic "core"

recent improvement in bilateral relations has yielded the signing of a number of agreements between the two countries on such things as culture, energy, trade, illegal migration and organized crime, economic and regional cooperation and tourism. These agreements facilitate the creation and establishment of an improved climate and institutional framework within which Greek-Turkish discourse can take place.[19]

However, as one progresses through the various layers of Greek-Turkish bilateral relations, the issues gradually start to fall within the realm of high politics and their resolution becomes more difficult. Thus, "hard issues," such as Cyprus and the Aegean, can be considered as the core of their relations, as these issues are clearly emotive for both sides and touch upon fundamental aspects of their respective national strategy and security policies. The fate of the Annan Plan for Cyprus exemplifies the difficulty inherent in these hard issues that are not easily amenable to resolution despite the fervent diplomatic efforts and encouragement by international actors such as the EU and the United States. In this regard, despite the remarkable progress achieved in recent years—at least in terms of the overall climate of bilateral relations—these issues of high politics remain largely unresolved (although some marginal progress, as compared to the long stalemate that was the previous *status quo*, has been made). In this context, from the Greek perspective, Turkish troops are still occupying part of Cyprus and the Turkish position that an extension of Greek territorial waters to 12 miles would constitute a *causus belli* has not been altered. There are violations of Greek airspace on a daily basis and subsequent dogfights over the Aegean that force the two air forces to remain on high alert—with the concomitant impact on the level of military tension. From a Turkish perspective, these or other issues, such as the Joint Defence Area doctrine declared by Greece and Cyprus,[20] also threaten its national security and interests.[21] It should be stressed that the aim of this contribution is not to delve into the substance of these issues but rather to point out that the inability to make substantial headway regarding these issues, let alone resolve them, may explain the continued upward trend in defense spending by Greece. The same applies, of course, in the case of Turkish defense expenditure. However, this does not fall within the main scope of this essay, which focuses solely on Greek military spending.

Defense planning takes place within a medium- to long-term time frame and is probably unaffected by fluctuations in bilateral relations that do not appear to lead to strategic shifts and to sustainable long-term solutions to the issues that form the strategic core of bilateral relations and are the sources of tension and friction. Therefore, current defense capability is the result of decisions made by defense planners in the past. Defense planning and decisions are made under conditions of uncertainty. If no observable change in the rival's long-term strategy is evident, then defense planners will tend, at least partially, to allocate spending based upon past experience. If the rival's behavior and/or actions in the past were—or were perceived to be—aggressive and hostile, then a "better safe than sorry" attitude will tend to dominate current defense planning and decisions, irrespective of the climate in which current bilateral discourse is conducted. If a rival has behaved aggressively in the past, defense planners will tend to assume that there is no reason to expect it will not do so again in the future if the issues that caused this aggressiveness remain unresolved. This is even more the case if in the past the rival has relied on or used its military strength either to extract concessions or to advance its interests by force.

Since the current improvement has thus far only affected the upper layers of Greek-Turkish relations—leaving the underlying strategic core essentially unaffected—one could suggest that the fundamental strategic issues that divide the two countries continue to partially drive and determine military spending and arms procurement decisions. If, indeed, this is the case, then in order to partly explain the upward trend of Greek military spending an index is required in order to quantify the underlying tension—particularly the underlying military tension, despite improvements in the climate in which Greek-Turkish discourse is currently taking place.[22]

Two of the fundamental issues that form the strategic core of Greek-Turkish relations are, as mentioned above, Cyprus and the Aegean. From the Greek defense planners perspective, such a "tension index"—reflecting the deep strategic divisions that still exist—could be the number of Greek airspace violations over the Aegean by the Turkish air force. Such activities maintain and increase the underlying military tension which, reasonably, will have a positive impact on the defense budget, either increasing it or at least rendering it more inelastic and therefore less prone to cutbacks.

Before proceeding with the use of this proposed tension index, a number of points of clarification are in order. In particular, it should be pointed out that this index, published by the Greek Ministry of Defense (MoD), is not independently verified by outside actors, such as NATO sources.[23] This, of course, raises issues concerning the validity of the index along with the methodological problems associated with what in fact constitutes an airspace violation. In brief, without delving into the technical substance of the issue, which is well beyond our scope, Greece claims a ten-mile airspace over the Aegean. Turkey disputes this claim and only recognizes a six-mile airspace—a measure equal to that of Greek territorial waters.[24] Thus, to a large extent, the reported violations concern the entrance of Turkish air force planes into the area between the six- and ten-mile zone. In essence, what is being proposed here is that once one of the two parties in a dyad of states perceives the actions of the other as infringements of its territory (in this case, airspace), such actions—irrespective of possible justification—generate tension, and particularly military tension since branches of their respective armed forces are involved (almost daily dogfights, mostly between the six- to ten-mile zone). Clearly, the reverse also applies to the other member of the dyad, who may very well perceive the size of national airspace claimed by the other party—again irrespective of possible justification—as inhibiting its right to free and unobstructed access to international airspace. Therefore, given the differences between the two parties on the size of the airspace, this issue becomes a source of tension and friction that has a military dimension built into it. One could then reasonably argue that this could have an impact, albeit indirect, on defense policy and therefore military spending.[25] Finally, it should be stressed that the index is not used to examine the presence of an armaments race between the two countries in the action-reaction sense, but rather to see whether it is possible to trace and establish a one-sided perception-behavior linkage in the case of Greek defense spending.

Turning back to the tension index, a graphical representation reveals that in the last 15 years or so the index shows an upward trend, seemingly unaffected by the rapprochement of recent years (Figure 7). Indeed, while allowing for a drop in 2000, the number of violations has increased substantially, especially between 2001–2, as seen in Figure 7. In fact, the number of violations reported by the Greek MoD in 2002 (a total of 3,240)

FIGURE 7
NUMBER OF VIOLATIONS OF THE GREEK AIRSPACE

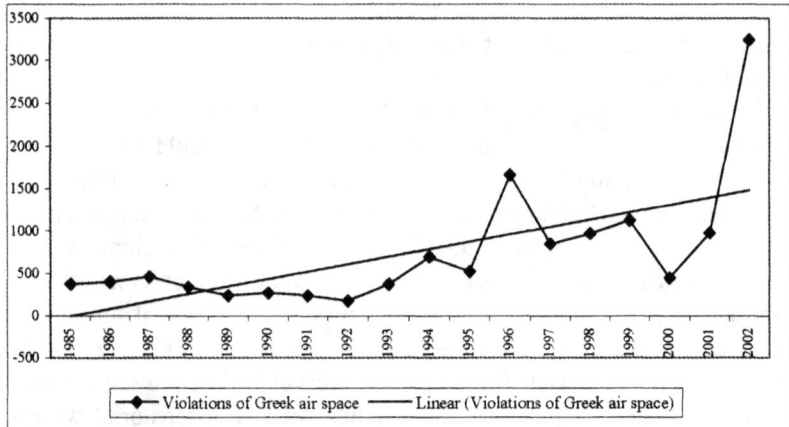

is greater than the number in 1996 (a total of 1,667), the year of the Imia/Kardak crisis that brought the two countries to the brink of war. Allowing for the undoubtedly important methodological weakness and unreliability of this data series, it is nevertheless possible to use it to capture the underlying divisions and concomitant tension in bilateral relations. The index seemingly encapsulates the military threat perceptions of one side in our dyad.

Following this line of reasoning, one may attempt to partially explain the upward trend of Greek military spending in terms of this underlying military tension, as illustrated by the aforementioned index. Again, without entering into the substance of the airspace issue, from a Greek defense planner's perspective the violations of Greek airspace by the Turkish air force offer ample evidence that there has been no marked change in the long-term strategy of Turkey. A graphical comparison of both this tension index and Greek military expenditure in Figure 8 reveals the parallel upward trends. Although this is by no means evidence of a causal relation and an armaments race, it may nevertheless help to explain why the Greek defense budget has continued to grow in real terms throughout the post-bipolar period.[26] In Figure 9, the rate of change of Greek military spending is plotted against the number of airspace violations and the common trend shared by the two time series is more pronounced.

Using regression analysis, the graphically observed relationship was examined to determine if it could be further corroborated. A number of different regression equations with different specifications were estimated

FIGURE 8
GREEK DEFENCE SPENDING AND AIRSPACE VIOLATIONS

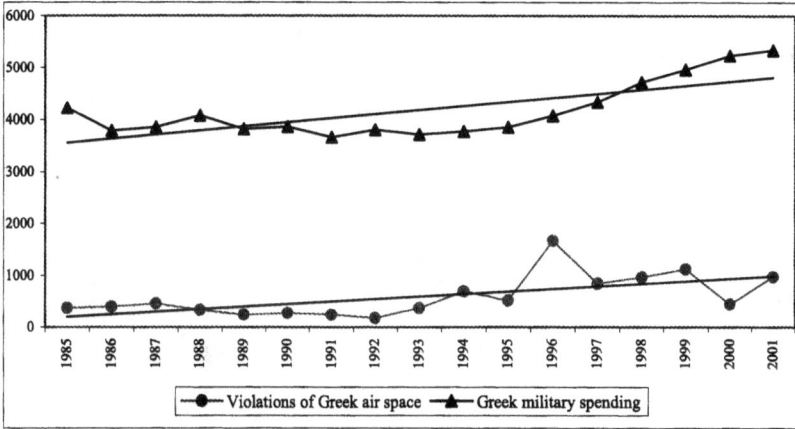

FIGURE 9
AIRSPACE VIOLATIONS AND THE RATE OF CHANGE OF GREEK
MILITARY EXPENDITURE

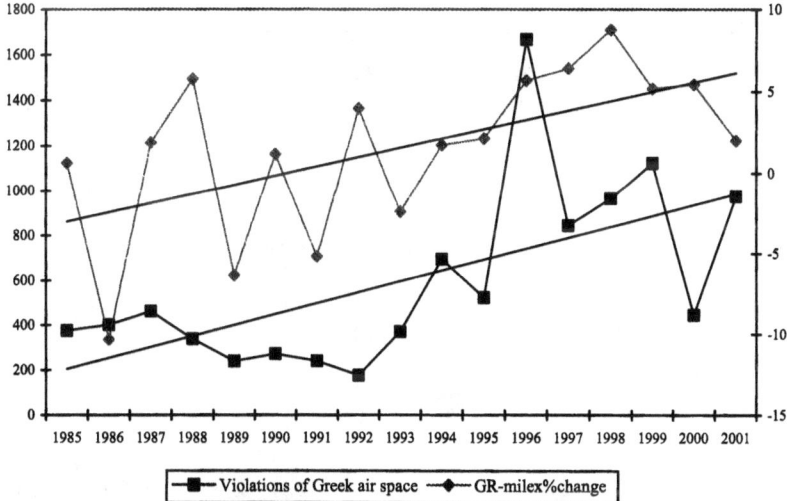

using Greek military spending, both in levels (MGR_t) and first differences (ΔMGR_t) as the left-hand-side dependent variable. The violations time series ($Viol_t$)—both in contemporaneous and lag form—as well as Turkish military spending ($MTUR_t$) were used as explanatory variables. The

TABLE 1

THE EFFECTS OF AIR SPACE VIOLATIONS ON GREEK MILITARY SPENDING

Dependent variable: MGR$_t$

Independent variables	(1.1)	(1.2)	(1.3)	(1.4)	(1.5)	(1.6)	(1.7)
Constant	7.654	7.497	6.241	5.64	5.622	0.056	0.416
	(29.08)	(29.48)	(6.51)	(6.50)	(6.76)	(0.06)	(0.42)
MTUR$_t$			0.196	0.244			
			(1.53)	(2.21)			
MTUR$_{t-1}$					0.258		
					(2.34)		
MGR$_{t-1}$						0.962	0.910
						(7.56)	(7.26)
Viol$_t$	0.109		0.063			0.044	
	(2.58)		(1.24)			(2.04)	
Viol$_{t-1}$		0.135		0.093	0.078		0.056
		(3.29)		(2.24)	(1.80)		(2.56)
Diagnostics							
R^2	0.31	0.44	0.41	0.59	0.60	0.87	0.89
D.W.	0.61	0.70	0.58	0.61	0.66	[1.49]*	[2.10]*
F-stat	6.68	10.85	4.80	9.36	9.90	44.67	51.80

Notes: * The value of the LM diagnostic test of residual serial correlation; *t-ratios in brackets.*

Dependent variable: ΔMGR$_t$

Independent variables	(2.1)	(2.2)	(2.3)	(2.4)	(2.5)	(2.6)	(2.7)
Constant	-95.519	-108.60	-77.272	-59.778	-51.403	-40.981	-67.43
	(1.07)	(1.31)	(0.87)	(0.72)	(0.75)	(0.53)	(0.95)
ΔMGR$_t$			-0.129				
			(1.32)				
ΔMGR$_{t-1}$				0.049	0.037		
				(0.56)	(0.45)		
ΔMGR$_{t-1}$						-0.010	-0.118
						(0.05)	(0.58)
Viol$_t$	0.271		0.289	0.241		0.233	
	(2.20)		(2.39)	(2.33)		(2.06)	
Viol$_{t-1}$		0.312			0.282		0.306
		(2.60)			(2.86)		(2.74)
Diagnostics							
R^2	0.25	0.33	0.35	0.31	0.41	0.30	0.41
DW	2.10	2.34	1.96	2.63	4.09	[2.84]*	[6.10]*
F-stat	4.85	6.78	3.49	2.73	3.13	2.51	4.20

Notes: * The value of the LM diagnostic test of residual serial correlation; *t-ratios in brackets.*

results, reported in Table 1, appear on the whole to be fairly consistent in terms of the impact of the violations variable on Greek defense spending. Generally, they appear to suggest the presence of a strong statistical link between the two time series.

In particular, on the basis of the results of regressions *(1.1)*, *(1.2)*, *(2.1)* and *(2.2)*, where the violations time series *(Viol$_t$* and *Viol$_{t-1}$)* is used as the only right-hand-side explanatory variable for both the levels of Greek defense expenditure *(MGR$_t$)* and its first difference *(ΔMGR$_t$)*, it has a positive and statistically significant coefficient (t-ratios in parentheses).[27] In all estimated regressions the coefficient sign and statistical significance of the violations variable is consistently positive and significant, with the exception of equation *(1.3)*. The same applies where first differences *(ΔMGR$_t$)* are used as the dependent variable. It should be stressed here, though, that the obtained results from the regression analysis should be treated cautiously since on the basis of the diagnostics it appears that the equations suffer from serial correlation problems.[28] However, these problems are not present in the case of regressions *(1.6)* and *(1.7)*. In fact, these equations appear to be the best specified with a high explanatory power (R^2=0.87 and 0.89 respectively)[29] and no evidence of serial correlation (LM=1.49 and 2.10 respectively).[30]

Nevertheless, despite, the evidence provided by the estimated regressions in favor of a strong statistical link between Greek defense spending and Greek airspace violations, the results reported in Table 1 should not be treated as anything more than a mere indication of the presence of a possible link between the two variables suggesting that the use of such a tension index may help in explaining Greek military expenditure. Naturally, this warrants further and more systematic econometric investigation. Similarly, the results do not offer evidence of an armaments race in an action-reaction sense. However, on the basis of these purely preliminary findings, one may argue that military tension indices should be introduced in efforts to statistically capture the action-reaction behavior of the defense expenditures by the two countries. However, this claim needs to be empirically tested via more rigorous statistical techniques that would determine the usefulness of such an index.

CONCLUDING REMARKS

As a number of studies have shown, Greek military spending is partly driven by acute external security considerations and, in particular, the ongoing conflict with Turkey. Mutual concern over each other's long-term strategy is an important determinant of military spending. This has attracted considerable attention in the relevant literature, which attempts to determine if an action-reaction behavior exists. In the case of Greece, such expenditure has continued to grow in real terms throughout the post-bipolar period. In this study, it was argued that the recent improvements in Greek-Turkish bilateral relations have not touched their strategic core. It is this core and the issues contained therein that, to a large extent, determine defense policy and planning and at least partially drive defense spending and arms procurement. Even if the climate in which the current discourse of their relations is conducted is not tense, the fundamental sources of their strategic division and conflict remain unaffected. Using an index that attempts to quantify the underlying military tension which stems from the major issues that form the strategic core of their relations, it was argued that Greece's military expenditure is partially driven by long-term threat perceptions *vis-à-vis* Turkey—maintained and reinforced by the underlying military tension. Preliminary econometric results from regression analysis appear to corroborate this argument. Defense planning and the concomitant outlays for arms procurement take place within a medium- to long-term time perspective. Thus, if no observable significant change in the strategy of an antagonistic power is evident, valuable resources will continue to be allocated to defense uses. This allocation can continue to take place largely unaffected by short-term fluctuations in the climate of the bilateral relations of two states.

NOTES

The author gratefully acknowledges useful and insightful comments and constructive suggestions by Ali Çarkoğlu on an earlier version of this contribution, as well as the valuable input by the participants of the workshop "Greek-Turkish Relations in the Aftermath of Copenhagen 2002: The End of Rapprochement or New Beginning," Faculty of Arts and Social Sciences, Sabancı University, Istanbul, June 13–14, 2003.

1. Christos Kollias, "Country Survey VII: Military Expenditure in Greece," *Defence and Peace Economics*, Vol.6, No.4 (1995), pp.305–19.
2. A comprehensive and critical survey of this literature is provided by Jurgen Brauer, "Survey and Review of the Defence Economics Literature on Greece and Turkey: What Have we Learned?" *Defence and Peace Economics*, Vol.13, No.2 (2002), pp.85–107. See also Jurgen Brauer, "Turkey and Greece: A Comprehensive Survey of the Defence Economics Literature," in Christos Kollias and Gülay Günlük-ᵃenesen (eds.), *Greece and Turkey in the 21st Century: The Political Economy Perspective* (New York: Nova Science, forthcoming).
3. See, for example, Keith Hartley and Todd Sandler (eds.), *The Economics of Defence Spending: An International Survey* (London and New York: Routledge, 1990), and Keith Hartley and Todd Sandler (eds.), *Handbook of Defence Economics* (North Holland: Elsevier, 1995a). Similarly, see Todd Sandler and Keith Hartley (eds.), *The Economics of Defence* (Cambridge: Cambridge University Press, 1995b). See also Ron Smith, "The Demand for Military Expenditure," *Economic Journal*, Vol.90, No.4 (1980), pp.811–20, and Ron Smith, "Models of Military Expenditures," *Journal of Applied Econometrics*, Vol.4, No.4 (1989), pp.345–59.

4. Sandler and Hartley (1995b), pp.52–72.
5. See Thanos Dokos, "Greek Security Policy in the 21st Century," in Christodoulos Yiallourides and Panayiotis Tsakonas (eds.), *Greece and Turkey After the End of the Cold War* (New York and Athens: Caratzas, 2001), pp.79–100, and Athanasios Platias, "Greece's Strategic Doctrine: in Search of Autonomy and Deterrence," in Dimitri Constas (ed.), *The Greek-Turkish Conflict in the 1990s* (London: Macmillan, 1991), pp.91–108.
6. See, for example: Christos Avramides, "Alternative Models of Greek Defence Expenditures," *Defence and Peace Economics*, Vol.8, No.2 (1997), pp.145–87; Panayiotis Kapopoulos and Sophia Lazaretou, "Modeling the Demand for Greek Defence Expenditure: An Error Correction Approach," *Cyprus Journal of Economics*, Vol.6, No.1 (1993), pp.73–86; Kollias (1995), pp.311–14; and Christos Kollias, "The Greek-Turkish Conflict and Greek Military Expenditure 1962–90," *Journal of Peace Research*, Vol.33, No.2 (1996), pp.217–28.
7. Nadir Öcal, "Asymmetric Effects of Military Expenditure between Turkey and Greece," *Defence and Peace Economics*, Vol.13, No.5 (2002), pp.405–16.
8. The war with the PKK guerillas can partially explain Turkish military spending trends, whereas in the case of Greece, fiscal problems may offer a possible explanation.
9. Christos Kollias, "A Look at the Methodological Issues Involved in the Greek-Turkish Arms Race Hypothesis," *Hellenic Studies*, Vol.9, No.2 (2001), pp.91–114.
10. Christos Kollias and Suzanna-Maria Paleologou, "Domestic Political and External Security Determinants of the Demand for Greek Military Expenditure," *Defence and Peace Economics*, Vol.14, No.6 (2003), pp.437–46.
11. See Gülay Günlük-Şenesen, "Turkish Defence Expenditures in View of the Ups and Downs in Turkish-Greek Relations: Is There a Reaction," *Hellenic Studies*, Vol.9, No.2 (2001), pp.73–89, and also Kollias (2001), pp.98–110.
12. Günlük-Şenesen (2001), pp.81–5.
13. See the surveys of the defense economics literature on Greece and Turkey by Brauer (2002), pp.85–107; Brauer (2003).
14. For the discussion and analysis of these methodological issues, see Michael Leidy and Robert Staiger, "Economic issues and Methodology in Arms Race Analysis," *Journal of Conflict Resolution*, Vol.29, No.3 (1985), pp.503–30, and Charles Anderton, "Arms Race Modeling: Problems and Prospects," *Journal of Conflict Resolution*, Vol.33, No.2 (1989), pp.346–67. For issues concerning the econometric estimation, see Ron Smith, Paul Dunne and Eftychia Nikolaidou, "The Econometrics of Arms Races," *Defence and Peace Economics*, Vol.11, No.1 (2000), pp.31–43. For the specific Greek-Turkish issue, see Brauer (2002), pp.89–91; Brauer (2003); Kollias (2001), pp.98–110; and Günlük-Şenesen (2001), pp.81–5.
15. For a comprehensive presentation see, *inter alia*, Christodoulos Yiallourides and Panayiotis Tsakonas (eds.), *Greece and Turkey After the End of the Cold War* (New York and Athens: Caratzas, 2001).
16. Günlük-Şenesen (2001), pp.79–81.
17. For the impact on Greek-Turkish relations see, for example, Panayiotis Tsakonas, "Turkey's Road Map to the European Union: Implications for Greek-Turkish Relations and the Cyprus Issue," *Hellenic Studies*, Vol.9, No.1 (2001), pp.71–100, and Panayiotis Tsakonas, "Turkey's post-Helsinki Turbulence: Implications for Greece and the Cyprus Issue," *Turkish Studies*, Vol.2, No.2 (2001), pp.1–40.
18. Thanos Dokos and Panayiotis Tsakonas, "Greek-Turkish Security Relations Reconsidered: A View from Athens," in Kollias and Günlük-Şenesen (2003).
19. See Alexis Heraclides, "Greek-Turkish Relations from Discord to Détente: A Preliminary Evaluation," *Review of International Studies*, Vol.1, No.3 (2002), p.23.
20. The JDA Doctrine is essentially the integration of military planning and operations by Greece and the Republic of Cyprus. In the context of Greek extended deterrence, it signifies the commitment by Greece to intervene militarily in case of Turkish military operations in Cyprus.
21. From a Turkish perspective, the JDA—and thus the active military engagement of Greece in Cyprus—as well as the possible future extension of Greek territorial waters to 12 miles in line with the international treaty currently in force, constitutes threats to its interests, rights and national sovereignty.

22. It should be stressed that any attempt to quantify bilateral relations of a dyad of nations and the underlying tensions between them has inherent difficulties and is subjective.

23. Reportedly, the Greek MoD directly relays the activities of the Turkish air force to NATO in real time, but since the official NATO position is that the problem of the length of Greek airspace is a purely bilateral issue the figures used here cannot be independently verified.

24. See Richard Clogg, "Greek-Turkish Relations in the post-1974 Period," in Constas (1991), p.15. The roots of this problem can be traced back to 1974; since then, Turkey has not accepted Greece's 1931 declaration that its national airspace extended to ten miles and only recognizes a six-mile airspace, arguing that airspace should be the same as territorial waters. Turkey has also declared a *causus belli* policy if Greece extends its territorial waters to 12 miles in line with the international treaty currently in force.

25. Defense expenditure is influenced by a multitude of both external and internal factors: the former include such factors as alliance and external threats; the latter include economic constraints, domestic political cycles, the interests of the military and internal repression. Thus, in the case of Greek military expenditure, it would be wrong to attribute its growth over the past few years solely to security and defense considerations *vis-à-vis* Turkey, let alone claim that the proposed tension index is its main determinant.

26. Again, this may be cited only as a partial explanation of Greek military spending and the trend it has exhibited. A number of other factors can be cited as determinants of such spending. See, *inter alia*, Avramides (1997), pp.145–87, and Kollias and Paleologou (2003).

27. The t-statistic determines whether or not the coefficient of each right-hand variable is equal to zero, individually. When this is true, from a statistical point of view the variable is insignificant. In our case the obtained t-statistics indicate that the coefficients of the violations are significantly different to zero and therefore partially explain the dependent variable. Similarly, the F-statistic determines whether or not the coefficients of all the right-hand variables are equal to zero. When they are, from a statistical point of view they are insignificant.

28. The observations of the variables of interest in our time series analysis contain error terms. This is because econometric models are unable to predict the exact values of the variables every time. However, sometimes the error terms in different observations of the variables are related and then the problem of serial correlation (autocorrelation) exists. Because of this problem, the most frequent and popular test is Durbin-Watson (DW), which takes the value from zero to four. Usually, a value around 2.00 suggests that there are no serial correlation problems in the estimated regression.

29. This statistic indicates how well the model performs: how well the right-hand variables (independent variables) "explain" the left-hand variable (dependent variable).

30. The type of regression models we are using in the case of (*1.6*) and (*1.7*) as well as (*2.6*) and (*2.7*) are autoregressive. This means that the lagged value of the dependent variable (MGR_{t-1} in our case) appears as a regressor in the estimated relationship. We chose this type of model as, based on the theory of military expenditure, this type of expenditure is affected by its own value in previous periods, that is, current defense spending is affected by its lagged values or, in other words, spending decisions in previous fiscal periods. Given that the lagged dependent variable appears as a regressor, the DW statistic is biased and therefore not appropriate to check for serial correlation. Thus, the LM diagnostic test was employed in the case of (*1.6*) and (*1.7*) as well as (*2.6*) and (*2.7*), as can be seen in Table 1. Results of the Durbin's h-test for serial correlation also yielded similar results, with a value of -0.27 for (*1.6*) and -0.50 for (*1.7*).

8

The View from Turkey:
Perceptions of Greeks and
Greek-Turkish Rapprochement by the
Turkish Public

ALİ ÇARKOĞLU and KEMAL KİRİŞCİ

Two disastrous earthquakes in Turkey in August and November and one in Greece in September 1999 caused massive damage to property and great loss of life on both sides of the Aegean. Unexpectedly, this precipitated a phenomenon that became known as "earthquake diplomacy" between the two countries.[1] Earthquake diplomacy, which was based on an upsurge in Greek and Turkish public empathy with the victims of the earthquakes in both countries, has since expanded to affect many levels of interaction. Civil society contacts between the two countries have grown tremendously over the course of just a few years. Sports-related contacts have not only increased but also ceased to be an extension of the enduring nationalist tensions between the two countries; friendship matches have become common. The media in both countries has started to adopt a much more positive outlook on bilateral relations. There has also been coverage of the emotional stories of groups of elderly people, who had been forcefully exchanged in the 1920s between the two countries (*mübadiller* in Turkish), and their descendents, who were visiting the towns or villages where they were born. Dialogue between the ministers of foreign affairs and cooperation at the governmental level has also significantly increased. The European Council's decision at its Helsinki Summit in December 1999 to recognize Turkey's candidacy for the European Union (EU), with significant help from the Greek side, helped to consolidate the gains of earthquake diplomacy.

Undoubtedly, Greek-Turkish relations since the beginning of earthquake diplomacy have come a long way. So much so, that the very newspaper in Turkey, *Hürriyet*, that had played a central role in galvanizing the Turkish public opinion into a belligerent mood during the Imia/Kardak crisis in 1996, reported the remarks of the Greek commander under huge banner headlines of "Winds of Friendship over the Aegean: Words that are closing an era."[2] Governmental relations have become much more cordial than what they were only a few years ago. Numerous cooperation agreements have been signed, ranging from combating illegal immigration to the prevention of double taxation; some have been ratified and others are waiting to be approved by respective parliaments. These are significant developments because no governmental agreements beyond "protocols" or "joint communiqués" had been signed between the two countries since the 1970s (and even those agreements had had little effect).

One area where visible improvement in governmental relations can be observed is in the treatment of each other's minorities. Traditionally, members of the Greek community in Istanbul and of the Turkish community in Western Thrace have suffered the most from the foul relations between the two countries. In the past, both governments implemented policies that denied the ethnic identities of these communities and instituted policies of harassment to force them to immigrate or become assimilated. Over the last few years, there has been a marked improvement in both countries' treatment of their respective minorities. Greece has also ceased vetoing decisions favorable to Turkey at the EU purely to discomfort Turkey, another indication of warming relations. Nevertheless, the long list of bilateral conflicts, including the question of Cyprus and the airspace issues over the Aegean, remains unresolved. Nationalists and hardliners on both sides regularly point to this fact and question whether the "dialogue" between the two countries is progressing. Typically, both sides suspect each other of taking advantage of the dialogue in order to enhance their own national interests at the expense of the other side. They continue to see relations between the two countries from a zero-sum game perspective.

For their part, advocates of the "dialogue" have propounded the virtues of low politics cooperation, as well as the expansion of inter-societal relations. They have claimed that dialogue is of paramount importance for at least three reasons. First, dialogue creates constituencies in both governments, as well as in the respective civil societies, with an interest in cooperation. Second, the dialogue helps to build mutual trust and good will, the two ingredients so critical for resolving the deeply entrenched conflict. Some even go so far as to argue that, once the dialogue progresses to a point where a sufficient level of mutual trust is obtained, many of the bilateral conflicts will actually become irrelevant. Third, dialogue also enables parties to discover that cooperation can be beneficial to both sides. These three points are critical in terms of mobilizing public support to favor the "dialogue" between the two countries, which is increasingly exposed to pressures from their respective mass publics.

In open societies, it is difficult, if not impossible, to envision a government that does not pay attention to public opinion concerning various policies. Decisions that are not supported by the public run the risk of undermining the legitimacy of the policies of a popularly elected government. Increasingly, this has become true for foreign policy as well. Hence, as decisionmakers embark upon a new policy of cooperation—or confrontation, for that matter—with another country, they must seek public support for their actions. As Robert Putnam has pointed out in his seminal work, diplomacy can be envisaged as two sets of games being pursued simultaneously.[3] Level I consists of negotiations between diplomats or between decisionmakers; Level II consists of negotiations between these decisionmakers and their respective national constituencies. In other words, these decisionmakers have to be able to "sell" the decision taken at Level I to the actors in Level II, or, in other words, to the public in the largest sense of the word.

Three more elements need to be added to these two-level games to make them more reflective of real world interactions. The first is the way decisionmakers in one country interact with the public of the other country. The second involves the interaction that takes place between the civil societies of the two countries. The third element concerns the way critical third party players relate or interact with the two main parties, for example, how the EU, the North Atlantic Treaty Organization (NATO) or the United States relate or interact with Greek and Turkish actors. These interactions can, of course, support, as well as discourage, cooperation. They are also expected to have a critical bearing upon the national decisionmakers' ability to "sell" a decision or a decision in the making. This, in turn, will determine whether the public will favor cooperation or confrontation.

Hence, as diplomatic negotiations between two countries progress, they are surrounded by this complex set of games—each with its own dynamic and each with its own particular impact on the diplomatic negotiations at Level I. It is the end product of this interaction that will be critical as to whether the decisionmakers of the two countries will be able to adopt a policy of cooperation or conflict. It will always be a difficult exercise to determine in which direction the influence flows. Is it the decisionmakers that will shape the public's view, or will it be the preferences of the public shaping the politicians'—and ultimately the diplomats'—reactions to one another at the Level I game table? The question is further complicated by the fact that public opinion is rarely homogenous. It is composed of different "pockets," sections or constituencies. Hence, all participants will have their own idiosyncratic reactions to each level of the game and their respective players.

Disentangling this complexity is inevitably an immense intellectual endeavor. However, the first important task is to obtain a picture of the public opinion in one particular country and to identify its dominant characteristics. Surprisingly, there has been practically no systematic study of the role of public opinion in Greek-Turkish relations and no comparative study of the composition and determinants of public opinion in both countries. However, given the heterogeneous nature of public opinion, determining its composition is critical for advancing policy positions—whether they entail cooperation or the escalation of hostilities or tensions.

In the ensuing sections we aim to examine Turkish public opinion towards foreign policy in general and Greek-Turkish relations in particular. Keeping the above outlined understanding of the dynamics of interaction between foreign policymakers and the domestic constituencies that constrain them in this endeavor, we aim to map the general attitudinal bases of foreign policy preferences among the Turkish electorate. First, we attempt to determine if there are countries or country groups that are perceived to be friendlier than others in the minds of the Turkish public. Which country or countries are perceived to be the best friend of Turkey in the international arena? Which country is perceived as the worst enemy? Among these countries, where does Greece stand? How do people perceive the threats to Turkey's security over the next couple of years? Where do the people perceive these threats to originate from? Given the longstanding conflicts over the Aegean and Cyprus, does the Turkish public perceive Greece as a military threat?

More specifically, we first provide a short descriptive account of the main issues on the agenda of Greek-Turkish relations from the perspective of the Turkish voters. How is the historical heritage perceived and how is it related to present-day issues? What are the main issues of conflict between the two nations? How should solutions be attempted? Is the current rapprochement perceived as successful and mutually beneficial? Do people approve of the way their government is handling Greek-Turkish relations? How do people view the conflict in Cyprus? What do they perceive as a viable path to its resolution?

TURKISH PUBLIC OPINION AND FOREIGN POLICY IN THE CONTEXT OF GREEK-TURKISH RELATIONS

Perceptions of Foreign Nationalities and Ethnicities

Perhaps the broadest impact of public opinion on foreign policy comes from attitudinal proclivities towards other nationalities and ethnicities. These are almost never discussed at the negotiation tables or even put on the agenda of the Level I diplomats nor even the representatives of the Level II constituencies. However, when the public evaluates a policy concerning a given state or ethnicity, some states or ethnicities are considerably disadvantaged compared to others in terms of negative perceptions. These negative perceptions of other nationalities and ethnicities reflect historical experiences, long-running conflicts and the impact resulting from negative socialization in formal as well as informal networks. Looking at these perceptions of friendship towards nations' or ethnicities' representatives, one is struck by the consistent regularities of negative as well as positive predispositions among the public.

Enduring rivalries, such as the one between Greece and Turkey or the longstanding animosity between the Armenians and Turks, lead one to expect the public to regard the representatives of these nations negatively when compared to others. If one accepts these null hypotheses, then continuing conflict in bilateral relations can be seen as a reflection of the public's preferences as well as other longstanding strategic issues between them. In order to achieve a simple comparative assessment of friendliness towards other nationalities and ethnicities among Turkish public opinion, a list of such nationalities and ethnicities was given to the respondents in our sample. These included long-time allies such as the Americans and the Europeans as well as traditional adversaries like the Greeks, Russians and Armenians.[4] Muslims of Sunni faith, such as Saudi Arabians and Palestinians, and the predominantly Shiite Iranians and Azeris were also included in the list. Kurds were included to evaluate the impact of a decade of bloody internal strife. Israelis were included to evaluate the possible impact of the Jewish-Muslim conflict in the Middle East. The Japanese were included in the list as representative of a nation that has relations with Turkey almost exclusively through commerce, the public images several famous Japanese products and, more recently, through tourism.[5]

Figure 1 clearly shows that among the Turkish public, not all nations are being perceived similarly. However, one pattern is very clear: when talking about a foreign country, nationality or ethnicity, the Turkish public is generally negatively predisposed towards them. On average all nationalities and ethnicities are ranked quite low on a friendship scale from 1 (totally unfriendly) to 10 (totally friendly). A typical Turk does not see an unknown representative of a nation or ethnicity as being friendly.

Nevertheless, not all nationalities or ethnicities are rated as equally unfriendly. The highest average friendliness score is given to the Azeris, followed by the Japanese. All others receive a score reflecting a generally unfriendly evaluation by usually remaining below 5 out of 10. Saudi Arabians and the Palestinians, as representatives of Sunni Islam, come next, followed by the Americans as the country with the highest average friendliness evaluation for a non-Muslim nationality.[6] Despite long-lasting ethnic terrorism in Turkey conducted by the Kurdistan Workers' Party (*Partiya Karkeren Kurdistan*—PKK), compared to long-time allies like

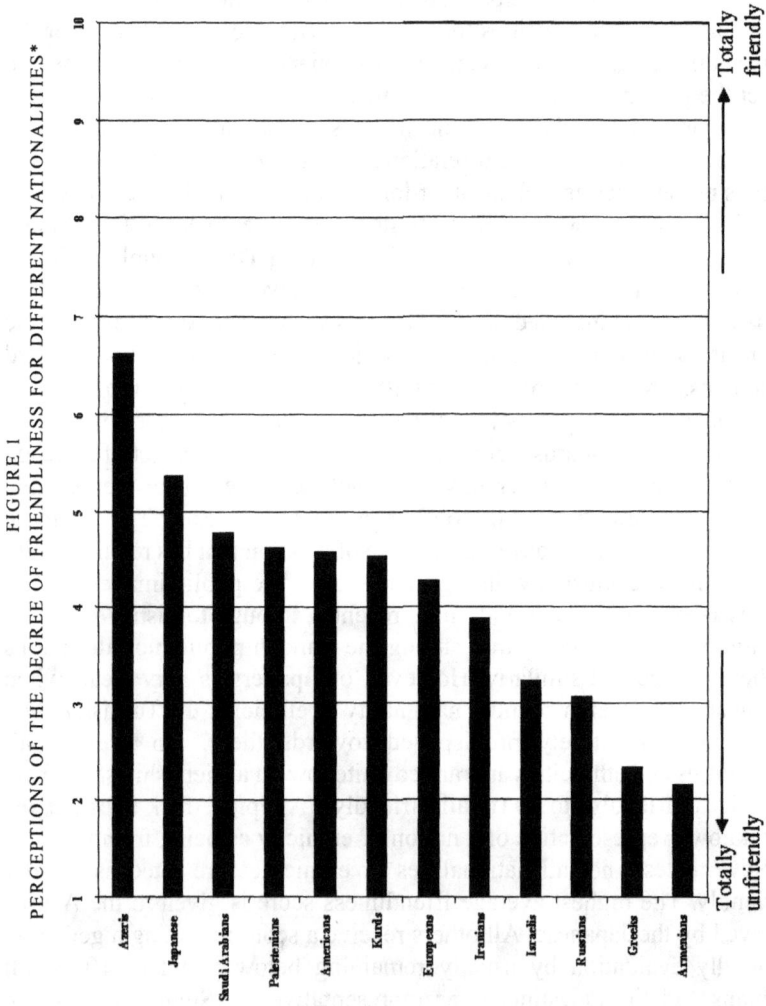

FIGURE 1
PERCEPTIONS OF THE DEGREE OF FRIENDLINESS FOR DIFFERENT NATIONALITIES*

Note: Mean values of the friendliness evaluations on a scale of 1 to 10.

the United States and Europe, Kurds are not viewed so negatively. However, Kurds received an average of 4 out of 10 and thus remain closer to the totally unfriendly side.[7] While predominantly Shiite Iranians come close to 4 on average, Jewish representatives from Israel, Orthodox Christian Russians, Greeks and the Armenians are lower on the scale.

Not surprisingly, these evaluations correlate quite highly across different nationalities and ethnicities. In other words, if an individual evaluated Americans negatively, then the likelihood that the same individual will negatively evaluate Europeans is higher. As more nationalities and ethnicities are evaluated, and the answers tend to have high instances of inter-correlation, there arises a possibility to simplify the underlying relationships. Therefore, a latent (unobserved) variable approach might be fruitful in characterizing the relationships among the variables. Taking the observed relationships as the starting point, the complex set of interrelations between large numbers of variables is used to derive a smaller number of unobserved variables. These latent variables help characterize the interrelationships among the observed variables. At this point, factor analysis can be used to derive artificial dimensions, or factors, through a complex algebraic method. These derived factors not only correlate well with a subset of the real variables included in the analysis but they can also be chosen to be independent of one another (or simply orthogonal), which helps in the complex statistical tests at the later stages of the analysis.[8]

Relatively high correlations appear between the respondents' evaluations of Americans and Russians, Russians and Armenians, Armenians and Greeks, Iranians and Saudi Arabians, Palestinians and Azeris, Palestinians and Saudi Arabians, and Greeks and Israelis. On the basis of these correlations, three latent dimensions are derived. The factor analysis results in Table 1 show that according to the first dimension, the evaluations of Armenians, Russians, Greeks, Israelis and Europeans load highly, while the rest of the group either loads low or, as in the case of Palestinian and Azeris, load negatively. In other words, the evaluations of Armenians, Russians, Greeks, Israelis and Europeans correlate highly with the latent variable derived from the factor analysis. Since high positive correlation means that as positive evaluations of these nationalities increase so does the value of the latent variable, we interpret the latent variable as reflecting the friendly evaluations of the "traditional foes." This dimension is thus called "traditional foes and rivals and non-Muslims." Indeed, no predominantly Muslim nationality appears to load highly in this dimension; rather, these help interpret the latent second dimension.

TABLE 1
DIMENSIONS OF PERCEIVED DEGREE OF FRIENDLINESS
(FACTOR ANALYSIS RESULTS)

	Traditional Foes	**Muslims**	**Distant Friends**	**Communalities**
Armenians	**0.78**	0.21	-0.17	0.49
Russians	**0.75**	0.03	0.23	0.61
Greeks	**0.74**	0.12	0.05	0.52
Israelis	**0.55**	0.06	0.41	0.45
Europeans	**0.47**	0.12	0.42	0.38
Iranians	0.17	**0.80**	0.05	0.50
S. Arabians	0.06	**0.75**	0.17	0.53
Palestinians	-0.05	**0.62**	0.39	0.54
Kurds	0.19	**0.55**	-0.01	0.22
Japanese	0.17	0.24	**0.69**	0.40
Azeris	-0.20	0.38	**0.67**	0.47
Americans	0.38	-0.16	**0.64**	0.32
% of variance				***Total***
explained	**29.80**	**15.40**	**10.20**	**55.40**

Notes: Extraction Method: Principal Component Analysis; Rotation Method: Varimax with Kaiser Normalization; Rotation converged in 12 iterations.

In the second dimension, Iranians, Saudi Arabians, Palestinians and Kurds appear to load highly, while others remain low. Since one commonality that brings these nations together is the predominance of Islam, we call this dimension "Muslim countries." The third dimension is harder to interpret since we observed three quite different nationalities grouped together. Japanese load highest on this dimension followed by Azeris and then Americans. One commonality between these groups seems to be that they constitute those nationalities that are not typically well known or closely observed by the general Turkish population. While Azeris, for instance, are neighbors, they are predominantly of Shiite origin and not too many live in Turkey. During the inter-war years, as well as the cold war years, there was little contact between Turkey and the Azeris in Azerbaijan. Furthermore, unlike the Balkans, Azeris did not immigrate to Turkey. It is only with the end of the cold war that contacts between the two countries have increased. Similarly, Turks are mostly acquainted with the Japanese and the Americans via television or commerce. During the cold war, only a very small percentage of Turks would have been exposed to American and Japanese tourists or American servicemen and their families in Turkey. This is in contrast to the much greater degree of exposure to Europeans, mostly Germans, through tourism, but—more importantly—through Turkish immigration to Europe, particularly to Germany. Accordingly, this dimension is called the "distant friends dimension." It should be noted that these three dimensions capture about

55 percent of the variation in the 12 evaluations, and the commonality of our variables with the three derived dimensions is quite high.[9]

Best Friend vs. Worst Enemy in the International Arena

Prior to obtaining the evaluations of different nationalities and ethnicities discussed above, an open-ended question was asked at the very beginning of the questionnaire to determine which countries the respondents saw as Turkey's best friend and worst enemy. Since the question format was open-ended, the respondents were not given any country names nor were they guided into thinking about the objectives of the researchers by being provided with a specific list of countries. Thus, the objective was to obtain which country first came to the minds of the respondents. The findings are quite interesting, especially if one evaluates them together with the closed-ended evaluations discussed earlier.

In exactly one-third of the responses, the respondents indicated that there was "no best friend of Turkey" in the international arena, implying that Turkey is either alone or simply "a lone wolf" (see Figure 2a). Since most of the respondents named a variety of countries in their other responses, the answer "no country" cannot be attributed to an inability to find a country to name as "best friend." It seems that these answers reflect a conscious choice that expresses a feeling of isolation and loneliness perceived by the electorate in the context of the international arena.

FIGURE 2a
WHICH COUNTRY IS TURKEY'S BEST FRIEND
IN THE INTERNATIONAL ARENA?*

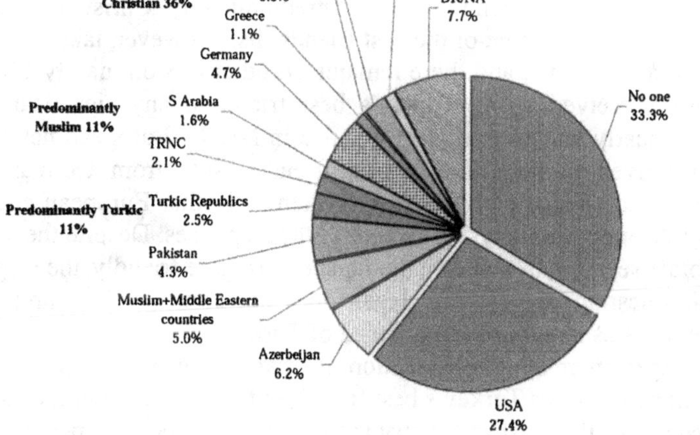

Note: *Open-ended question format.

FIGURE 2b
WHICH COUNTRY IS TURKEY'S WORST FRIEND
IN THE INTERNATIONAL ARENA?*

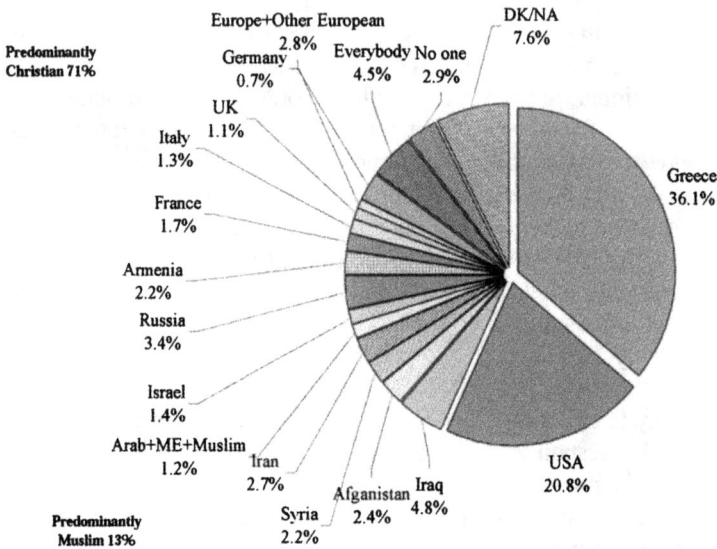

Note: * Open-ended question format.

Perhaps not surprisingly, the United States, after nearly half a century of intense cooperation between the two countries, was perceived to be Turkey's best friend by about 27 percent of the respondents. Interestingly, if one includes the United States, predominantly Christian countries occupy about 36 percent of the best friends' list. However, take the United States out of the list, and there remains no other predominantly Christian country perceived to be Turkey's best friend in any significant way. Despite nearly half a century of alliance in NATO, European nations are not perceived to be Turkey's best friend. Aside from Germany (4.7 percent) and Greece (1.1 percent), Balkan and other European countries constitute approximately 2.8 percent of the responses. Despite the Turkish electorate seeming to perceive the Japanese as quite friendly, the responses to this question suggest that Japan does not come to the mind of the respondents as an ally or close friend of Turkey.

Another interesting observation is that not many people mention Muslim countries as Turkey's best friends in the international arena either. A predominantly Muslim country is found in only about 11 percent of the responses. Turkic countries such as Azerbaijan, the Turkish Republic of

Northern Cyprus (TRNC) and the Turkic Republics of Central Asia form about 11 percent of the answers. Since these Turkish-speaking countries are also predominantly Muslim, it is fair to suggest that while the Christian country group—including the United States—comprises about 36 percent, the Muslim countries group draws about 22 percent support overall.

The same open-ended type of question was also asked concerning perceptions of the electorate as to Turkey's worst enemy. The results are again quite revealing for our purposes (see Figure 2b). Greece tops the list by a large margin (36.1 percent). The United States is also regarded as the worst enemy by a large group of respondents (obviously separate from the group who regarded the United States as Turkey's best friend in the earlier question).

It is noteworthy that only a small marginal group of respondents named a predominantly Muslim country as the worst enemy, while about 71 percent picked a predominantly Christian country. In short, the Turkish electorate seems to perceive a Christian country as Turkey's worst enemy. Moreover, despite long-lasting alliances and cooperation within the EU, about 7.6 percent of the respondents picked a European country as the worst enemy of Turkey.

Another interesting result is that if Armenia is not mentioned in the question, it does not seem to occur to the respondents as a possible worst enemy. This is in stark contrast to the low friendliness scores that Armenians received in the earlier close-ended question. Such a finding suggests that only when Turks are provided with a reminder on judging the friendliness of the state or ethnicity in question do they immediately respond with their negative predispositions—ones supported by the official lines.

Afghanistan and Iraq also make the enemies list. This finding is partially due to the fact that the survey was being conducted in the field just about when the decision to send Turkish troops to Afghanistan was taken. At the time of the survey, there was a great deal of uncertainty as to how the situation in Afghanistan would develop, how many soldiers would stay there and for how long. We suspect that all of these factors encouraged the respondents to fear that a military threat could easily come from some source in Afghanistan. Iraq, on the other hand, was not as prominently on the world agenda during the time the survey was being implemented in the field as it became later on during the fall of 2002 and the winter of 2003, but apparently it was a matter of great concern among its neighboring countries (after Greece). It is noteworthy that without scratching the surface of neighborly relations and increasing cooperation in the aftermath of the earthquakes of 1999, our respondents' first and predominant choice for the worst enemy of Turkey appears to be Greece.

Threat Perceptions: Where Greece Stands

Now that some general predispositions for or against different countries and their residents have been discovered from the list of countries, it is appropriate to identify the "threats to the national security of Turkey over the next five years" as perceived by the public. For this purpose, a simple scale evaluation, ranging from 1 ("not a threat at all") to 10 ("could be a big threat"), was used for ten different types and sources of threats to the national security of Turkey. When simple mean evaluations are taken, it becomes obvious that there are distinct sources perceived as a threat to Turkey's national security over the next few years. The highest average grade on the ten-point scale appears to be the "corruption problem in Turkey with political connections," followed by "radical religious terror," "ethnic based terror" in the country and domestic "political uncertainty and chaos" (see Figure 3). It seems that threats to Turkey's security are mostly perceived as originating from within, rather than from outside, the country. It is not clear how these threats could materialize. Nevertheless, these threats are clear reminders of the reasons for the security rhetoric adopted during the infamous February 28 process.[10] Therefore, they could be interpreted as a reflection of the official line of argument as perceived and understood by the public.

Regional threats are rated the lowest likely developments. Weapons of mass destruction (WMD) in neighboring countries and international terrorism are rated between the regional threats and threats from within. Table 2 illustrates the results of the two-dimensional factor analysis based on replies to these questions. The first dimension clearly captures the threats originating from outside of the country while the second dimension captures the domestic threats. From a factor-analysis perspective, the Turkish electorate also perceives security threats to originate either externally or internally. Domestic threats are rated relatively higher than external threats. Regional uncertainty and chaos in the Middle East, the Caucuses and the eastern Mediterranean (stemming from the Cyprus issue) dominate this first dimension. The two derived factors capture about 61 percent of the variation in the ten variables included in the analysis.

The obvious next question in this context is whether or not respondents are worried about Turkey being attacked over the next five years. Figure 4a demonstrates that while about 47 percent of the respondents are not worried about Turkey being attacked militarily *per se*, about 51 percent are worried to some degree. Obviously, answers to this question are very much context dependent. For instance, by the winter of 2003 when Turkish involvement in military action against Iraq was put on the parliamentary agenda, these sorts of worries are more likely to have increased. Those respondents who were somewhat worried about Turkey being attacked

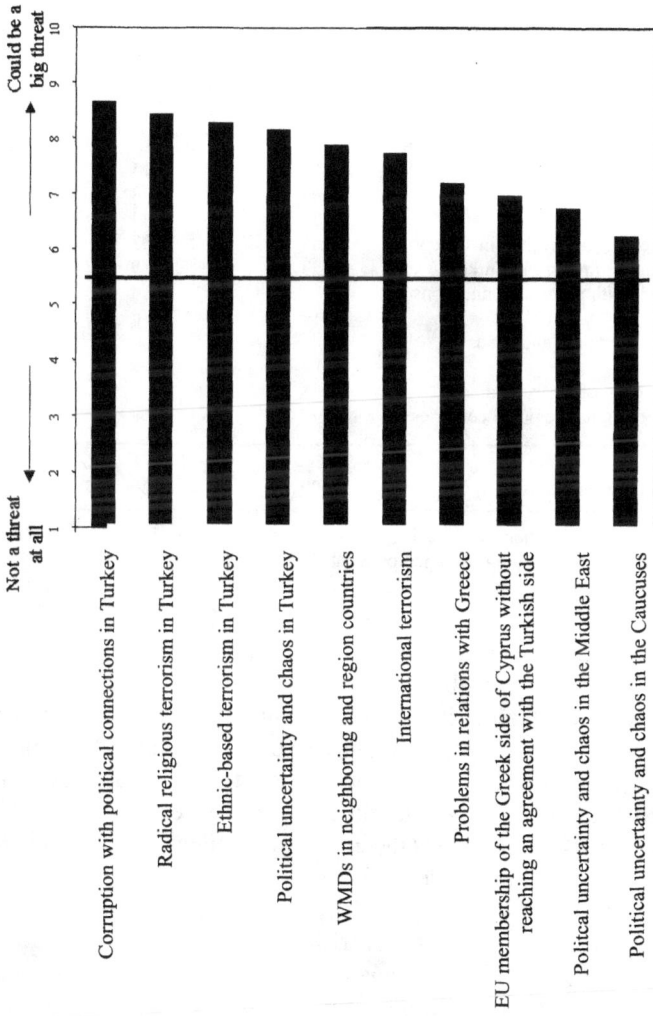

FIGURE 3

FACTORS THAT COULD CAUSE A THREAT TO TURKEY'S SECURITY DURING THE NEXT FIVE YEARS*

Not a threat at all

Could be a big threat

Corruption with political connections in Turkey

Radical religious terrorism in Turkey

Ethnic-based terrorism in Turkey

Political uncertainty and chaos in Turkey

WMDs in neighboring and region countries

International terrorism

Problems in relations with Greece

EU membership of the Greek side of Cyprus without reaching an agreement with the Turkish side

Political uncertainty and chaos in the Middle East

Political uncertainty and chaos in the Caucuses

Note: * Mean values of the friendliness evaluations on a scale of 1 to 10.

TABLE 2
TWO-DIMENSIONAL REPRESENTATION OF THREAT PERCEPTIONS TO TURKEY
OVER THE NEXT FIVE YEARS (FACTOR ANALYSIS RESULTS)

	Threats from the outside world (Dimension 1)	Internal threats (Dimension 2)	Communalities
Political uncertainty and chaos in the Middle East	**0.84**	0.19	0.75
Political uncertainty and chaos in the Caucuses	**0.83**	0.17	0.71
EU membership of the Greek side of Cyprus without reaching an agreement with the Turkish side	**0.76**	0.15	0.60
Problems in relations with Greece	**0.67**	0.28	0.54
International terrorism	**0.55**	0.44	0.50
Radical religious terrorism in Turkey	0.09	**0.83**	0.70
Ethnic-based terrorism in Turkey	0.23	**0.80**	0.70
Corruption with political connections in Turkey	0.19	**0.70**	0.53
Political uncertainty and chaos in Turkey	0.34	**0.69**	0.60
Weapons of mass destruction in neighboring and regional countries	0.49	**0.50**	0.50
			Total
% of variance explained	**47.90**	**13.20**	**61.10**

Notes: Extraction Method: Principal Component Analysis; Rotation Method: Varimax with Kaiser Normalization; Rotation converged in three iterations.

militarily were asked a follow-up question asking who is most likely to attack Turkey. Figure 4b shows the distribution of the answers to this second question. Greece is seen as a potential attacker by 29 percent of the 51 percent who were worried about Turkey being attacked. In other words, about 15 percent of the entire sample seem to think that Turkey might be attacked and that that attack might come from Greece.

Following Greece, Iraq is the country perceived as most likely to attack with 16 percent of respondents fearing an attack. The fear of attack list is rounded out by Afghanistan at 15 percent and the United States at 12 percent. Although somewhat surprising that Afghanistan appears on this list, one should bear in mind again that at the time the survey was being conducted Turkish troops were getting ready to be sent to Afghanistan for peacekeeping operations. Therefore, it is not surprising that people were worried that Turkish troops might be attacked in Afghanistan. While it may be argued that the potential attackers in Afghanistan were not—in all likelihood—going to be Afghani forces, this information was too

FIGURE 4a
HOW WORRIED ARE YOU THAT TURKEY COULD BE ATTACKED OVER THE
NEXT FEW YEARS?

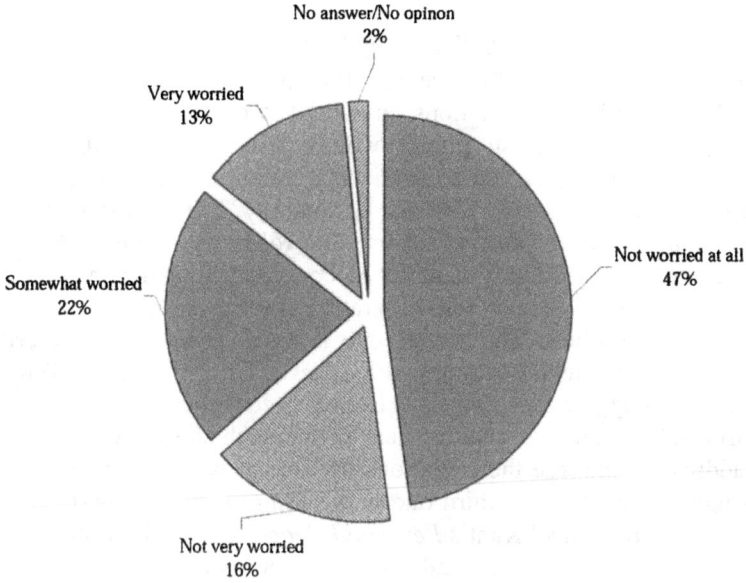

No answer/No opinon
2%

Very worried
13%

Not worried at all
47%

Somewhat worried
22%

Not very worried
16%

FIGURE 4b
IF THERE WERE TO BE A MILITARY ATTACK, WHICH COUNTRY DO YOU THINK
IT IS MOST LIKELY TO COME FROM?

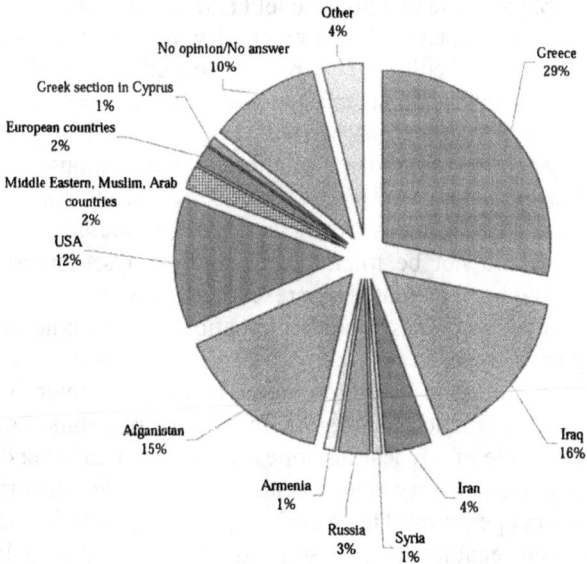

Other
4%

No opinion/No answer
10%

Greek section in Cyprus
1%

European countries
2%

Middle Eastern, Muslim, Arab
countries
2%

USA
12%

Greece
29%

Afganiotan
15%

Iraq
16%

Armenia
1%

Iran
4%

Russia
3%

Syria
1%

complicated to be digested by the respondents. The presence of the United States on this list of potential attackers reflects a deep-rooted suspicion among some circles in Turkey regarding this country.[11]

Diagnosing the Broad Policy Guidelines of Foreign Policy Preferences

Before we delve into the specific foreign policy issues concerning Greek-Turkish bilateral relations, an overall assessment of foreign policy options by the Turkish public would provide a useful point of comparison. It is possible to argue that relations between states are shaped by three distinct "cultures of anarchy."[12] The first one is the *Hobbesian* culture (derived from the ideas in Thomas Hobbes' *Leviathan*, 1651) characterized by deep mistrust of the international system and the reliance on self-help rather than any cooperative schemes for solving conflicts. The second one is the *Lockean* culture (derived from the ideas in John Locke's *Two Treaties of Government*, 1690) where states do recognize each other's existence even if they may have serious conflicts. The Lockean analogy here is that such states are also willing to address or manage their relations by way of negotiating "contracts" through diplomacy. The third one is the *Kantian* culture (derived from the ideas in Immanuel Kant's *Perpetual Peace*, 1795) where states share a body of common values and norms—often associated with pluralist democracies—and enjoy friendly societal relations. The relationship between such states is characterized by cooperation and a general sense of security and stability.

It is possible to argue that both Level I and Level II players of Putnam's two-level games interact with the external world after having filtered it through one of these "cultures." A player steeped in a Hobbesian culture will visualize the international arena as one where one can trust no one but oneself. The international arena will be seen as being anarchic or dominated by conflict. This vision of international relations would, in turn, be supported by a domestic political structure that emphasizes national unity, national security and national sacrifice. Questioning and criticizing these tenets would not be tolerated. In many ways, domestic political structures would be perpetuated by presenting a view of an anarchic world. In other words, the domestic and international environments would be reinforcing each other.

A Lockean culture is likely to emerge in an environment where some dissent and argumentation is possible. In other words, some Level I and II players are capable of advocating policy options to achieve ends desirable to more than one country and are able to mobilize support for some international cooperation. The world is still seen to be anarchic, but a Lockean culture enables at least some decisionmakers to believe in the possibility of achieving some cooperation to manage this anarchy for national benefit. This may be supported by a partly democratic political structure or at least by a political structure that offers some competition between views. However, these views would be competing against Hobbesian ones, hence the advocates of a Lockean world would have a vested interest in achieving some level of controlled cooperation at the international level to be able to defend themselves against Hobbesian arguments and policy options.

A Kantian culture is clearly associated with a world of "democratic peace." In a country whose decisionmaking culture is dominated by a Kantian one, there may well be advocates of policies that are derived from Hobbesian and Lockean considerations. However, such Level I and II policy advocates would not be in a situation to undermine the dominant culture and the domestic political structures associated with it. The domestic system would always be capable of questioning the wisdom of such policies and, while it might fail to prevent their adoption on one or two occasions, the other states in a Kantian system of cooperation would tolerate it. The level of security and trust in the system would be capable of resisting such occasional challenges. Furthermore, the very nature of a Kantian system would be one where states would be linked with each other through extensive inter-societal contacts and cooperation. These interactions and the level of interdependence between Kantian states would constitute another set of safety mechanisms against the intrusions of Hobbesian thinking.

Policy Guidelines

In order to evaluate the broadest foreign policy preferences of the Turkish electorate we asked a series of questions using the same set of options while addressing different contexts of conflict. At the most general level of analysis—independent of an historical context—our question was worded in the following way: "In your opinion, what is the most effective way of creating trust between two societies that have had problematic relationships with one another?" The options given were as follows:

1. Diplomatic negotiations between two governments;
2. Lifting of existing military threats;
3. Development of economic relations;
4. Development of social and cultural relations between civil society organizations;
5. Development of relations through membership in international organizations like the EU; and
6. Other (to be specified by the respondent).

When no country-specific historical context was specified in the question, the answers strongly favored the diplomatic negotiations option (about 49 percent of the respondents). The second most supported option in this case was the development of economic relations (17.5 percent). Development of social and cultural ties through civil society organizations appears to be the third most supported option with about 15 percent. The last two were the lifting of the existing military threats (8.8 percent) and membership in an international organization like the EU (6.4 percent). It is striking that the Turkish public does not recognize the EU as a peace-promoting institutional framework.[13] Hence, the results suggest that the Turkish public is more inclined to support a Lockean "peace" (51 percent), where emphasis is on intergovernmental deals, while a significant group (29 percent) attributes importance to transnational or inter-societal relations via civil society and trade. It should be underlined, however, that little support is given to policies that would typically be associated with a Hobbesian world, such as the use of force or the threat of the use of force.

The overall picture of preferences remains more or less unchanged when the respondents are asked the same question concerning conflicts between Greek and Turkish, as well as Armenian and Turkish, societies. Respondents were slightly more supportive of diplomatic negotiations in the conflict between Armenian and Turkish societies. However, the relative standings of the rest of the options remain almost stable compared to the more general case—where no specific reminder of the conflicts between two societies is included in the question. As such, it seems that Level I diplomatic negotiations between the two sides in a conflict is seen by almost half of the respondents as the most acceptable way to create trust between two societies in conflict. However, nearly 30 percent of the responses also underline that development of Level II relations, either in economic or in cultural terms between the civil societies, is also important in creating trust between societies in conflict. A perhaps more realist approach is reflected in the responses by nearly ten percent of the respondents stressing the necessity of the revocation of military threats on one another. The impact of a third-party influence, such as the EU, is last in the minds of the Turkish public in resolving longstanding conflicts and creating trust between two societies.

The same question-formulation strategy was followed in the next set of questions, which address the preferences for a tough and non-conciliatory tone as opposed to a flexible and conciliatory one. First, a general statement of Turkey's policy options towards another unnamed country is given. At a later stage in the questionnaire, the same policy options are offered in the context of Greek-Turkish relations. The question format adopted here offered two extreme foreign policy stands. The respondent was then asked to evaluate which end s/he feels closer to by picking a point on the 1-to-10 scale where 1 represented one extreme (totally non-conciliatory and tough policy) and 10 the opposing extreme (totally conciliatory and flexible policy).

The first question in this set of questions concerned Turkey's policy towards other countries: "In your opinion, should Turkey follow a totally non-conciliatory and tough policy or totally conciliatory and flexible policy towards other countries?"[14] About 69 percent of the respondents placed themselves at points closer to the conciliatory and flexible policy end of the spectrum while roughly 31 percent took a stand closer to the inflexible policy end. When the same question was asked within the context of Greek-Turkish relations concerning a general policy stand towards Greece, about 34 percent chose a position closer to the tough and non-conciliatory end of the spectrum. The rest, a clear majority of about 66 percent, were closer to the cooperative, conciliatory end of the spectrum.

In order to determine the public's preferences for diplomatic negotiations on the one hand and the use of military power on the other (total dependence on either being the two extremes of the spectrum), the following question was asked: "In your opinion, what is the best way to guarantee peace?" Again, we observed very little difference between the general context and the Greek-Turkish conflict context. Similar to the finding above of a high rate of trust in diplomacy, we find about 63 percent closer to the diplomacy side than the military power side. When the question is asked in the context of Greek-Turkish relations, almost the same percentage of respondents favors the diplomacy side as opposed to the military power side.

In order to contrast preferences for diplomacy versus civil society initiatives (again, total dependence on either being the two extremes of the spectrum) and rapprochement, the following question was asked: "In your opinion, what is the best way to resolve conflicts between two countries in peaceful ways?" When diplomatic negotiations are presented in contrast to civil society relations, the preference in favor of either end disappears; while 49 percent place themselves closer to the diplomatic negotiation side, 51 percent are closer to the civil society relations side. In the case of Greek-Turkish relations, however, the diplomatic end once again dominates, with 55 percent placing themselves closer to that end.

In short, the general trend in preferences, regardless of context, is not in favor of a tough and inflexible stand on foreign policy. Similar to the finding above, the overall preference is in favor of diplomatic negotiations in this format of questioning. The only time diplomatic negotiations are not clearly preferred over the alternative is when civil society relations were offered in contrast to diplomacy. In that case, civil society relations and diplomatic negotiations were seen as of almost equal importance by the respondents. In this format of questioning, there also does not seem to be a very significant difference between preferences in the general context and those in the context of Greek-Turkish relations. The only exception to this pattern was when the two policy options were diplomacy and civil society relations in the context of Greek-Turkish relations. There, once again, diplomacy gains importance as opposed to the general case, where there was a 50:50 split in the answers.

PUBLIC PERCEPTIONS CONCERNING
GREEK-TURKISH RELATIONS

Having seen how the Turkish public perceives the representatives of the outside world and the threats they pose, as well as the overall policy preferences exhibited with or without a historical context, we now move into an analysis of the specificities of Greek-Turkish bilateral relations. Figure 5 presents the descriptive findings of the aspects of Greek-Turkish relations that directly touch individuals' lives. The results are mixed with encouraging as well as discouraging observations about the personal basis for cooperation between the two countries. For instance, there is not much support for the idea that Greeks who had left Turkey in the past might return to Turkey. The average agreement score on a 1 to 10 scale is barely above 5. When we aggregate those who are closer to being fully in agreement with the statement that the return of Greeks who, for one reason or another, had left Turkey has many drawbacks, and those who are closer to being in full disagreement, we get an almost equally split picture—47 percent disagree and 51 percent agree. Obviously, we do not specify what we mean by "returning." For instance, would they be living together as they used to in Istanbul up until the late 1950s or like they did up until 1922 primarily in the Aegean coastal towns? Would they return and claim whatever property they had left behind? None of these issues were specified to the respondents. However, "many drawbacks" presumably does hint to or indicate some, or all, of these concerns, and the statement does tend to be favored by a slight majority.

Responses to the other assertions reflect a declining degree of indecisiveness. For example, 52 percent disagree with the statement that Greek churches still in existence should be repaired. However, those who do not want a Greek to be their neighbor and who think that Turks and Greeks could never be friends rise to 43 percent and 41 percent respectively, showing clearer majorities who disagree with negative statements about Greeks. People also seem to feel comfortable going to

FIGURE 5
GREEK-TURKISH RELATIONS FROM A PERSONAL PERSPECTIVE

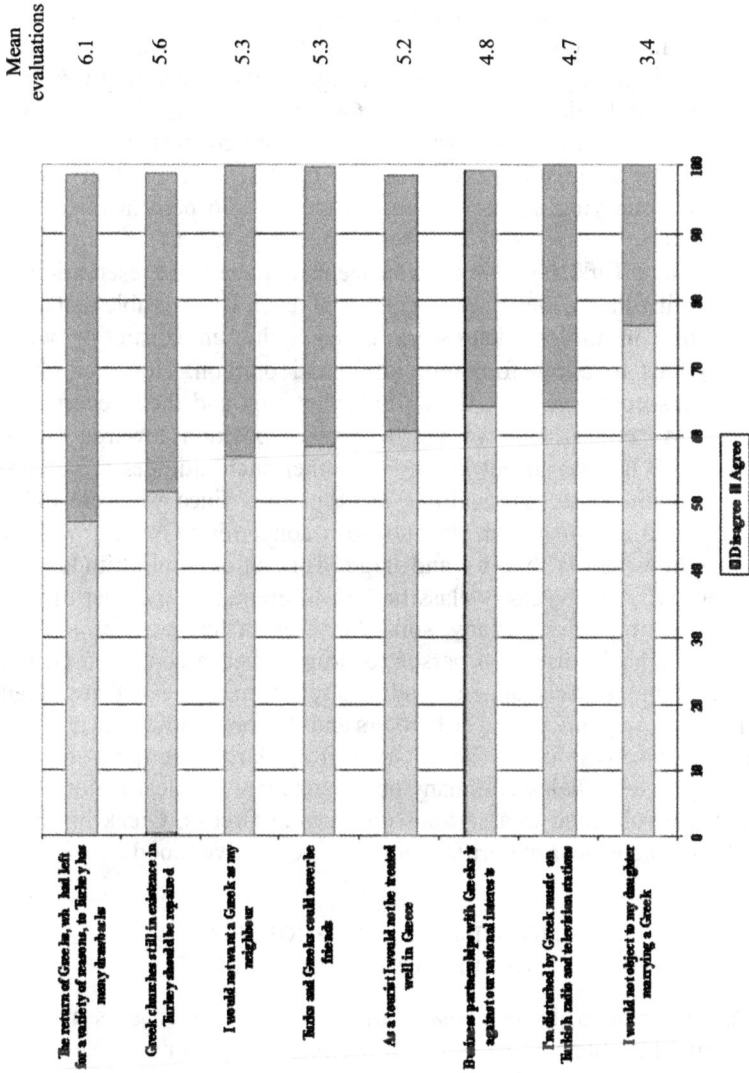

Greece as a tourist—60 percent indicate that they disagree with the statement that they would not be treated well in Greece. Only about 35 percent seem to justify lack of economic relations between Turks and Greeks on the grounds that such partnerships are against Turkish national interests (64 percent in disagreement). Considering that many radio stations in big cities and tavernas actually play Greek music, there is an unsurprisingly high rate of approval regarding broadcasting Greek music on radio and television stations—64 percent argue that they are not disturbed by these broadcasts. However, the highest rate of rejection comes, not surprisingly, in response to the assertion that someone's daughter marrying a Greek is not disturbing—76 percent reject such an assertion.

In short, Turkish public opinion seems to have some reservations about reconciling their differences at a personal level. It is possible that all of our questions in this module were either quite unrealistic or were too ambiguous to allow formation of a real opinion. However, these are questions commonly asked in similar settings and they nevertheless do reflect a certain sense of negative predisposition towards Greeks in general. What we do not know is whether such attitudes are commonly shared about other nationalities or ethnicities since we were only in a position to ask such in-depth questions concerning Greeks. What we do know, however, is that, by and large, Turkish cultural attitudes towards anyone who can be easily classified as different, as a member of a clearly identified minority of any sort—be it a different race, a drunk, a psychologically disturbed person, a drug addict, a convicted criminal, a homosexual, a Christian, etc.—attracts rejection. It seems that tolerance is in short supply among Turkish voters and that only those who are insularly like themselves attract acceptance from large segments of Turkish society.[15] Nevertheless, on many occasions there are clear majorities in the responses obtained to assertions concerning Greeks, Greek business and culture where clear majorities reflect a cooperative mood.

THE MOST IMPORTANT PROBLEMS FACING GREEK-TURKISH RELATIONS

We now turn to discuss what Turkish public opinion sees as the most important problem to be resolved between Greece and Turkey. Figure 6 shows that three problems emerge as the most important ones. By far the largest group thinks that the Cyprus problem is the most pressing issue in bilateral relations (53 percent pick this option); problems concerning the Aegean Sea (20 percent) and lack of trust between the two countries (15 percent) rank second and third. This ranking of the pressing issues in

FIGURE 6

WHAT IS THE MOST IMPORTANT PROBLEM IN GREEK-TURKISH RELATIONS?

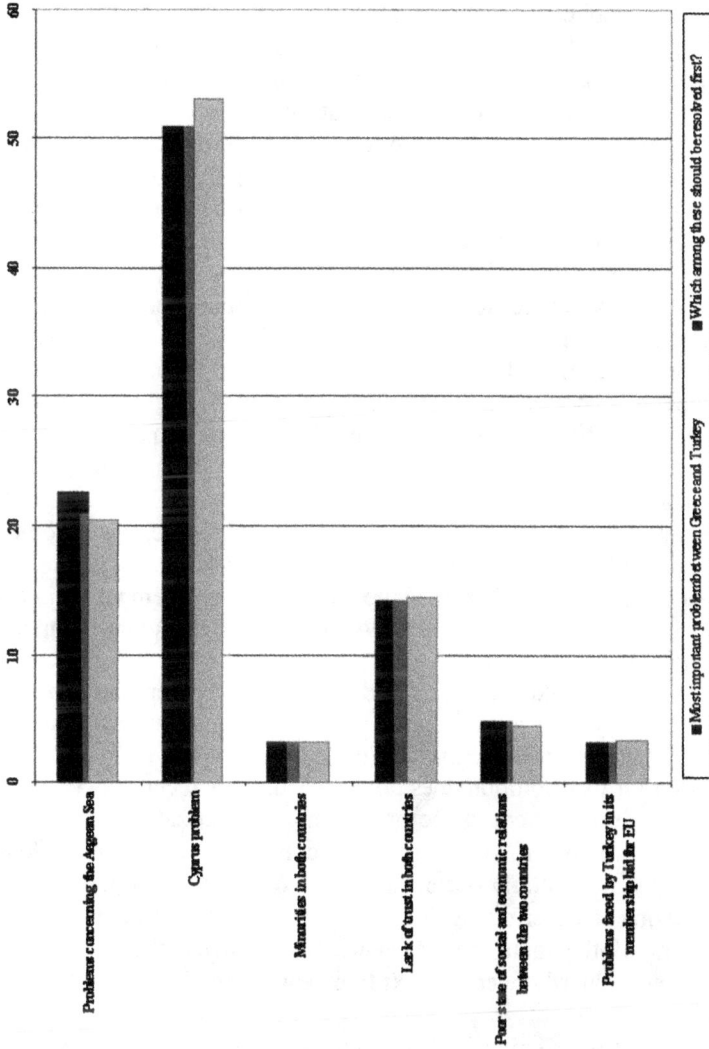

Greek-Turkish relations is quite understandable. Nevertheless, it is noticeable that minority issues and the problems Turkey faces in its membership bid for the EU do not seem to be important in the minds of the public. One reason might be that these issues did not feature prominently in the press at the time of the survey and were thus absent from the public mind. Moreover, perhaps, at least as far as public opinion is concerned, these are issues that have largely been resolved over the past couple of years. However, equally important for our purpose is the low relevance attributed to the poor state of social and economic relations between the two countries. In other words, improved Level II relations do not seem to be a big concern of the Turkish public. Again, one reason for this occurrence might be that after the earthquake diplomacy and the ensuing events, it is possible that such difficulties are no longer perceived as pressing in bilateral relations.

The same figure demonstrates that the public believes that the most important and pressing issue should be solved first. We also observe that the problem respondents view as most pressing among the Greek-Turkish issues is expected to be resolved via "diplomatic negotiations" (57 percent). "Lifting of military threats" also has some support (about 11 percent). However, support for Level II-type relations such as developing economic relations or developing socio-cultural ties between the two countries loses some strength for the most pressing problem case compared to the case of the most pressing problem in bilateral conflicts. This is hardly surprising since the most urgent problem might in the minds of the public involve serious diplomatic give and take that cannot wait for Level II rapprochement.

When we asked our respondents as to whether they think that the conflict they have chosen as the most urgent and important one could get out of hand and become militarized in the event that the method they have chosen for its resolution does not succeed, 37 percent answer in a positive way—indicating acceptance of potential militarization of the conflict in question. In other words, military confrontation between Greece and Turkey is not entirely out of the minds of the Turkish public. This is not surprising considering the fact that 29 percent of the 51 percent (about 14.8 percent of the total sample) who were worried that Turkey could be attacked militarily over the next five years chose Greece as the most likely attacker.

Equally interesting is that when the respondents were asked whether they think these problems could be resolved by a military confrontation, only a small minority (approximately 16 percent) answered affirmatively and about ten percent did not provide an answer. In other words, an overwhelming majority seems to be quite confident that militarizing this

FIGURE 7
SUPPORT FOR VARIOUS POLICY ISSUES

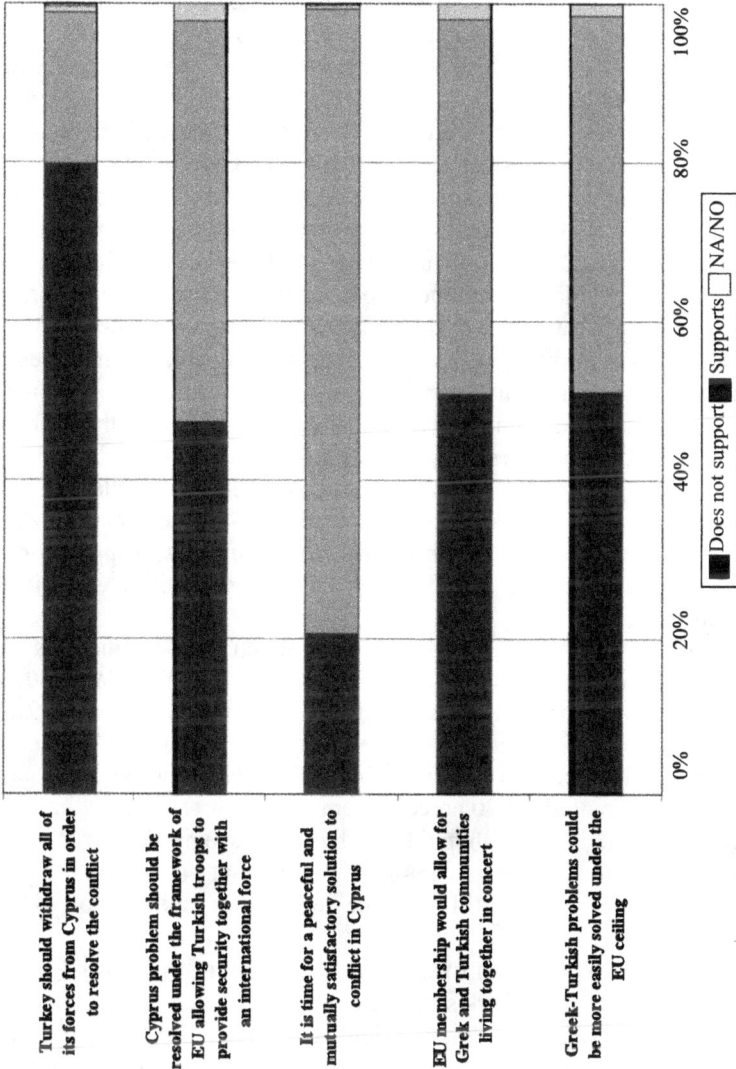

Turkey should withdraw all of its forces from Cyprus in order to resolve the conflict

Cyprus problem should be resolved under the framework of EU allowing Turkish troops to provide security together with an international force

It is time for a peaceful and mutually satisfactory solution to conflict in Cyprus

EU membership would allow for Grek and Turkish communities living together in concert

Greek-Turkish problems could be more easily solved under the EU ceiling

0%   20%   40%   60%   80%   100%

■ Does not support ■ Supports □ NA/NO

conflict is not going to resolve much, despite the fact that such a development is still a highly likely one. One further complicating factor in this set of questions is whom the respondents see as the most likely victor in a military confrontation. Given the patriotic feelings among the respondents, it is no surprise that roughly 67 percent indicated that Turkey would win in a confrontation with Greece. However, a sizable 29 percent indicated that both sides would incur losses in the event of a military confrontation.

We asked a number of questions about how some of the policy issues that exist in Greek-Turkish relations could be resolved with some aid from the EU. The sample is almost split evenly, one side supporting the view that under the EU umbrella, the problems could be more easily resolved (48 percent) and the other that disagrees with this assumption (51 percent) (Figure 7). Would EU membership be a catalyst to resolve the problems? We asked to what degree respondents would agree with the statement that EU membership would allow for Greek and Turkish communities to live together peacefully in Cyprus. A sizable 47 percent agreed, while 51 percent disagreed. Thus, the role of the EU in resolving the problems on the island does not seem to win a clear majority. Nevertheless, it is worth noting that nearly half of the respondents believe that the EU umbrella would bring peaceful coexistence to Cyprus. We believe that for a country gripped by a severe suspicion towards foreigners, such support for the EU as a catalyst for resolving conflicts in Cyprus is still a very significant result.[16]

Finally, we wanted to know how much support there is for the proposition of withdrawing all military forces from the island: 80 percent of the respondents did not support this assertion, while only 19 percent agreed. Therefore, one is led to conclude that the preferences at the aggregate level cannot be said to be cooperative. However, once again, a sizable group of about 20 percent seems to support an option that is almost never voiced in Turkish public debates. It seems that even when the official position is overwhelmingly dominant, a radical proposal to withdraw troops can still win the support of one out of every five respondents.

In order to obtain an overall evaluation we asked to what degree the respondents support Turkish policy towards Greece and Cyprus over the period of the year preceding the fieldwork, that is, from the fall of 2000 to 2001. The support for Turkish policy towards Greece (53 percent) is significantly lower than the one towards Cyprus (67 percent). However, we observe that a clear majority in both cases supports the government policy. In the Greek case, the margin in favor of the majority is slimmer and thus leaves room to examine the reasons for such hesitation.

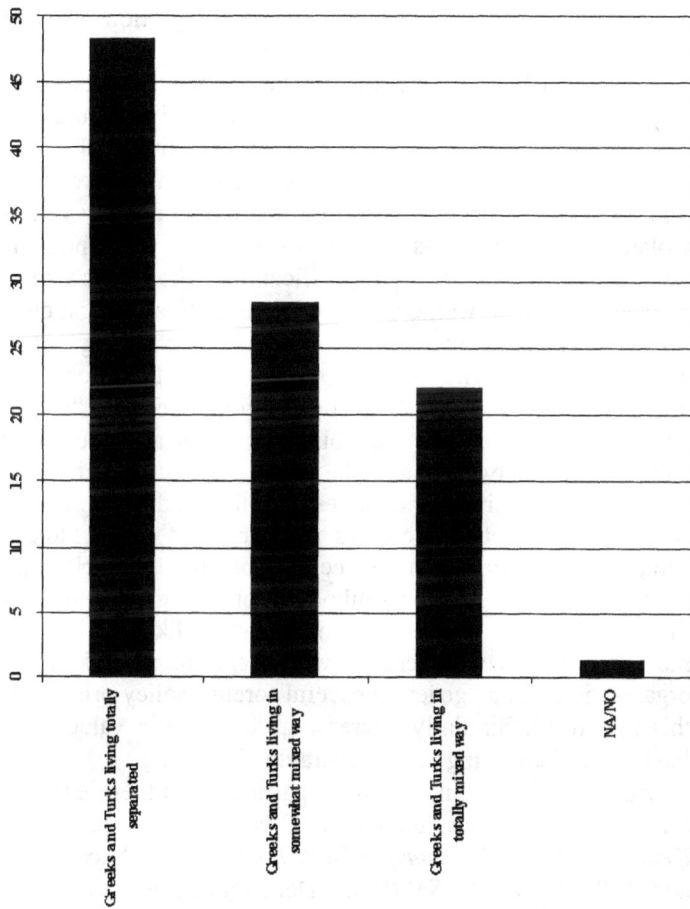

FIGURE 8

THE BEST WAY TO ENSURE GOOD RELATIONS BETWEEN THE TWO SIDES IN CYPRUS IS TO HAVE ...

In order to get a feeling for the preferred ultimate solution to the problem on Cyprus, we asked whether the respondents see the future of the island communities as living "totally mixed together again," "totally separated from one another, as they are today," or "a mixed solution" between the two extremes. Figure 8 indicates that approximately 48 percent see the two communities on the island living totally separated from one another in the future, while only 21.9 percent see a total mixture of both sides. About 28 percent support a solution in between, suggesting that a plurality supports some degree of integration between the two communities.

For a detailed picture of the determinants of these choices, we separated those who thought that the best way to insure good relations between the two sides in Cyprus was that they live totally separately with a dummy variable that takes the value of 1 for this choice and 0 otherwise. The dependent variable is specified as a binary dummy variable and thus violates the assumptions of the conventional regression methods. We accordingly use a binary logit specification.[17] The results are given in Table 3. Men, more than women, tend to choose "total separation" and, as the "years of schooling" increase, the likelihood of choosing "total separation" declines. Those who tend to "trust the international and Islamic organizations," tend to choose some option other than "total separation," while those who "trust the political parties and the parliament" are increasingly likely to make the "total separation" choice.[18] Similarly, increasing "perceived friendliness of the traditional foes and distant friends," as expected, decreases the likelihood of the "total separation" choice. In the same vein, as feelings of "patriotic self-importance and confidence" increase, the likelihood of choosing "total separation" of the Turkish and Greek communities on the island likewise increases, whereas more "cooperative tendencies within the framework of international organizations" and "general peaceful foreign policy principles" decreases this likelihood. Similarly, increasing "democratic values" decreases the likelihood of choosing "total separation."

Additionally, we find that three parties' constituencies are significantly differentiated in their likelihood of choosing a foreign policy option. Center-left CHP (*Cumhuriyet Halk Partisi*—Republican People's Party) and DSP (*Demokratik Sol Parti*—Democratic Left Party) and center-right DYP (*Doğru Yol Partisi*—True Path Party) supporters all are significantly more likely to choose "total separation" over some kind of mixed coexistence on the island. We seem to be getting a first glimpse of an unpredictable tendency where it is evident that it is not the right-wing extremist parties like MHP (*Milliyetçi Hareket Partisi*—Nationalist Action Party), SP (*Saadet Partisi*—Felicity Party) or AKP (*Adalet ve*

TABLE 3
DETERMINANTS OF CHOICE FOR GREEKS AND TURKS
LIVING TOTALLY SEPARATED IN CYPRUS

Variable	Coefficient	Standard Error	Significance Level
Age	0.00	0.00	0.86
Sex (Male=1, Female=0)	**0.38**	**0.11**	**0.00**
Years of schooling	**-0.07**	**0.02**	**0.00**
Immigrant background (MB) (Dummy variable)	-0.01	0.18	0.96
Socio-economic status (ownership dimension)	0.01	0.08	0.90
Region variable (Region) (West=1, East=0)	-0.05	0.20	0.81
Urban/Rural (Dummy Variable)			
(Urban=1, Rural=0)	0.26	0.20	0.20
Region × (Urban/Rural)	-0.36	0.23	0.12
Life satisfaction (Dummy Variable)			
(Satisfied=1, Otherwise=0)	-0.17	0.11	0.12
Credible trust in International			
Organizations (Factor scores)	**-0.19**	**0.06**	**0.00**
Credible trust in the political system			
(Factor scores)	**0.11**	**0.05**	**0.03**
Credible trust in Islamic organizations			
(Factor scores)	**-0.11**	**0.05**	**0.05**
Credible trust in local and central government			
(Factor scores)	0.08	0.05	0.12
Perceived threat dimension (External threats)			
(Factor scores)	0.07	0.05	0.18
Perceived threat dimension (Internal threats)			
(Factor scores)	-0.02	0.06	0.73
Perceived friendship dimension			
(Traditional foes) (Factor scores)	**-0.26**	**0.06**	**0.00**
Perceived friendship dimension (Muslim			
countries) (Factor scores)	-0.07	0.06	0.21
Perceived friendship dimension (Distant			
friends) (Factor scores)	**-0.18**	**0.06**	**0.00**
Security Trust in other countries (Factor scores)	0.05	0.06	0.37
Use of international organizations for			
foreign policy (Factor scores)	**-0.14**	**0.06**	**0.02**
Patriotic self-importance and confidence			
(Factor scores)	**0.22**	**0.06**	**0.00**
General peaceful principles of foreign policy			
(Factor scores)	**-0.17**	**0.05**	**0.00**
Patriotism dimension (Factor scores)	**0.18**	**0.07**	**0.01**
Xenophobia dimension (Factor scores)	0.06	0.06	0.30
Democratic values (Factor scores)	**-0.17**	**0.06**	**0.01**
Left-Right ideology self-placement scores	-0.01	0.08	0.94
ANAP (Dummy variable)	0.45	0.25	0.07
CHP (Dummy variable)	**0.50**	**0.21**	**0.02**
DSP (Dummy variable)	**0.61**	**0.31**	**0.05**
DYP (Dummy variable)	**0.59**	**0.18**	**0.00**
SP (Dummy variable)	0.49	0.36	0.16
MHP (Dummy variable)	0.12	0.22	0.59
HADEP (Dummy variable)	0.49	0.28	0.08
AKP (Dummy variable)	0.20	0.15	0.20
Turk as primary identity (Dummy variable)	0.04	0.12	0.74

TABLE 3 (CONTINUED)

Variable	Coefficient	Standard Error	Significance Level
Age	0.00	0.00	0.86
Religiosity attitudes (Factor scores)	0.14	0.07	0.06
Worried about Turkey being attacked			
(Dummy variable)	0.15	0.15	0.32
Supporters of EU membership			
(Dummy variable)	-0.14	0.14	0.32
Economic condition evaluations	0.03	0.05	0.46
Constant	0.14	0.43	0.74
	Predicted 0	**Predicted 1**	**Percent Correct**
Observed 0	684	326	67.70%
Observed 1	319	623	64.10%
		Overall	66.90%
Nagelkerke R-square	0.22		

Kalkınma Partisi—Justice and Development Party) that are more likely to support "total separation" on the island but rather the constituencies of the centrist parties. However, with the exception of CHP, all of these parties did not fare well in the November 2002 elections, and thus the present situation may not be adequately reflected here. Nevertheless, we at least observe that in November 2001 the present AKP government did not have an isolationist constituency.

In order to get some feeling for the mass support for and the evaluation of the recent rapprochement between Greece and Turkey, a number of questions were asked. According to the results, Turkish public opinion sees the Turkish side as being closer to cooperation and the Greek side as being furthest away from it. Who then benefits more from this dialogue between Greece and Turkey is an interesting question. The public opinion is split on this issue as well. Approximately 39 percent of our respondents claim that Turkey benefits more, while about 31 percent claim that both sides benefit equally. Accordingly, nearly 69 percent see Turkey benefiting from the rapprochement, while those who think that Turkey does not benefit from it are a mere 14 percent of our respondents. Relative perspectives on this question also do not seem to be very important. While about 11 percent think that Greece benefits relatively more than Turkey, roughly four percent think that Turkey loses relatively more. In short, there seems to be comfortable support for continued rapprochement between the two countries.

CONCLUSION

Our analyses provide a rich array of empirical findings concerning Greek-Turkish relations. This makes it quite difficult to discern an underlying theme that is valid and relevant both conceptually and policy wise. Our data reveals that Turks perceive Greeks as unfriendly in comparison to other nationalities and ethnicities. Their negative predispositions from a personal perspective are less apparent but still quite salient in their answers. However, we should underline that this unfriendliness is not solely directed towards Greeks. It is all a question of relativity: overall, Turks distrust the external world, but happen to distrust Greeks relatively more than they do many other nationalities. Similar to the overall cultural traits that emerge from past research in World Values Surveys that reveal a very low degree of interpersonal trust and tolerance among Turkish voters, our findings about Greeks and other nationalities and ethnicities should not be surprising.[19] It should be emphasized that when diagnosing the bilateral problems and the solutions that Turkey should follow, we observe glimmers of hope for a more cooperative Level II environment. First, Turks see the Cyprus and the Aegean Sea issues as the most important problems between the two countries. They tend to prefer Level I diplomatic negotiations for their solutions. Despite deep mistrust in the political system—in terms of foreign policymaking—Level I still appears as the dominant legitimate authority for a solution.[20] Nevertheless, nearly one in four respondents picked Level II-based solutions for bilateral problems.[21]

Given these overall tendencies, one is led to believe that Level I initiatives to take the lead in promoting friendly relations with Turkey's traditional foes like Russia, Armenia and Greece will pay off in the end by increasing the support for a Level II engagement with Greece as well. On the other hand, since religiosity appears to dominate these evaluations, utmost care to not offend the religious sensitivities of the voters must be taken—and is one important policy implication. Equally important is an intensified relationship with non-Muslim religious groups within the country. Again, recognition by the Turkish leadership of Judeo-Christian religious leaders is expected to be helpful in establishing understanding and tolerance towards "traditional foes."

In addition, we observe that Turks predominantly perceive Greece as the most likely country to attack Turkey and that if the existing problems are not solved, then, according to Turkish public opinion, war might be inescapable. This fits with our finding that the Turkish public is not particularly Hobbesian; in other words, it does not believe in the use of force in international affairs. However, given this diagnosis, we should stress that a very significant group also indicates that there will be no winners of a military conflict between the two countries.

The immigrant backgrounds of the respondents turn out to be significant as such backgrounds make them more likely to have friendly perceptions of the Greeks in general. From a policy perspective, we also observe that respondents with immigrant backgrounds tend to disapprove of Turkish foreign policies towards Greece and Cyprus. More educated respondents tend to see Greeks as less friendly but have a lower tendency to support total separation of the two communities in Cyprus. As such, education in the traditional official manner seems to breed separation and dislike between the two nations. However, in other policy issues, higher levels of education lead to more cooperative attitudes.

What is most striking is that party-based preferences are not present in Greek-Turkish or for that matter in general foreign policy attitudes either. Hence, Level I leadership cannot target a certain party constituency. Rather, it has to target constituencies in terms of general attitudinal characteristics, on the basis of reducing inherent cynicism towards foreigners or of religious reactions or geography. As such, the creation of a more cooperative environment becomes more difficult and more risky since the leader cannot simply depend on his/her power to win support on the basis of partisanship.

We also observe that EU-related positions have a significant impact on the preferences concerning Greek-Turkish relations. If individuals "trust in international organizations and the EU," they tend to be more supportive of the EU's role in mediating the Greek-Turkish conflict as well as the Cyprus issue. Pessimistically, long-term cultural traits seem to be the most influential on attitudes and preferences, and these support negative predispositions. On a more optimistic note, Turkish voters tend to see efforts seeking a Level I-dominated diplomatic solution as trustworthy. They are thus open to the efforts of the leadership of the political elite to create a more cooperative environment in bilateral relations and they seem to significantly support recent policies pursued along this line.

Lastly, our optimism derives from the fact that even for the most controversial and "sensitive" issues, we observe a significant constituency in favor of a more cooperative outcome. These constituencies are amenable to influence from Level I actors. It remains to be seen if the Turkish political elites will choose to continue pursuing the recent opportunities for mutual cooperation and lead the masses to mobilize behind this rapprochement, which, ultimately, could eliminate the most important hurdle in the way of Turkey's bid for membership of the EU. Finally, there is also an important Kantian perspective among the Turks who support Level II contacts. They may also be a source of influence on Level I actors.

APPENDIX

A total of 3,086 subjects from urban and rural areas over the age of 18 were interviewed between November 8–30, 2001; Frekans Research Company conducted the face-to-face interviews. The target group was the voting-age population in both the rural and urban settlements. Collective places of residence like prisons, hospitals and student dormitories were excluded from the study. Provinces were used as the primary sampling units and the interviews were carried out in 20 provinces: Manisa, Gaziantep, Şanlıurfa, Malatya, Bursa, Ankara and Istanbul were selected to represent themselves, and Sinop, Yalova, Aydın, Burdur, Sakarya, Samsun, Adana, İzmir, Kars, Diyarbakır, Karaman, Osmaniye and Konya were selected to represent the clusters they belong in. Province clusters were formed on the basis of socio-economic indicators and election results.[22]

According to the sampling plan, a total of 3,021 face-to-face interviews were planned, and 3,086 subjects were interviewed during the application stage. In samples of this size that are selected by a simple random sampling procedure, the maximum margin of error is expected to be 1.8 percent at a 95 percent confidence level.

Summary Descriptions of the Variables Used in the Analyses

Variables	Descriptions
Age	Age of the respondent in years.
Sex (Male=1, Female=0)	Sex of the respondent (DV, Male=1, Female=0).
Years of schooling	Years spent in schools.
Immigrant background (Dummy Variable)	If the respondent comes from an immigrant background, that is, his/her parents or grandparents, then the DV=1, otherwise DV=0.
Socio-economic status (ownership dimension)	Ownership dimension of socio-economic status, factor scores. Increased values indicate better ownership status.
Region variable (Region) (West=1, East =0)	Dummy Variable separating Western and Eastern provinces. West includes Adana, Ankara, Aydın, Burdur, Bursa, Istanbul, İzmir, Manisa, Osmaniye, Sakarya, Samsun, Sinop and Yalova.
Urban/Rural (Dummy Variable) (Urban =1, Rural=0)	Settlements with a municipality are considered urban, villages and settlements without a municipality (*bucaks*) are considered rural.
Region × (Urban/Rural)	Interactive Dummy Variable separating western urban settlements from western rural and eastern settlements.
Life satisfaction (Dummy Variable) (satisfied=1, otherwise=0)	Life satisfaction Dummy Variable, DV=1 for those who are satisfied, equals 0 otherwise.
Credible trust in International Organizations (Factor scores)	Factor scores of knowledge × trust in institutions, dimension 1 indicating "credible trust" in international organizations. Increasing factor scores indicate higher friendliness evaluations for these institutions/organizations.*
Credible trust in political system (Factor scores)	Factor scores of knowledge × trust in institutions, dimension 2 indicating "credible trust" in domestic political institutions. Increasing factor scores indicate higher friendliness evaluations for these institutions/organizations.*
Credible trust in Islamic organizations (Factor scores)	Factor scores of knowledge × trust in institutions, dimension 3 indicating "credible trust" in Islamic organizations. Increasing factor scores indicate higher friendliness evaluations for these institutions/organizations.*
Credible trust in local and central government (Factor scores)	Factor scores of knowledge × trust in institutions, dimension 4 indicating "credible trust" in local and central government. Increasing factor scores indicate higher friendliness evaluations for these institutions/organizations.*

Perceived friendship dimension (Traditional foes) (Factor scores)	Factor scores of friendliness evaluations for different nationalities and ethnicities, dimension 1 indicating "friendliness of traditional foes" such as Russia, Armenia and Greece. Increasing factor scores indicate higher friendliness evaluations for these countries.*
Perceived friendship dimension (Muslim countries) (Factor scores)	Factor scores of friendliness evaluations for different nationalities and ethnicities, dimension 2 indicating "friendliness of Muslim countries" such as S. Arabia, Iran and Kurds. Increasing factor scores indicate higher friendliness evaluations for these countries.*
Perceived friendship dimension (Distant friends) (Factor scores)	Factor scores of friendliness evaluations for different nationalities and ethnicities, dimension 3 indicating "friendliness of distant friends" such as the US, Japan and the Azeris. Increasing factor scores indicate higher friendliness evaluations for these countries.*
Security Trust in other countries (Factor scores)	Factor scores of general foreign policy preferences, dimension 1 indicating "security trust in other countries" such as the US, EU and NATO. Increasing factor scores indicate higher trust in foreign policy for these countries/institutions.*
Use of international organizations foreign policy (Factor scores)	Factor scores of general foreign policy preferences, for dimension 2 indicating "security trust in other countries" such as the UN, EU and NATO. Increasing factor scores indicate higher trust in foreign policy for these countries/institutions.*
Patriotic self-importance and confidence (Factor scores)	Factor scores of general foreign policy preferences, dimension 3 indicating "patriotic self-importance" (Turkey is seen as an important country in the world and European system) "defense confidence" (Turkey can defend herself). Increasing factor scores indicate higher self-importance scores and confidence in self-defense capacity.*
General peaceful principles of policy (Factor scores)	Factor scores of general foreign policy preferences, dimension 4 indicating "peaceful principles for foreign policy" (inclination for cooperation, conciliatory and compromising approach). Increasing factor scores indicate higher cooperation tendency.*
Perceived threat dimension (External threats) (Factor scores)	Factor scores from threat perceptions, dimension 1 indicating threats from the outside world.*
Perceived threat dimension (Internal threats) (Factor scores)	Factor scores from threat perceptions, dimension 2 indicating threats from inside the country.*
Patriotism dimension (Factor scores)	Factor scores from patriotic attitudes. Increasing factor scores indicate increasing tendency to support patriotic assertions.*
Xenophobia dimension (Factor scores)	Factor scores from xenophobic attitudes. Increasing factor scores indicate increasing tendency to support xenophobic assertions.*
Democratic values (Factor scores)	Factor scores from democratic attitudes. Increasing factor scores indicate increasing tendency to support democratic assertions.*
Left-Right ideology self-placement scores	Self-placement scores on a 1 to 10 left-right scale.*
ANAP (Dummy variable)	Dummy variable separating ANAP voters in November 2001.*
CHP (Dummy variable)	Dummy variable separating CHP voters in November 2001.*
DSP (Dummy variable)	Dummy variable separating DSP voters in November 2001.*
DYP (Dummy variable)	Dummy variable separating DYP voters in November 2001.*
SP (Dummy variable)	Dummy variable separating SP voters in November 2001.*

MHP (Dummy variable)	Dummy variable separating MHP voters in November 2001.*
HADEP (Dummy variable)	Dummy variable separating HADEP voters in November 2001.*
AKP (Dummy variable)	Dummy variable separating AKP voters in November 2001.*
Turk as primary identity (Dummy variable)	Dummy variable separating those who choose Turk as a primary identity.
Religiosity attitudes (Factor scores)	Factor scores from religious attitudes. Increasing factor scores indicate increasing tendency to support religious assertions.*
Worried about Turkey being attacked (Dummy variable)	Dummy variable separating those who are worried that Turkey could be attacked militarily.
Supporters of EU membership (Dummy variable)	Dummy variable separating those who support Turkey's EU membership.
Economic condition evaluations	Additive measure of economic evaluations of the respondents. Increasing values show deteriorating economic condition evaluations by the respondents.*

Note: * See A. Çarkoğlu and K. Kirişci, *Two-Level Diplomatic Games: The Role of Public Opinion in Greek-Turkish Relations* (unpublished manuscript, 2003) for details.

NOTES

This study was made possible by a generous grant from the United States Institute of Peace (USIP), which was matched by the Research Fund of Boğaziçi University. We would like to thank those scholars and retired officials who kindly gave of their time to evaluate our survey questions and offer their opinions and suggestions. We are particularly grateful to the Turkish Economic and Social Studies Foundation (TESEV) for organizing a brainstorming session on our survey questionnaire. The grant also enabled us to be in touch with our Greek colleagues Theodore Couloumbis, Ilias Nicolacopoulos and Thanos Dokos in order to exchange views and ideas about the questionnaire.

1. Steven Kinzer, "Earthquakes Help Warm Greek-Turkish Relations," *New York Times*, Sept. 13, 1999.
2. Nur Batur, "Winds of Friendship over the Aegean: Words that are Closing an Era," *Hürriyet*, Jan. 13, 2003, pp.1, 26.
3. Robert Putnam, "Diplomacy and Domestic Politics: The Logic of Two Level Games," *International Organization*, Vol.42, No.3 (1988), pp.427–60.
4. Perceptional differences between different European nationalities were not investigated in our questionnaire due to space limitations; only an overall judgment on Europeans was requested.
5. From a methodological perspective such questioning has inherent problems. One is the impossibility of asking for an evaluation of all relevant nationalities and ethnicities in a survey setting. The other is the difficulty of coming up with encompassing criteria for determining the relevant nationalities and ethnicities in the questionnaire. Nevertheless, our expectation is that over repeated samples with different sets of nationalities and ethnicities, a similar picture of evaluation characteristics would emerge. A test of this assumed stability of evaluations remains, however, beyond the scope of this essay.
6. It should be noted that these perceptional evaluations of friendliness were obtained in November 2001, about 18 months prior to the problematic bilateral relations between the United States and Turkey in the context of the Iraq War.
7. Of the sample, 363 respondents—about 11.8 percent of the sample—claimed to speak Kurdish. Those who spoke Kurdish evaluated Kurds, on average, as seven out of ten; significantly closer to the friendly side. It is, therefore, those who cannot speak Kurdish, about 4.2 out of ten, who push this average evaluation down to the unfriendly side. In a similar vein, those who speak English or French or German evaluate Americans and

Europeans as more friendly while perceiving Saudis, Iranians and Kurds as less friendly when compared to those who cannot speak those languages. Those who speak Arabic, however, evaluate Americans and Europeans as less friendly, while perceiving Saudis, Iranians and Kurds as more friendly when compared to those who cannot speak Arabic. It seems, then, that language education—and the cultural socialization that it brings—has a significant impact on people's perceptions of nationalities and ethnicities.

8. On the methodology, see Ali Çarkoğlu and Kemal Kirişci, *Two-Level Diplomatic Games: The Role of Public Opinion in Greek-Turkish Relations* (unpublished manuscript, 2003) for a more in-depth explanation of the factor analysis, its justification for our purposes, its use and interpretation. See also, Paul Kline, *An Easy Guide to Factor Analysis* (London and New York: Routledge, 1994) and Richard L. Gorsuch, *Factor Analysis* (Hisdale: Erlbaum, 2nd Edn. 1983) for details about the techniques of factor analysis.

9. Factor-loading plots are not shown here due to lack of space. However, they help us to pictorially interpret the results. The first and second dimensions of the evaluations are clearly separated from one another. Non-Muslim, traditional foes and rivals stand separated from the Muslim group, in between which the Japanese are located. First and third dimensions somewhat overlap since Americans, Europeans and Israelis load relatively high on both dimensions. Saudi Arabians, Iranians and Kurds are located close by the origin and thus are not differentiated on both of these dimensions. The second and third dimensions, however, show a distinct pattern that separates the Muslim group from what is called the "distant friends," such as the Japanese, Americans, Israelis and Europeans. Azeris are highly loaded on both of these dimensions. Russians, Greeks and Armenians appear close by the origin on these two dimensions.

10. See Ümit Cizre, "Demythologizing the National Security Concept: The Case of Turkey," *The Middle East Journal*, Vol.57, No.2 (2003), pp.213–29.

11. Considering that, early in July 2003, US troops raided a Turkish liaison office in Suleimania in northern Iraq and arrested 11 Turkish soldiers, these respondents' fears were not that unrealistic.

12. Alexander Wendt, *Social Theory of International Politics* (Cambridge: Cambridge University Press, 1999), *passim*.

13. These options do not seem to leave any other significant option out of the preference options made available in the questionnaire since the "Other" option covers only about two percent of the respondents.

14. During the testing phase of the questionnaire it became evident that answers obtained to this question are very dependent on wording. We tried "mutual compromise" and "mutual cooperation" as opposed to "conciliatory." Compromise wording was observed to push the answers away from the mutual compromise option. It was being perceived to be a weakness in international relations and the respondents did not want to support a weak policy position as a general guideline for foreign policy. Cooperation in Turkish (*kooperasyon, işbirliği* or *uzlaşma*) was also not understood by all types of respondents. The first option was a foreign word used in Turkish and thus people with low education levels did not understand it and most probably felt alienated from the questionnaire as a result. The second option was a so-called "pure Turkish" word that required high education levels for proper understanding. Consequently, the researchers opted to use "*hiç anlaşmaya yanaşmayan katı bir politika*" (totally non-conciliatory and tough policy) instead of "*tamamen anlayışlı ve esnek bir politika*" (totally conciliatory and flexible policy) as the opposing ends of the scale.

15. See Yılmaz Esmer, *Devrim, Evrim, Statüko: Türkiye'de Sosyal, Siyasal, Ekonomik Değerler* [Revolution, Evolution, Status Quo: Social, Political and Economic Values in Turkey] (Istanbul: Turkish Economic and Social Studies Foundation [TESEV] Publications, 1999), pp.22–6, 85–92.

16. We also asked whether it is time for a peaceful and mutually satisfactory solution to the conflict on the island: 79 percent supported this option. Nevertheless, a sizable group of 21 percent did not support such an assertion.

17. See Scott J. Long, *Regression Models for Categorical and Limited Dependent Variables* (Thousand Oaks, CA: Sage Publications, 1997) for an accessible review of the methods used here.

18. For these variables, see the Appendix.
19. See Esmer (1999), pp.22–6, 85–7.
20. Concerning lack of trust in the political system see, among others, Fikret Adaman, Ali Çarkoğlu and Burhan Şenatalar, *Hanehalkı Gözünden Türkiye'de Yolsuzluğun Nedenleri ve Önlenmesine İlişkin Öneriler* [Causes and Policies against Corruption in Turkey from the Perspective of Households] (Istanbul: TESEV Publications, 2001), pp.40–45 (in Turkish).
21. Among the determinants of this choice of Level II initiatives for a solution, we see that "religiosity," "perceptions of distant friends" and "patriotic self-importance and confidence" are all exerting negative influences. On the positive side, we see "friendliness perceptions of the traditional foes" and "general peaceful principles of foreign policy" as the most important factors.
22. Details on the sample selection procedures, questionnaire design and testing and data analysis can be found in Çarkoğlu and Kirişci (2003) and can be obtained from the authors.

9

Conclusion

ALİ ÇARKOĞLU

Essays in this volume have taken shape in a period when Turkish domestic politics and foreign policy were being hurriedly reshaped under the influence of several new developments. As a result of the September 11 terrorist attacks in the United States, American-led international forces took the initiative in toppling the Taliban regime of Afghanistan. Turkey supported this intervention and actively participates in peacekeeping operations. A number of momentous reforms were also passed in the Turkish Grand National Assembly (TGNA) in an attempt to comply with the Copenhagen Criteria set as a prerequisite for EU membership negotiations. These legislative adjustments overhauled the way politics are organized and conducted in the country and expanded democratic rights. The pro-Islamist Justice and Development Party (*Adalet ve Kalkınma Partisi*—AKP) came to power following a deep economic crisis and years of failing centrist party-dominated governments. As a result, the secularist bureaucracy and the military's opposition to the popularly elected government with pro-Islamist roots increased.

Simultaneously, the United States headed for an almost unilateral engagement with Iraq and removed the Saddam Hussein regime that it claimed to have been hiding a massive arsenal of weapons of mass destruction, had alleged links to the September 11 plotters and a proven record of human rights violations. The Western alliance against Iraq began to reflect signs of divergent interests and preferences concerning the conflict as Britain, Spain and Italy sided with the United States, while France, Germany and Russia coalesced into an opposition front in the UN Security Council. Signs of divergence were even present in the North Atlantic Treaty Organization (NATO), where a number of allies hesitated to offer their support—especially concerning the deployment of military aid to Turkey. The Turkish parliament, unexpectedly, failed to support the AKP government's recommendation to allow the United States to deploy troops to northern Iraq through Turkish territory. The following months witnessed rising tensions between Ankara and Washington, which peaked in July 2003 when US troops arrested a small Turkish military liaison unit in northern Iraq. The strategic alliance between Turkey and the United

States that had once seemed rock solid was now, at best, questionable. Unable to depend fully on NATO when the need arose to defend Turkey, having at best a shaky security engagement with the new Europe and now passing through the most difficult period in its relations with the United States since the arms embargo of the late 1970s, Turkey seemed a true "lone wolf" in its neighborhood.[1] The recent rapprochement with Greece seemed of secondary importance amidst the chaotic uncertainty that surrounded Turkish foreign policy. However, as these earth-shaking developments occurred, Turkey was also faced with increasing pressure from the international community to facilitate the resolution of the Cyprus conflict. As such, Greek-Turkish relations continued to play a central role in Turkey's relations with the West and its foreign policy in general.

As usual, making sense of the distant past is relatively simpler than focusing on and making sense of the recent past with an eye towards gaining some insight regarding the future. Perhaps, from a systems perspective, the international arena is becoming more and more complex over time. However, more often than not, from the perspective of its participants, while the past looks tranquil and simple, the present appears to be terribly turbulent and complex. Those who analyze the players in the international system are challenged to look at this complexity and to decipher possible long-term trends and currents with potentially significant systemic impact.

Our challenge in this collection of essays has also been one of distinguishing the shifts and changes in the fundamental long-term direction of the foreign policies of Greece and Turkey from developments with little long-term significance. In parallel to this concern about diagnoses of long-term vitality is also a more conceptual one focusing on the interplay between the domestic dynamics of international players and their foreign policy. More specifically, a two-level game perspective underlines the foregoing discussions where the more formal diplomatic negotiations of Level I simultaneously—if not directly interacting with the more informal, grass roots and civil society interactions of Level II— shape foreign policies.

Faced with these two exceptional tasks, several accomplishments nevertheless become apparent after the discussions of our contributors. Some of the points touched upon below are commonalities shared by a number, if not all, of the contributors, and some are reflected more prominently in some contributions than in others. The continual interplay between domestic politics and foreign policy is reflected to varying degrees in all of the contributions. As to diagnoses of long-term relevance, each contribution has its own perspective. While Kostas Ifantis and Othon Anastasakis conceptualize the bilateral relations between Greece and

Turkey as part of regional developments that have long-term implications for both countries' future policies, Gülay Günlük Şenesen and Christos Kollias focus on the long-term trends in military expenditures of the two countries as they relate to their bilateral relations. While Ahmet Evin focuses on Greek perceptions of Turkey, Ali Çarkoğlu and Kemal Kirişci look at Turkish perceptions of Greeks that reflect long-term accumulated stereotyping and hostile policy positioning on both sides, as well as recent cooperative maneuvering with a clear policy objective. Ahmet Sözen's appraisal of the recent developments in the constitution-building debates in Cyprus clearly reflects the legal challenge that has divided the two communities on the island for the last five decades. In Sözen's account we also find reflections not only of the domestic politics and foreign policy interactions on both sides of the island but on both sides of the Aegean as well—with considerable long-term implications for all the parties involved.

GREEK-TURKISH RELATIONS FROM A LONG-TERM PERSPECTIVE

Greek and Turkish foreign policy objectives and the visions of the two countries of their place in the future international arena seem to have been on a convergent path for roughly the last decade. This rising wave of harmonious neighborly relations might potentially culminate in a peaceful and cooperative coexistence within the EU. The chaotic international environment in the aftermath of the Iraq War, however, is constantly exerting treacherous pressures on both countries' foreign policies. There is always the risk that the Greek-Turkish rapprochement of the past decade will be dashed to pieces on the rocky coasts of the Aegean or Cyprus. Taking a pessimistic long-term perspective, a widening rift may be forming not only between Turkey and Greece but also between Turkey and Europe and, in consequence, a solidification of the rift between East and West, and the Middle East and Europe, as well as Islam and Christianity.

What is at stake in Greek-Turkish relations, beyond the potential militarization of conflicts between the two countries, is, first, the resolution of ethnic and religious conflicts and the creation of a basis for peaceful coexistence on the island of Cyprus, perhaps becoming a model of multi-ethnic and multi-religious governance within the framework of the new Europe. The ability of the EU to absorb this quandary and transform it into a new regime of conflict resolution as well as an example of cooperative governance is being tested. From the Greek perspective, a failure to resolve these conflicts with Turkey may mean, on the one hand, that it remains a borderline state having to cope with guarding the fringes of the new fortress of Europe; on the other hand, more optimistically, the successful resolution of the current conflicts may mean a Greece that is a key player in shaping the EU's proactive foreign policy—a policy that can credibly solve conflicts and maintain orderly governance in an expanding union with an increase in southern Mediterranean members (with the inclusion of Turkey).

From the Turkish perspective, a collapse of the momentum to resolve the ongoing disputes over the Aegean and Cyprus means first and foremost the closure of a potentially promising new security environment as part of Europe. Perhaps equally off-putting would be that Turkey would remain an integral part of the future of Europe only as the continually stereotyped antagonist, the "other" of the new Europe. However, achieving success in the recent rapprochement between the two countries may mean accession to the EU and consolidation of European identity for Turkey. Even without the coherence of a European security framework, Turkey—as an integral part of the new Europe—would see itself as a more confident player in the chaotic Middle East and Caucasus and, together with Greece, a central player in the dynamics that shape the EU in general.

Ahmet Sözen's contribution to this volume is a short summary of an extremely complex legal battle over the future of the island of Cyprus. Sözen underlines the characteristics of the only remaining proposal on the table for the resolution of the conflict—the Annan Plan. From the perspective of conceptual discussions on constitution building and conflict resolution, his emphasis on the failure of the 1960 consociational democratic system on the island and the new shift to a power-sharing mechanism similar to the 1960 arrangement in a bi-zonal form contributes to the discussions of the viability of consociational arrangements in conflict-ridden societies. Since Cyprus is also on the road to full membership of the EU, Sözen argues that if a solution is actually reached it would demonstrate the capacity of the EU to resolve conflicts in multiethnic societies. As such, this experience could provide clues as to the long-term trends in conflict management in the expanding new Europe.

Both Kostas Ifantis' and Othon Anastasakis' contributions to this volume share a common diagnosis that could potentially play an instrumental role in shaping the strategic dynamic both in the Balkans and the Middle East. Anastasakis rightly points to the *status quo* tendencies in both Greek and Turkish foreign policies towards the Balkans, especially during the chaotic days at the time of the fall of Yugoslavia. Within this turbulence, the two countries were successful in finding ways in which they could generate a positive-sum game in the Balkans for all involved.

Ifantis' account of the very recent row between Turkey and the United States, as well as between Europe and the United States, over the future of Iraq, provides similar clues as to the foreign policy preferences of all three of the involved parties concerning the Middle East. It is worthy of note that divergent interests on both sides of the Atlantic peaked during the Greek presidency of the EU. Although Ifantis underemphasizes Turkey's hesitation regarding active involvement in the Iraq War, which caused rising tensions between Washington and Ankara, this could very well be interpreted as a new European flavor to Turkish foreign policy. Turkey's obvious preference for the preservation of the territorial integrity of Iraq provided, aside from the French and German opposition, the only strategically significant resistance from within the Western alliance to American ambitions to reshape the Middle East. Such defiance on the part of Turkey, and unsupported by the European security circles, could hardly be durable. However, chaotic divisions within the national parliaments of EU members (as well as within the European Parliament) over the war in Iraq that did not lead to a pressing, united and credible European voice for or against the war in Iraq are in sharp contrast to Turkey's position after the TGNA's momentous rejection of active involvement. Speculatively, it may well be that the resulting "irrelevance" of Europe to the future reshaping of the most important strategic region of the world may be the most significant story that comes out of the recent developments surrounding the Iraq War.

Initial Turkish indecisiveness and eventual refusal to take an active part in the Iraq War resulted in a dangerous crisis with the United States. The long-term roots of this indecisiveness can be found in Turkey's historic sensitivities towards the West concerning regional security in the Middle East, and especially the Kurdish groups in the region. From an institutional perspective, Turkey was also discomforted by the fact that its involvement in Iraq would have had no international support within the UN or NATO and thus could potentially have put it in a very awkward position *vis-à-vis* northern Iraq. Given the rifts in Europe concerning Iraq and the resulting signals from Europe, opposing the active involvement of Turkey in northern Iraq could have been linked to the continuing debate over Cyprus—where international recognition of the Turkish legal position is not firm.[2] Turkey's insistence on multilateral initiatives in Iraq with solid internationally recognized legal bases clearly reflects the relation of these concerns to the Cyprus issue.

Those who have argued that US support for Turkish membership in the EU is given with the intention to turn Turkey into a "Trojan Horse" within the newly forming European security regime have so far been proven wrong. Instead, Turkey's ambitions to ascend to the EU have proven to be more effective in pushing Turkish strategic preferences to favor Europe, while leaving the short- and potentially long-term strategic ambitions of the United States behind. Turkey in this sense has proven to be a European

Trojan Horse within the Atlantic alliance rather than the other way around. The implications of Turkey's shifting strategic preferences could be tremendous for the Middle East policies of the EU as well as for the United States. As Ifantis rightly underlines, the immediate implications of these shifting balances in US-Turkish relations for Greek-Turkish relations and Greek-Turkish-EU relations are also considerable.

Focusing on the specifics of Greek-Turkish relations, the contributions by Günlük Şenesen and Kollias stress an ambiguity in the way both countries' defense expenditures react to one another. Despite continuing high levels of defense spending on both sides of the Aegean (which deplete both countries' scarce resources and could be used for catching up with their development objectives instead), each country's defense expenditures do not seem to be the driving force behind the other's expenditures. Given common data problems in such evaluations, however, Kollias claims that threat perceptions on the part of Greece that are shaped by alleged Turkish violations of Greek airspace over the Aegean drive the Greek determination to arm itself in excess of many of its comparable allies in Europe. Given empirical difficulties in substantiating his claim, Kollias' contribution is nevertheless significant as it underlines the perceptual bases of arms races.

GREEK-TURKISH RELATIONS FROM A TWO-LEVEL GAME PERSPECTIVE

If all politics are local, so are foreign policy decisions. Although a claim that domestic local political concerns are the sole source of foreign policy decisions is certainly an exaggeration, more often than not domestic policy matters and pressures from domestic constituencies shape foreign policy decisions. Ahmet Evin's contribution to this volume, together with Ali Çarkoğlu and Kemal Kirişci's, provide conceptual justification and ample examples for a two-level game perspective of Greek-Turkish relations. Since Robert Putnam's seminal essay, a growing body of literature has claimed that foreign policy is not devoid of domestic political concerns. In fact, in many instances, formal interest groups as well as the informal pressures of public opinion have had impacts on the way foreign policy decisions are made.[3] Evin emphasizes, for instance, that EU membership has shifted Greek domestic concerns to a new European playing field, diverting attention from Turkey to more European concerns—which conveniently allows Greek politicians to cooperatively maneuver their policies towards Turkey.

Undoubtedly, such policy shifts as the recent Greek-Turkish rapprochement are not the result of a uni-variate interaction between diplomatic initiatives on both sides. Domestic political concerns as reflected in the amorphous pressures of public opinion concerning foreign policy are increasingly seen as a crucial factor in shaping foreign policy initiatives. Çarkoğlu and Kirişci point to the long-term consequences of historical conflicts among the Turkish public in their perceptions of the Greeks and Greek foreign policy. While the negative perceptions concerning the Greeks and Greek foreign policy still continue in Turkey, no matter how imperative the rapprochement might be for Turkish short- or long-term policies, the policymakers will find it difficult to convince their relevant constituencies to accept the collaborative and cooperative foreign policy initiatives and to provide much needed support for them. When such support is lacking, or at best shaky, substantiating the rapprochement from the so-called *"sirtaki"* policy, the resolution of conflicts at the negotiating table and further developing social, economic and political cooperation between the two countries will be very challenging. Nevertheless, the methodology presented by Çarkoğlu and Kirişci, that is, the use of mass public opinion surveys which can diagnose pockets of resistance as well as groups that are likely to enthusiastically provide the much needed popular support for specific foreign policy initiatives, also gives a basis for hope in the short term. Such groups in Turkey, supportive of Greek-Turkish rapprochement, do exist and in some cases could be productively mobilized to increase cooperation and reduce tensions. From a pessimistic perspective, however, the same methodology also diagnoses pockets of severe and potent resistance to further development of the Greek-Turkish rapprochement.

Returning to our challenge of discerning long-term relevance from short-term excitement over memorable developments with little long-term consequences, this collection of essays does provide us with some artillery. Greek-Turkish relations are of potent significance to the way Turkey relates to the West, and, in that respect, they exemplify the way East meets West and how Islam relates to European Christianity. For Greece and Turkey, these relations define their future role in global politics. For global politics, these relations have consequences for the future shape of the Balkans and the Middle East—not so insignificant regions of the world.

From the perspective of two-level games, the long-term consequences of accumulated Turkish negative perceptions of the Greeks and Greek policies are quite relevant for the future of Greek-Turkish relations. A similar negative perception of the Turks and Turkish foreign policy in Greece, which can be diagnosed with opinion surveys similar to the one presented here about Turkey, would complicate the matter even further. To manage the two-level interactions between Greece and Turkey, what is needed is a careful analysis of the two public opinions concerning their perceptions of one another and then the formulation of the necessary cooperative policy initiatives that can gather significant support behind them or that can at least avoid being buried by strong popular resistance to such initiatives.

NOTES

1. Soli Özel, "Of Not Being a Lone Wolf: Geography, Domestic Plays and Turkish Foreign Policy in the Middle East," in Geoffrey Kemp and Janice G. Stein (eds.), *Powder Keg in the Middle East: The Struggle for Gulf Security* (Lanham, MD: Rowman and Littlefield, 1995), pp.161–94.
2. See Sedat Ergin's report in *Hürriyet* concerning then Prime Minister Abdullah Gül's remarks in a meeting with Pentagon officials and American diplomats. Sedat Ergin, "Pazarlık Başlıyor" [Negotiations Begin] <http://www.hurriyetim.com.tr/haber/0,,sid~1@w~1@ tarih~2003-09-19-m@nvid~314039,00.asp>, *Hürriyet*, Sept. 19, 2003.
3. See Robert Putnam, "Diplomacy and Domestic Politics: The Logic of Two Level Games," *International Organization*, Vol.42, No.3 (1988), pp.427–60, and essays in P. Evans, K.H. Jacobson and Robert Putnam (eds.), *Double-Edged Diplomacy: International Bargaining and Domestic Politics* (Berkeley, CA: University of California Press, 1993).

Index

Abramowitz, Morton 39
Adalet ve Kalkinma Partisi (AKP) *see*
   Justice and Development Party
Aegean Sea, disputes 10–12, 19n10,
   106–7
Afghanistan, Turkish perceptions 127,
   130
airspace, disputes 11, 36, 107–8,
   109–113, 116nn23-4, 159
Akiman, Nazmi 35–6
Albania 46, 51, 54, 56, 58, 59n1
Americans
   Turkish perceptions 120–25
   see also United States
Annan, Kofi 36, 62
Annan Plan, Cyprus 62, 63, 65–75, 157
Armenians, Turkish perceptions 120–25,
   127
arms race
   literature 79–80
   see also defense spending
arms trade 87, 98n20
Azeris, Turkish perceptions 120–25

Balkan Pact (1934) 46, 59n1
Balkans, Greek and Turkish involvement
   45–58, 157
bilateral relations
   cycle 105–6
   and European Union (EU) 32–7,
      41–2, 49, 73–5
   history 5–8, 80–82
   improvements 117–20
   layers of 106–8
   long-term perspective 156–9
   problems of 138–46

tension index 108–9
Turkish perceptions 136–46
two-level game perspective 159–61
and United States 21–4, 27–8,
   38–42
see also disputes
Black Sea Economic Cooperation
   initiative 53, 58
Bosnia-Herzegovina 52, 56
Boutros Ghali, Boutros 71, 76n5
Brauer, Jurgen 79–80
Bulgaria 46, 51, 52–3, 56, 59n1
Bush, George W. 26

Cem, İsmail 8, 45
coexistence, Greece and Turkey 5, 18n1
cold war 22–4, 46
collegial dialogue 8–9
conflicts *see* disputes
consociational democracy 62, 76n1
Conventional Armed Forces in Europe
   (CFE) Treaty 86
Couloumbis, Theodore 23
cultures of anarchy 132–3
Cumhuriyet Halk Partisi (CHP) *see*
   Republican People's Party
Cyprus
   agreement plans 76n5
   Annan Plan 62, 63, 65–75, 157
   consociational democracy 62, 76n1
   disputes 12–14, 37, 61–75, 107
   EU membership 13–14, 37, 61, 75,
      142
   history of conflict 62–3
   Joint Defence Area (JDA) doctrine
      108, 115nn20-21

For Product Safety Concerns and Information please contact our EU
representative GPSR@taylorandfrancis.com
Taylor & Francis Verlag GmbH, Kaufingerstraße 24, 80331 München, Germany

www.ingramcontent.com/pod-product-compliance
Lightning Source LLC
Chambersburg PA
CBHW050716280326
41926CB00088B/3059